GOVERNMENT
IN GREAT BRITAIN,
THE EMPIRE, AND THE
COMMONWEALTH

T0384631

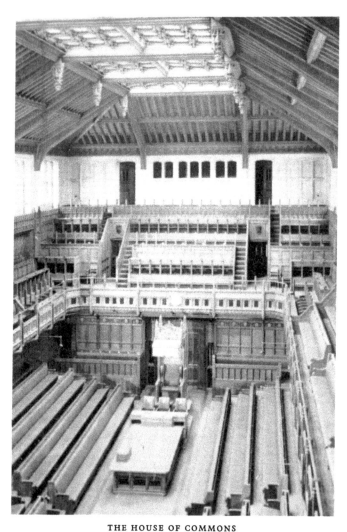

THE HOUSE OF COMMONS

(The new House retains the form of that destroyed
by enemy action on 10 May 1941)

GOVERNMENT
IN GREAT BRITAIN,
THE EMPIRE, AND THE
COMMONWEALTH

BY

L. W. WHITE, M.A.
Headmaster of Beckenham and Penge Grammar School

AND

W. D. HUSSEY, M.A.
Senior History Master, Whitgift School, Croydon

CAMBRIDGE

AT THE UNIVERSITY PRESS

1958

CAMBRIDGE
UNIVERSITY PRESS

University Printing House, Cambridge CB2 8BS, United Kingdom

Cambridge University Press is part of the University of Cambridge.

It furthers the University's mission by disseminating knowledge in the pursuit of education, learning and research at the highest international levels of excellence.

www.cambridge.org
Information on this title: www.cambridge.org/9781107587052

© Cambridge University Press 1958

This publication is in copyright. Subject to statutory exception and to the provisions of relevant collective licensing agreements, no reproduction of any part may take place without the written permission of Cambridge University Press.

School edition 1957
Library edition 1958
First paperback edition 2015

A catalogue record for this publication is available from the British Library

ISBN 978-1-107-58705-2 Paperback

Cambridge University Press has no responsibility for the persistence or accuracy of URLs for external or third-party internet websites referred to in this publication, and does not guarantee that any content on such websites is, or will remain, accurate or appropriate.

CONTENTS

PART I. GREAT BRITAIN

CHAPTER I. THE NATURE OF THE BRITISH CONSTITUTION (*page* 17)

CHAPTER II. THE SOVEREIGN (*page* 22)

CHAPTER III. PARLIAMENT—ITS ORIGINS AND DEVELOPMENT (*page* 31)

CONTENTS

CHAPTER IV. THE PARTIES, THE ELECTORS
AND THE ELECTED (*page* 39)

CHAPTER V. THE HOUSE OF COMMONS, ITS CUSTOMS
AND ITS PRIVILEGES (*page* 53)

CHAPTER VI. THE HOUSE OF COMMONS—TIMETABLE, THE PASSING OF A LAW AND THE ELEMENTS OF PROCEDURE *(page 66)*

CHAPTER VII. THE HOUSE OF LORDS *(page 85)*

CHAPTER VIII. THE PRIME MINISTER AND THE CABINET *(page 92)*

CONTENTS

CHAPTER IX. THE DEPARTMENTS OF STATE AND THE CIVIL SERVICE (*page* 104)

CHAPTER X. FINANCE AND GOVERNMENT (*page* 116)

CHAPTER XI. THE COURTS OF LAW, THE JUDGES AND THE MAGISTRATES (*page* 125)

CONTENTS

CHAPTER XII. THE POLICE AND THE ARMED FORCES (*page* 140)

CHAPTER XIII. LOCAL GOVERNMENT I. ITS DEVELOPMENT AND PRESENT-DAY ORGANISATION (*page* 148)

CHAPTER XIV. LOCAL GOVERNMENT II. ITS SCOPE, FINANCE, AND RELATIONS WITH THE CENTRAL GOVERNMENT (*page* 166)

CHAPTER XV. THE GOVERNMENT AND THE CITIZEN (*page* 181)

PART II. THE EMPIRE AND THE COMMONWEALTH

INTRODUCTION (*page* 193)

CHAPTER XVI. THE CONSTITUTIONAL DOCTRINE OF THE

FIRST BRITISH EMPIRE (*page* 194)

CHAPTER XVII. THE OLD REPRESENTATIVE

SYSTEM OF GOVERNMENT (*page* 205)

CHAPTER XVIII. THE AMERICAN REVOLUTION (*page* 214)

CHAPTER XIX. CONSTITUTIONAL DEVELOPMENTS,

1763-1815 (*page* 221)

CHAPTER XXIII. THE DOMINIONS IN THE
TWENTIETH CENTURY (*page* 261)

LIST OF ILLUSTRATIONS AND DIAGRAMS

*This map is available for download from www.cambridge.org/9781107587052

14

PREFACE

The purpose of this book is to describe the main features of government in Great Britain, the Empire and the Commonwealth, to show the influence of tradition, precedent and proper procedure, and to illustrate the fluidity of the constitution. It is hoped that the book will make clear the duties and responsibilities of democracy as well as its privileges.

In part I, which is the work of L. W. White, the emphasis throughout has been on present-day practice. It has been possible in this part to include only such references to the historical development of institutions as are essential to an understanding of the position to-day. In part II, which has been written by W. D. Hussey, the approach has necessarily been different, and the constitutional development of the British Empire from its beginnings in the seventeenth century down to the present day is described. This part relates how English representative institutions were carried overseas and adapted to the needs of government of the colonies. The institution of Crown Colony government is also described and its development is traced from non-representative forms to those leading finally to self-government. Because of the limitations of space, emphasis throughout part II has been on general principles rather than on detailed descriptions of constitutions; constitutional change to-day is so frequent that accounts of constitutions quickly become out-of-date.

The authors, who have collaborated closely in the planning and writing of this book, acknowledge with gratitude the assistance they have received from many friends, especially on special points and technicalities regarding the courts of law, local government and parliamentary procedure. They are particularly indebted to Mrs Marjorie McIntosh of the Department of Social Studies at Bedford College, University of London, who read the manuscript of part I and made many valuable suggestions, to Mr N. H. Brasher who read the proofs and gave much help, to Mr E. W. Woodhead, County Education Officer of Kent, and to the Borough Treasurers of Croydon and

Bromley. Thanks are also due to H.M. Stationery Office, the Home Office, the Central Office of Information and *The Times* for permission to quote from official documents and to use diagrams. The authors have, as is inevitable, made much use of many of the works mentioned in the book list.

Finally, the authors wish to thank the publishers for their patience and forbearance during the long period this book has been in preparation, and for their helpfulness at all times.

L.W.W.
W.D.H.

September 1957

PART I: GREAT BRITAIN

CHAPTER I

THE NATURE OF THE BRITISH CONSTITUTION

The meaning of the term 'Constitution'

The term 'Constitution' means the system of laws, or of laws and customs, in accordance with which a country is governed, and by which all its citizens are bound. When a country has a written constitution, the fundamental laws can be discovered by reading the constitutional act and its amendments. Great Britain has no written constitution. It is therefore impossible to name any one document which a person may consult and from which he can hope for enlightenment. Indeed the very term 'Constitution' means something different to every thinking Briton, for each one will place more emphasis on one function of government than on another. A famous Frenchman, de Tocqueville, realising this expressed the view that the English constitution did not exist at all.

The functions of government and the separation of powers

There is, however, a substantial basis of agreement on essentials between responsible citizens. The essential powers of government are held to include legislative, executive and judicial functions. It is also recognised that these powers should largely be exercised by different people or groups of people, but that a rigid separation of powers is impracticable. Thus the ministers who form part of the executive should not be excluded from Parliament, the executive should not be barred from influencing legislation, and the judges, while freed from parliamentary and executive control, should not be prevented from questioning the acts of the executive. All are agreed on the supremacy of Parliament, through which the will of the people is expressed, and all uphold the rule of law, that is, the application of the same law to all citizens and the equality of all citizens before the law.

B

The legislative functions in Great Britain are exercised by the Queen-in-Parliament; the executive functions by the Queen's ministers, the Civil Service and the local government authorities; the judicial functions by the judges and the magistrates. Standing aside are the police and the armed forces, who have special duties in the maintenance of law and order and the defence of the country respectively, but who are subject to the rule of law. The link between all the functions of government is the monarchy.

The British Constitution has evolved step by step through the centuries. Though there have been civil wars and rebellions in Britain like the Civil War between Charles I and Parliament, and the Revolution of 1688, there has never been a complete, lasting break with traditions of the past. The British Constitution has been worked out by trial and error. Some institutions have been tried and discarded; others have been developed as the conditions of life and the social structure have changed.

Constitutional landmarks

Because the British Constitution has developed in this way, we have to consider many documents and influences when we attempt to answer the question: 'What is the British Constitution?'

There are certain great landmarks along the path of progress: Magna Carta, an agreement between King John and the barons in 1215, which was later held to guarantee certain privileges for all Englishmen; the Petition of Right of 1628, by which Parliament won from Charles I the recognition of certain essential liberties; the Habeas Corpus Act of 1679, by which the citizen's right to protection against imprisonment without any cause being shown was reaffirmed; the Bill of Rights of 1689 and the Act of Settlement, which established the supremacy of Parliament and gave the monarchy a title based on Act of Parliament, and which together incorporated many of the principles on which the modern constitution has been founded; the Catholic Emancipation Act of 1829, by which the civil disabilities of Roman Catholics were removed; the Reform Act of 1832, which began the long process of the extension of the franchise; and the

Parliament Act of 1911, which limited the powers of the House of Lords. These are just a few of the measures which mark the evolution of the British system of government.

Custom and convention

Side by side with the laws passed by Parliament, there have accumulated many customs and conventions which are necessary to the well-being and working of the constitution, but which have never been put into writing in an Act of Parliament. These conventions are the maxims, practices and rules which regulate much of the conduct of the sovereign and her ministers, and also the procedure of Parliament. Although they are not strict law, they are obeyed as if they were laws, because there is in Britain a strong tradition of obedience to law and custom, and also a clear realisation of the part these customs and conventions play in making democratic government work smoothly and effectively. Foremost among these conventions is that which enables the Prime Minister and his cabinet to conduct the policy and business of Her Majesty's Government.

Sources of the Constitution

Where then shall we find the British Constitution? First it is to be found in numerous Acts of Parliament: in some the workings of Parliament are made clear; by some the powers of the sovereign are defined; by others the position of the judges and the courts of law has been safeguarded; by still others the individual citizen is protected. Secondly, it is affected by documents like Magna Carta, which was drawn up before Parliament existed. Thirdly, it has been influenced by the commentaries written by great constitutional lawyers and historians, in which are to be found interpretations of acts and customs. Fourthly, it has been modified by the verdicts of juries of ordinary men and the decisions of learned judges, and finally it includes customs as old as, or older than, history, derived from the common law, the ancient custom of the realm. It is clear, therefore, that no one, not even in a life-time of study, could read the whole of the British Constitution.

Features of the Constitution

Great Britain is a monarchy. The whole work of legislation and government is carried out in the Queen's name. The Army, Navy and Air Force are hers, and the law is her law. But in her capacity as head of the state she always acts through her ministers, as will be explained in chapter II. The Queen's ministers at the head of the executive are dependent upon parliamentary support, but in their turn control the programme of Parliament, and initiate most of the legislation. Thus, the functions of legislature and executive are so interwoven that it is impossible to disentangle them.

The Government is further controlled by the rule of law. This means that it and its officials are bound by the ordinary law like other citizens. There is no special code of rules that applies to them only, and there are no special courts to hear cases arising from the actions of officials in the discharge of their duties.

The judges and the courts of law are independent of the Government. Their independence was established long ago by the Act of Settlement of 1701. No judge need fear dismissal for political reasons, nor will he be asked to express political opinions. He holds his office during good behaviour, and such is the tradition of his high office that he gives his judgments without fear or favour.

Great Britain, being a small country, can easily be governed as a unit—it is a 'unitary' state. There is no special Parliament for Scotland or Wales, though there is a Parliament for Northern Ireland with considerable powers, and there is a Secretary of State for Scotland and a Standing Committee of the House of Commons which deals with all Scottish matters. As a result of increasingly strong demand a minister has been appointed to look after Welsh affairs, and it may not be long before there is a Secretary of State for Wales.

There is nothing in the British Constitution that cannot be changed by the passing of an Act of Parliament. No special machinery is necessary; there is no referendum to the people; there is no court that can declare illegal any Act passed by Parliament. The constitution is quite fluid or flexible. Thus the British Constitution is designed for practical government rather than to conform to theoretical principles.

Constitutions in the Commonwealth and Empire

Within the Commonwealth and Empire there are countries in every stage of development. The great countries of the Commonwealth are sovereign states united through common allegiance to the monarch. They are governed in accordance with constitutions originating from acts of the Parliament at Westminster. But, as will be shown in part II of this book, they are free to develop their own way of life and traditions, and to set up their own machinery for constitutional change if they so desire. In the Crown Colonies, and in those parts of the Empire whose stage of development is approaching Dominion status, a wide variety of forms of government is to be found. These will also be examined in part II.

The British and American Constitutions contrasted

A contrast of the British Constitution with that of the United States of America will serve to emphasise the constitutional points made in the foregoing paragraphs. The American Constitution is written. Its framers had before their eyes the Britain of the eighteenth century, and incorporated in the clauses of their constitution what they thought to be the best of the principles of British government. They were much influenced by the treatises on government and the natural rights and liberties of man of the great English philosopher, John Locke.

We can see at once how the American Constitution differs from the British. We can read it in a few hours. The original constitution and all its amendments would fill only a dozen or so pages of this book. We should, of course, have to read many more books to know how its clauses have been interpreted, but we should find the first impressions we had gained were little changed. Some of its features could not be applicable to Britain, for America is a vast country, too big an area to be ruled as a single unit. Even at its beginning the United States consisted of thirteen states, all jealous of their rights and proud of their origins. It therefore had to be a federation whose organisation and institutions made it easy for new states to be admitted on equal terms with the old. The desire of the states to preserve their individuality made them suspicious of the power of the central government. They therefore limited its powers to those given it in the constitution, and checked its activities by rigidly separating the legislative, executive and judicial functions. Further, they gave to the highest court of law of the federation, the Supreme Court of Justice, the duty of watching over the constitution, and declaring illegal any law which conflicted with it. The separation of legislature and executive was accomplished by forbidding the President's ministers to sit in either house of the legislature. This prevented the development of anything like the British cabinet system. The President was established as the executive; his ministers were his personal nominees and responsible to him; he was invested with very wide powers, much more extensive than those exercised by the sovereign in Great Britain even in the eighteenth century. Finally the constitution can only be changed by an elaborate process including a referendum to the people.

CHAPTER II

THE SOVEREIGN

The Crown and the Sovereign

The sovereign represents all aspects of government, since all government is in her name. The powers of the sovereign are twofold: those that appertain to the Crown, and those which the sovereign possesses as a person. The term 'Crown' itself is sometimes used to mean 'the sum total of governmental powers', and sometimes it is applied to the kingly power itself, so that we have to be very discerning both in the use and in the understanding of the term.

The Crown in its widest sense represents all that is essential for the administration of the state, its legislative, executive and judicial

functions. These functions have in the course of centuries been transferred from the sovereign to the nation, which in turn acts through a
ministry dependent on a parliamentary majority. Parliament, the
Government, and even the Opposition are the Queen's, and so are
the laws and the judges, and all acts of government are carried out in
her name. The majority of the powers that hundreds of years ago were
exercised personally by the sovereign are now used on her behalf. But
while surrendering direct power, the sovereign has retained influence
derived from convention, prerogative, respect, and the personality
and character of the sovereign herself.

In law, the Queen can do no wrong. Whatever functions she performs, except on purely ceremonial and social occasions, she carries
out at the request and on the responsibility of her ministers. There is,
therefore, a wide divergence between the nominal and the actual
powers of the sovereign. The powers of the Crown are related in the
chapters that follow. In this chapter we shall examine the influence
and prerogatives that remain with the Queen as a person.

The title to the Crown

The Queen's title to the Crown is derived from the Act of Settlement 1701 which said, 'The Crown shall remain and shall continue
to the said most excellent Princess Sophia and the heirs of her body
being Protestant.' The following is the text of the proclamation read
at the accession of Queen Elizabeth II:

Whereas it has pleased Almighty God to call to his mercy our late
Sovereign Lord King George VI, of blessed and glorious memory,
by whose Decease the Crown is solely and rightfully come to the
High and Mighty Princess Elizabeth Alexandra Mary:

We, therefore, the Lords Spiritual and Temporal of this Realm,
being here assisted with these His late Majesty's Privy Council, with
representatives of other Members of the Commonwealth, with other
Principal Gentlemen of Quality, with the Lord Mayor, Aldermen,
and Citizens of London, do now hereby with one Voice and Consent
of Tongue and Heart publish and proclaim, That the High and
Mighty Princess Elizabeth Alexandra Mary is now, by the death of

our late Sovereign of happy memory, become Queen Elizabeth II by the Grace of God, Queen of this Realm, and of Her other Realms and Territories, Head of the Commonwealth, Defender of the Faith, to whom Her Lieges do acknowledge all Faith and constant Obedience with humble Affection, beseeching God by whom Kings and Queens do reign, to bless the Royal Princess, Elizabeth II with long and happy Years to reign over us. God save the Queen.

The Queen and the executive

The executive government is the Queen's agent; all its actions are performed in her name and all its powers derive from her. But such is the practice of the constitution that she performs no executive act except through a minister, who is personally responsible to Parliament for that act.

When William III and Mary II became joint sovereigns after the abdication of James II, they chose as their ministers whomsoever they wished, irrespective of party. As the cabinet system developed in the eighteenth century, the custom grew up of the monarch's choosing a Prime Minister who in turn selected his ministers from his own party and submitted their names to the King for approval. Even in his choice of Prime Minister the sovereign was not unrestricted, for the government of the country could not long be carried on unless the man he chose commanded a majority in the House of Commons. Today the Queen must in practice choose the leader of the most powerful party in the House of Commons as her Prime Minister. She may offer objections to a minister whose name the Prime Minister submits to her, in which case he may substitute another. But persistence in such an objection on the part of the sovereign would produce a serious constitutional crisis.

Walter Bagehot in his famous book *The English Constitution* wrote, 'The constitutional sovereign is understood to have three rights, the right to be consulted, the right to encourage, and the right to warn.' The Queen has opportunities of influencing policy before the final decision has been reached. A note of cabinet proceedings, and also all documents of importance are submitted to her. The sovereign thus has the opportunity of becoming better informed on matters of state than many cabinet ministers, as her understanding of affairs widens with experience. Her ministers will not set her advice aside rashly, but once the policy has been decided upon, she will not interfere with the responsibilities of her ministers.

The sovereign's views are expressed in private in the course of her frequent contacts with her ministers, especially with the Prime Minister, whose duty it is to keep the Queen informed of events, and where necessary to explain and amplify the information given to her in official documents. Her opinions must not be made public, for, if she were drawn into the arena of public controversy, constitutional monarchy in its British form could not continue. That the sovereign often has opinions, likes and dislikes, has been made very clear by the publication of the letters of Queen Victoria, who at first regarded the Whigs as 'her' party, and later entered heart and soul into partnership with the conservative Disraeli, whom she had once referred to as 'detestable'. No doubt other instances of the sovereign's personal influence will be revealed when the inner secrets of the reign of King George V are made known.

There has been no clear case of the dismissal of a ministry by the personal action of the sovereign since 1783, when the efforts of George III to rule through the King's Friends were drawing to a close. Even Queen Victoria had to accept as ministers those whom the electorate favoured.

The Queen and the legislature

The sovereign law-making body is the Queen-in-Parliament; no Act is valid until it has received the royal assent. There is no law that forbids the Queen to exercise her right of veto, or refusal to sign, but as it is 250 years since the right was exercised, custom has established that it shall not be used. As the Queen's ministers now control the passage of all legislation, it is clear that refusal to sign a bill would be tantamount to the rejection of her ministers' advice and would precipitate a grave crisis which might be fatal to the monarchy. The signing of a bill constitutes a legislative act by the Queen. She also performs legislative acts within certain fields by proclamation and orders in council, but these too are only made upon the advice of the ministers.

Parliament is nominally dependent upon the sovereign since she summons it and dissolves it, and may prorogue it at the end of a yearly session, but in each case she acts on the advice of the Prime Minister. The needs of government require money, which can only be obtained by the passage of the yearly Finance Bill, and the maintenance of the Army and Air Force is also dependent upon an annual bill, so that there is no possibility that there will be a long gap between the sessions of Parliament.

There was a time when the sovereign could sustain the Government of the day in its hour of need by the creation of peers. This was done by Queen Anne to secure the passage of the Treaty of Utrecht in 1713. It was threatened on the advice of the King's ministers in 1832 at the time of the Great Reform Bill, and again in 1910–11 when it seemed that the Lords might throw out the Parliament Bill.

The Queen, the judges and the administration of justice

In the earliest days of kingship, one of the most important functions of the monarch, perhaps the most important, was the dispensing of justice. In medieval times the executive, legislative and judicial functions were indivisible and indistinguishable, and were all exercised by the King and his immediate advisers, but gradually the powers came to be separated. In early Stuart times, when the courts of law had long been firmly established, there were instances of royal pressure upon judges to obtain decisions favourable to the Crown, and these became a major issue in the struggle between King and Parliament. In the Act of Settlement (1701) it was enacted that the judges should hold office during good behaviour: 'quamdiu se bene gesserint', and that they could only be removed on an address by both Houses of Parliament. The judges to-day are still Her Majesty's judges, but the sovereign appoints them on the advice of the Prime Minister or the Lord Chancellor.

Criminal prosecutions, or prosecutions by the state, are still conducted in the Queen's name. Action is taken in such cases by the Director of Public Prosecutions, or on the advice of the chief law officer of the Crown, the Attorney-General.

One remaining fragment of the once extensive royal dispensing power is the right of the sovereign to grant a pardon, either freely or on conditions, to a convicted person, but this power is exercised on the advice and responsibility of the Home Secretary and only in a limited field. It has been retained to rectify mistakes or to soften the action of the law where it has appeared too harsh.

The Queen and the Church

The Queen is supreme head of the state in 'Matters ecclesiastical as well as civil'. The sovereign's powers in ecclesiastical matters were defined at the time of the Reformation in England, and her position with regard to the Church of England in England, and the Church of Scotland in Scotland, which are Established Churches, is regulated by law. The sovereign, by the Act of Settlement, may not be a Roman Catholic or marry a Roman Catholic, and must swear to maintain the Established Church. Queen Elizabeth II became Queen from the moment of her predecessor's demise without the blessing of the coronation ceremony. Among her titles is that of Defender of the Faith. This was bestowed upon Henry VIII by the Pope before the Reformation and has ever since appeared among the royal titles, and may be seen upon the coin of the realm.

The Queen appoints the highest dignitaries of the Church of England upon the advice of the Prime Minister. She may express her personal wishes with regard to certain appointments, but in the last resort she must accept the advice of her ministers in this as in other matters.

The Queen and the bestowal of honours

The royal right to bestow honours was one of the last to come under the control of her ministers. We have already seen that the appointment of ministers, of judges, and even of archbishops and bishops and other church dignitaries, is made on ministerial advice.

So is appointment to such offices as the Governor-Generalship of a Dominion, when the advice of the Prime Minister of the Dominion is sought. Important posts in the colonies are filled on the advice of the Prime Minister or the Colonial Secretary.

The bestowal of peerages, baronetcies and knighthoods is also made only on the advice of the ministers. Twice yearly, at the New Year and on the occasion of the sovereign's birthday, such honours are conferred. The Prime Minister himself is now restricted in his recommendations, for since 1922 the lists have been submitted to the scrutiny of a committee of three privy councillors whose duty it is to see that there are no abuses, such as the conferring of honours as rewards for donations to party funds.

All minor honours and decorations are also conferred on the recommendation of ministers, with the sole exception of appointments to the Royal Victorian Order, which remain the sovereign's means of rewarding personal services to her or the royal family.

The personal position and influence of the Sovereign

Although the sovereign reigns but does not rule, yet her example and that of her family is of great influence in the country's, and the Commonwealth's life. It is above all an example of service. Such service includes the signing of the mass of papers that require the sovereign's personal signature or sign-manual, the reading of and commenting upon state papers, the receiving of ambassadors, the granting of audiences to ministers and others of her citizens, the performance of functions like the opening of Parliament, participation in great spectacles of pageantry like the Trooping of the Colour, and humbler duties like visiting hospitals or the laying of foundation stones, and above all the cementing of the ties of the Commonwealth by receiving Commonwealth ministers and by visiting the Dominions and Colonies. Whatever the function, the sovereign must give it her close study and attention, for it must be performed with due ceremonial and exactitude. She must show interest, knowledge and that graciousness which is the characteristic of royalty.

The Civil List

Up to the time of Charles I the King was expected by his subjects to bear the whole cost of government from the royal revenues and those traditionally granted him by Parliament. The growing cost of government and the inability of the King to meet it from the resources at his disposal were largely responsible for the Civil War. It was not until after the Revolution of 1688 that Parliament fully realised its responsibilities for the finance of government, and made more proper provision for the sovereign's personal needs. George III surrendered to the nation his interest in the hereditary revenues of the Crown and received in return a fixed Civil List. The process, whereby the sovereign receives a sum of money from which the expenses of the royal household are defrayed, was completed in the reigns of William IV and Queen Victoria. Soon after the accession of Queen Elizabeth II, a committee representative of all parties was set up to examine the question of the Queen's Civil List. It had before it the precedents of the grants made to previous sovereigns, for example the Civil List of King George VI, which amounted to £410,000 (£110,000 for the King's Privy Purse and £300,000 for the expenses of the Royal Household) together with additional sums voted for other members of the royal family. The recommendations of this committee were accepted by a resolution of the House of Commons in July 1952 and the Civil List Consolidated Fund (Appropriation) Bill, founded on the report and resolution, became law in August of the same year. This gave the Queen a Civil List of £475,000 a year and her husband the Duke of Edinburgh an annuity of £40,000. The Queen retains the revenue of the royal estates of Balmoral and Sandringham, and the private royal fortune that has been bequeathed to her.

The royal household

Much of what is private life for a private citizen becomes public life for a sovereign. The great offices of the royal household are now political appointments, for the importance of the influence of the sovereign's immediate circle of advisers is fully realised. Sir Robert Peel's earliest disagreement with Queen Victoria arose in 1839, when he insisted on substituting for her Whig Ladies of the Bedchamber other ladies more favourably disposed to the Tory Government. There are nevertheless personal influences that are beyond the cabinet's control. The Queen will in many matters rely greatly on the advice and support of her husband, for with him almost alone can she discuss affairs of state without reserve. The influence of the Queen Mother is also likely to be great. Of obvious importance too is the Queen's personal private secretary, who is called upon to display discretion and impartiality in his advice. The personal entourage of the Queen can have a great influence on her in her personal relationships with her ministers, but is unlikely to have any measurable political influence.

The Regency Acts of 1937 and 1953

The Regency Acts of 1937 and 1953 have made standing provision for the infancy, incapacity or temporary absence from Great Britain of the sovereign. In the event of illness not amounting to incapacity, or in the case of her absence from the realm, the Queen can by letters patent delegate to counsellors of state certain royal functions. Certain matters, however, are withheld under these Acts viz., the dissolution of Parliament except on the express instructions of the sovereign, the creation of peerages, and some matters relating to the Dominions, who enact their own legislation with regard to a regency. Counsellors of state were appointed in 1951 during the illness of King George VI, when they were Her Majesty the Queen, the Princess Elizabeth, the Princess Margaret, the Duke of Gloucester, and the Princess Royal. Counsellors of state were also appointed when the Queen and the Duke of Edinburgh visited the Federation of Nigeria in January and February 1956.

The Queen and the Commonwealth and Empire

There is no sphere in which the personal influence of the sovereign is of more importance than in relations with the Commonwealth and

Empire. The Preamble of the Statute of Westminster 1931 describes the Crown as the symbol of the free association of the members of the British Commonwealth of Nations. It is the common tie of personal loyalty to the Queen herself, not to the abstract idea of the Crown, that links together Britain and the great Dominions and the Empire, and provides a common allegiance for her subjects throughout the world.

CHAPTER III

PARLIAMENT—ITS ORIGINS AND DEVELOPMENT

The supremacy of Parliament

The whole structure of the British Constitution rests on the supremacy of Parliament. Parliament comprises three elements, the Queen, the House of Commons and the House of Lords. No Act of Parliament becomes law until it has received the Queen's assent; this assent, as has been explained in chapter II, is a formality. The House of Commons, now the predominant partner in Parliament, initiates all important legislation and is solely responsible for bills dealing with finance; the House of Lords, though deprived of any powers in respect of finance bills and limited in its powers in respect of other bills, is still an important part of Parliament, as will be explained in chapter VII. There is no subject in the sphere of internal government on which Parliament cannot legislate; there is no existing law that it cannot repeal; there is no unwritten undertaking that it is compelled to honour; there is no court of law that can declare its actions illegal. Thus, though there are many things which Parliament would not do, because they would be inexpedient or foolish, there are no things which it is legally prohibited from doing.

The origins of Parliament

The English Parliament is an ancient institution, with seven hundred years of history. It has had a profound influence on government in the Commonwealth and Empire, and far beyond. On its methods and procedure have been based those of the many legislatures that have been formed on the British model. Throughout its long life it has been changing and adapting itself to the circumstances and conditions of the age. It began in medieval days, as the Great Council of barons, whom the King rather unwillingly had to consult. To this Council the term 'Parliament' or 'meeting for discussion' came to be applied. In 1295, in the reign of Edward I, the 'Model' Parliament met, including barons, higher clergy (bishops and abbots), knights of the shire, burgesses and representatives of the lower clergy. In the fourteenth century the presence of the knights and burgesses, as representatives of the commons of the shires and the boroughs respectively, was accepted as essential. The earliest Parliaments were not organised into Houses, but by the middle of the fourteenth century the Lords (i.e. the barons and higher clergy) were meeting together in one assembly, and the knights of the shire and burgesses in another, the representatives of the lower clergy having ceased to attend. The sole business of the knights and burgesses in these early days was to agree to the royal demands for taxation; they were not even supposed to deliberate before agreeing. But before long they began not only to deliberate but also to present petitions to the King. In the course of time a regular procedure came to be adopted which ultimately led to the enactment of parliamentary statutes. The Commons' petition or bill was passed to the Lords, the formula in old French being 'Soit baillé aux Seigneurs', i.e. 'Let it be passed on to the Lords.' When the bill was passed on to the King by the Lords and he agreed to it, the words were 'Le roy le veult', i.e. 'The King wishes it.' If the King refused the bill it was returned with the words 'Le roy s'avisera', i.e. 'The King will think about it.' The same process is followed to-day, except that no King has refused a bill for 250 years. During the fifteenth century the right of the Commons to be consulted about taxation was established, and the qualification for voting for the knights of the shire was fixed at the holding of freehold land worth 40s. a year, a considerable sum in those days; this remained the qualification for four centuries. The qualification for the vote in the boroughs or towns varied from place to place.

Parliament under the Tudors and Stuarts

Parliament, like the country as a whole, passed through a period of obscurity during the long Wars of the Roses in the middle part of the fifteenth century. But when at length a line of strong monarchs, the Tudors, put an end to anarchy, Parliament came out into the light, for the Tudors found it a convenient weapon for use first against the surviving barons and later against the Church. It was Henry VIII who first made full use of Parliament, for he made it his partner in bringing about the Reformation and ending the power of the Pope in England. He kept one Parliament together for eleven years, and thus enabled the House of Commons to gain a sense of continuity and a feeling that it was helping to shape policy. It even dared on occasions to refuse to grant the taxes demanded, and to criticise the King's ministers.

The long reign of Elizabeth I showed both the strength of the Queen's control over Parliament and the growing boldness of the Commons, who criticised the Queen for her unwillingness to marry and also objected to her religious and foreign policy. The Queen handled the Commons firmly, but nevertheless they gained in corporate feeling and importance in her reign. Through the creation of boroughs the number of members also greatly increased from 296 in 1500 to 462 in 1600, and membership became highly prized both for itself and also for the influence derived from it. The Tudors used Parliament to assist them in government and law-making without allowing it to decide policy or to originate legislation; the former was a matter for the sovereign, the latter for the Council. In the sovereign's eyes, agreement to taxation was still the chief function of Parliament.

When Queen Elizabeth I died, and the Scotsman James I came to the throne, a very different situation soon developed, for the new King had no knowledge of English affairs and blundered in his dealings with Parliament. Quarrels arose over important matters: taxation, the liberty of the subject, the privilege of members, and above all the increasing demand of the Commons to have a hand in the framing of policy. These differences became more and more acute until they led, in the reign of James I's successor, to the Civil War between Charles I and Parliament. In the Civil War, Parliament was victorious: the King was executed, the House of Lords and the Church of England were abolished. But the victory did not result in the supremacy of a freely elected Parliament. Instead, power passed to Oliver Cromwell and the army, which began as an ally of Parliament and ended by overthrowing it. Thus the army became more hated than Charles I had been, and the lessons learnt during the short period of army control have never been forgotten. When the monarchy was restored in 1660 in the person of Charles II, Parliament came back too. It was relatively more powerful, for its old rival the King's Council never recovered the wide powers it had exercised under the Tudors and early Stuarts.

Parliament after the Revolution of 1688

A final attempt at absolute government by James II brought about a bloodless revolution and the abdication of that sovereign. The Revolution settlement, largely incorporated in the Bill of Rights and Act of Settlement, not only established a monarchy which owed its title to Parliamentary enactment, but also began the process which has led to supremacy of Parliament and the responsibility of ministers to Parliament. The army was subjected to parliamentary control through the passage of the annual Mutiny Act. The judges alone were independent of Parliament, though they too were removable in the last resort on joint petition of the two Houses. The Lords as a House remained important, but the prestige of the House of Commons was enhanced. It was unrepresentative of the people, as it was still elected on the old fifteenth-century franchise, but nevertheless it often showed itself sensitive to such public opinion as then existed.

34

The balance and composition of Parliament was changed in the early eighteenth century by the legislative union with Scotland in 1707 by which 45 Scottish members sat in the House of Commons and 16 peers representative of the Scottish nobility in the House of Lords. A similar union with Ireland in 1801 brought into being the Parliament of the United Kingdom of Great Britain and Ireland and added 100 Irish members to the House of Commons and 28 lay and 4 spiritual peers to the House of Lords.

The eighteenth century saw the beginning of a great change in the relations between Parliament and the King's ministers. The increasing power of the Commons and the complete dependence of the Crown on the Commons for money led to the sovereign's choosing ministers who were acceptable to Parliament and who could command a majority in the Commons. This century thus saw the beginnings of the cabinet system of government and the establishment of the two great parties, the Whigs and Tories. In this century too came the first criticisms of the unrepresentative nature of the House of Commons and the first proposals for parliamentary reform.

Transition to the nineteenth century

At the end of the eighteenth century there were few constituencies in which electors were not dominated by aristocratic influence, and the House of Commons itself was an aristocratic body. The franchise remained as it had been for centuries, yet social conditions had greatly changed. In the villages, the ancient pattern of life had been disturbed by the enclosure of commons and open fields, and the introduction of new methods of farming. There was also a movement of population towards the Midlands and the North of England, where industry was expanding as a result of new inventions, new wealth and increased trade. As a result of the movement and growth of population, Parliament became more unrepresentative than ever. Further, the French Revolution stirred the hearts and minds of men so powerfully that even the repressive measures introduced during the long Revolutionary and Napoleonic Wars did not wholly prevent the spread of liberal ideas. In the years of unrest after the wars, the

Radicals maintained a campaign for parliamentary reform. In the shires, only the forty-shilling freeholders had the vote; in many of the boroughs, 'rotten' or 'pocket' boroughs as they were called, there was a handful of voters who were easily influenced by bribes or threats. Voting was, of course, open, i.e. by word of mouth. At length the Radicals triumphed and brought about the passage of the Reform Act of 1832, which began the transformation of the House of Commons. From this point the history of Parliament is bound up with the extension of the franchise which revolutionised both the electorate and the membership of the House of Commons.

Parliamentary reform, 1832-85

The great Reform Act of 1832 was carried only after bitter opposition from those who considered they had property rights in the 'rotten' and 'pocket' boroughs. As a result of its passage many people of the middle classes in the towns, such as the professional men and shopkeepers who had houses worth £10 a year, and the bigger tenant-farmers in the country districts received the vote, but the total number of voters was still only one million out of a population of twenty-four million. The total number of members of Parliament remained the same, but great changes were made in the distribution of seats. Fifty-seven of the smallest boroughs lost the right to send any members of their own to Parliament. Many others lost one of their two members. Many big towns, e.g. Manchester, Birmingham and Leeds, which had previously had no member of their own were now given representation, and the populous counties of the North got more seats. To the people of those days the Act appeared revolutionary, but it was only the beginning of a series of changes spread over a hundred years, which by peaceful means transferred political power from the landowning to the middle and working classes. The years that followed 1832 saw much unrest in Britain and on the continent of Europe. A body of men known as the Chartists demanded rapid political changes, some of them advocating violent action, but in spite of the influence of revolutions on the continent, Britain did not depart from her usual method of doing things

36

gradually and through Parliament. It was not until 1867 that the next franchise act was passed, this time by the Conservative Government, of which Disraeli was a member. It gave the vote to all male householders and male lodgers paying £10 a year in rent in the towns, and to middle-class people in the villages. For the Conservatives it was a 'leap in the dark' but it did not disturb the old system of party politics. The Liberals and Conservatives remained the predominant parties for another fifty years. Before the passage of the next franchise act two important measures were passed. In 1872 the Ballot Act made voting secret, and in 1883 the Corrupt Practices Act was passed, which imposed heavy penalties for bribery and other corrupt practices (see p. 50).

In 1884 came the next important step. The vote was given to male householders in the country, among them the miners and agricultural labourers, who had not previously received it. Most men of twenty-one and over except bankrupts, criminals, paupers and lunatics now had the vote, but there was as yet no thought of giving it to women. In 1885, another necessary measure was passed; there was a further redistribution of seats, this time roughly in proportion to population. Towns with between 15,000 and 50,000 inhabitants were given one member, those between 50,000 and 100,000 two members, and towns with over 100,000 were to have three or more.

Changes in the twentieth century

The next big step forward came in 1918, when, at the close of the First World War, age and residence became the qualifications for the franchise, men of twenty-one and over and women of thirty and over who were ratepayers or the wives of ratepayers being given the vote. This was in part a tribute to the assistance women had given in the war efforts, and in part the result of the campaign known as the Suffragette Movement which many prominent women had carried on in the years before the First World War. In 1928, women were at last given equal voting rights with men, the age for both being twenty-one. The total number of those entitled to vote in 1951 was over thirty-four million.

There have been minor changes since 1948. In 1948, special qualifications, like the University vote which gave to some men and women graduates an extra vote, were abolished, and provisions were made to allow absent and disabled voters to use their votes. The country was divided into one-member constituencies, and the Universities and the City of London lost their members. In all there were then 625 members for Great Britain and Northern Ireland, the latter being the only part of the British Commonwealth which had its own Parliament and was also represented at Westminster. As a consequence of the revision of the boundaries of certain constituencies, the number of members in 1955 had been increased to 630.

The composition of the House of Commons

The Act of 1832 had little effect upon the social composition of the House of Commons. In 1833 there were in the House of Commons 217 sons of peers and baronets and in 1865 180; in 1833 there were 500 members representative of the landed interest and in 1865 400. Nevertheless the small but persistent band of Radicals continued to exercise a great influence, the result of which was seen in the spate of reforms of the 1830's. Increased parliamentary business as well as somewhat changed membership made the House of Commons less of a leisurely club than formerly. Gradually Peel, Gladstone and Disraeli, all representative of new influences and opinions, made their way to the position of Prime Minister. Liberals and Conservatives took the places of Whigs and Tories, but both parties were equally reluctant to encourage direct working-class representation.

Even after adult male suffrage had been brought about by the Acts of 1867 and 1884, the composition of Parliament was affected only slowly. Lawyers, businessmen and the aristocratic element predominated. At the very end of the century, the Independent Labour Party was formed, and the Trade Union Congress began to interest itself in increasing the number of Labour members. Labour representation grew from two members in 1900 to twenty-nine in 1906, when the Parliamentary Labour Party was formed, and forty-two in 1910. From that time the power and influence of the Labour Party steadily grew until it overtook the Liberal Party in 1923. Thereafter, with some fluctuations, it continued to grow until it obtained a clear majority for the first time in 1945.

Another important change in the composition of the Commons resulted from the establishment of the Irish Free State in 1922, after which only Northern Ireland sent members to Westminster.

The House of Commons and the House of Lords

The revision of the franchise in the nineteenth and twentieth centuries and the changed composition of the House of Commons widened the gulf between the two Houses. Clashes occurred in the nineteenth century, and, in the early twentieth century, the incompatibility of the Liberal majority in the Commons and the Conservative majority in the Lords was soon apparent. The result was the Parliament Act of 1911. Nearly forty years later irreconcilable differences between the Labour majority in the Commons and the Conservative majority in the Lords arose during the third Labour Ministry and led to the Parliament Act of 1949. These measures, and proposals for the reform of the House of Lords, will be discussed in chapter VII.

CHAPTER IV

THE PARTIES, THE ELECTORS AND THE ELECTED

The party system

British government is based on the party system, with the stronger party governing and the party in the minority exercising constant watchfulness and subjecting the Government to searching criticism. Further it can be said that the British way in politics depends on a two-party system. Thus, with the continued strength of the Conservatives and the growth of the Labour Party, the Liberal Party, so powerful in the nineteenth and early twentieth centuries, has been eliminated as a strong political force though it is not without importance in days of small majorities. The whole tradition of our political life has prevented the development of many groups and parties as in France, and has also worked against coalitions, except in times of national stress and peril.

The development of the parties

The faint beginnings of parties can be seen in the disputes before the outbreak of the Civil War in the reign of Charles I, and become clearer in the reigns of Charles II and James II. Before the end of the seventeenth century, two groups of aristocratic politicians emerge; the Whigs, the party of the great landowners and the wealthy merchants, and the Tories, representing the smaller landowners or squires, and the lesser clergy of the Church of England. Though Whigs and Tories united to invite William III and Mary to come to England, it was the Whigs who got the credit and advantages from the establishment of a parliamentary monarchy, and they remained the predominant party, except for a short period in the reign of Queen Anne, until the accession of George III in 1760. George III set to work to break the supremacy of the Whigs, and formed a group of members known as the King's Friends in a last attempt to assert the personal power of the King, which had diminished during the reigns of the first two Hanoverians. Though he succeeded in weakening the Whigs, he failed to shake the power of Parliament. When the Revolutionary and Napoleonic wars were over and the country had settled down to peace, it was the Whigs who carried the Reform Bill and other great reforms in the years 1832 to 1835. It required an imaginative statesman like Peel to put new life into the Tories, who had been discredited as the upholders of repression and the opponents of reform; they became known as Conservatives. Under the leadership of the energetic and progressive Gladstone, the Liberal party took the place of the aristocratic Whigs. These parties, continually adapting themselves to new social and political conditions, held the political stage, occasionally disturbed by the Irish Nationalists, until the 1906 election, when the Labour Party appeared as a new political force.

After a long period of Conservative rule, Liberals of a new and more radical school took power in 1905 and startled Britain by their intensive social policy. They seemed to have entrenched themselves for a long period of power when war broke out in 1914. A split in the party and bad political management led to the complete rout of the Liberals after the First World War in 1918, a defeat from which the party has never recovered. This gave the Labour or Socialist Party the opportunity to make such rapid strides that it was able to take office between the two World Wars for two short periods, firstly in 1924, when it was dependent on Liberal support, and secondly from 1929 to 1931, when it was the biggest party in the House of Commons. A schism in the Labour Party at a time of national crisis in 1931 brought about a predominantly Conservative coalition government, though for a time the Socialist Ramsay MacDonald continued as Prime Minister. This coalition, from 1935 under a Conservative Prime Minister, lasted until 1940, when the disasters of that year led to the formation of a wider coalition under Winston Churchill.

Recent party fortunes

The war-time coalition came to an end in 1945, by which time the main parties, the Conservatives and the Socialists, were anxious to get back to party government. The 1945 election gave the Labour Party a clear majority for the first time, and enabled it to take power unfettered by the need to conciliate Liberal opinion. It seemed that the Conservatives with only 189 seats to the Socialists' 396 had suffered a defeat from which they could never recover, yet in 1951 they were in power again with a small majority, and in 1955 they strengthened their position. The figures for the last four general elections are instructive, not only because they illustrate the fortunes of the parties, but also because they show some of the results of the British system of single-member constituencies:

41

		Conservatives	Labour	Liberals
1945	Votes	8,693,000	11,985,000	2,253,000
	Seats	189	396	25
1950	Votes	12,475,000	13,265,000	2,637,000
	Seats	297	315	9
1951	Votes	13,700,000★	13,900,000	720,000
	Seats	320	296	6
1955	Votes	13,311,938★	12,369,532	722,395
	Seats	344	277	6

★ Conservatives and Supporters

Total membership 1951 – 625: 1955 – 630.

(For 1951 and 1955 add the Speaker and 2 Irish Nationalists to the number of members shown in the table above.)

In 1951, the Liberals had one member for each 120,000 votes, whereas the Conservatives had one member for 42,000 votes, and Labour one member for 47,000 votes; in 1955 there was still one Liberal member for each 120,000 Liberal votes, while the Conservatives had one member for 38,600 votes, and Labour one member for 44,600 votes.

Other electoral systems

Various systems in force in other countries aim at avoiding anomalies like those mentioned above. One is the transferable vote, which enables the voter to state an order of preference in a single-member constituency. The candidate with the lowest number of first-preference votes is eliminated, and the votes of his supporters are distributed according to their second preferences. This system was tried out experimentally in the University constituencies before their abolition. Another system is proportional representation which is in some countries used in large constituencies returning several members. This involves a complicated system of vote transfer. It has the advantage of making it more possible for minority parties to obtain a fair representation, and it also influences parties towards

avoiding extreme policies, in the hope of winning the second preference of the 'middle' voters. Fully to understand proportional representation and similar systems it would be necessary to read a detailed
work upon them.

Though there are undoubted anomalies and injustices arising from
the British electoral system, there is one great and all-important
advantage. It avoids the many parties or groups of the French
system, and it usually gives one party a majority that makes the work
of government possible.

The policies of the parties

There is nothing fixed or rigid about the policies of the three chief
parties in British politics. The programme of the Conservative Party
at the 1955 election was vastly different from the Conservatism first
developed by Sir Robert Peel; the Socialist programme to-day would
seem mild to many of the more extreme members of the Labour
Party in the 1920's; the Liberal programme of 1955 showed how far
that party has moved from the programmes of Gladstone.

The chief issues between the parties are capitalism and socialism,
or perhaps it would be more true to say the extent and nature of
control over public services and industries, for the Conservatives
have accepted the nationalisation of the Bank of England, of the coal
mines and of the railways, as well as the need for extensive social
services. They believe that except in well-defined spheres, capitalism
and private enterprise provide the best hope of improved conditions
for the whole population. The Socialists hold that the means for the
production of wealth should belong to and be controlled by the
nation, and that the country's wealth should be more equally shared.
In their opinion, capitalism is out-of-date in the modern world and
planned economy inevitable whatever party is in power. The Liberals
put their faith in the development of social services, the stressing of
the value of individual freedom and toleration of minorities, and the
advocating of lower tariffs as a spur to the improvement of international trade and relations.

The two most powerful parties are less widely separated in practice

43

than in theory. World conditions force upon the Conservatives restrictions and controls which they opposed when the Socialists were in power. Socialists are forced by economic circumstances to make less sweeping changes in the structure of industry than they would wish.

It is customary to talk of the Right and Left in politics, the Right representing the Conservative, the Left the more progressive elements. Further left than the Labour Party in Britain is the Communist Party, which believes that true Socialism cannot be achieved by gradualism. It polled only 33,144 votes in the 1955 General Election and had no candidate elected. But the Right and Left have a constantly changing significance, as the social structure of the modern world changes. The terms Right and Left are borrowed from the French Chambre des Députés where the members sit in a semi-circular arena. In the British House of Commons the Government sits on the Speaker's right and the Opposition on the Speaker's left.

The organisation of the parties

Each of the political parties has a national headquarters in London, which directs research and propaganda and prepares the ground for electoral campaigns. The Conservative and Liberal Parties are made up of local associations affiliated to the national organisations. These local associations send delegates to the annual National Conference at which the National Executive is elected. The Labour Party is differently composed. It consists not only of local parties, but also of Trade Unions and other Socialist bodies which are affiliated to it. The executive committee elected at the annual conference is made up of members representing the different organisations affiliated to the party.

The methods employed by the Conservatives and Liberals on the one hand, and the Labour party on the other, in the choice of candidates in the constituencies, also differ. The local Conservative and Liberal associations are somewhat similarly organised. They are run by executive committees elected at the annual meetings. The local associations through their executives choose the candidates for parliamentary elections. They may ask the assistance of the Central Office if there are no strong local candidates. After interviewing the prospective candidates the local executive makes a recommendation to a general meeting, or leaves the general meeting to make the final choice. In making the final choice the local association may be influenced by the candidate's personality, his acceptability in the constituency, the strength of his party conviction, and residence in the constituency. His ability to assist with the campaign expenses will count much less than formerly, as experience has shown that the party fortunes will be better served by a 'live' candidate rather than by one whose chief qualification is his wealth. The recommendations of the party headquarters will be considered, but the local associations sometimes select 'unknowns' and pass over well-known figures.

The choice of a Labour candidate is achieved differently. The local Labour Party consists not only of individuals holding labour views, but also of Trade Union branches, Co-operative Societies and other Socialist organisations. When it becomes necessary to select a candidate, the local executive committee asks the affiliated bodies to submit names, makes a selection and submits its choice to a general meeting. The local association's choice must then be endorsed by the National Executive Committee, which will not give the endorsement unless the candidate agrees to abide by the standing orders of the Parliamentary Labour Party, including a rule that prevents a Labour member from voting in a parliamentary division in a manner contrary to the decisions of a private meeting of the party.

Nominations of candidates are not the monopoly of political parties. At each election there are a number of independent candidates, but few of them have more than a forlorn hope, and almost all forfeit their £150 deposit.

Party discipline in the Commons

Rigid party discipline in the Commons is a development of the twentieth century. In the eighteenth century, the predominant Whig party was composed of small groups, who were often almost as bitterly opposed to one another as to the Tories. In the nineteenth

45

century, the Tory or Conservative Party and the Liberal Party suffered serious splits, and individual members often voted or abstained from voting as their conscience or personal feelings and not as their parties demanded. Moreover, they did not consider themselves bound to constant attendance at the House. During the twentieth century, and more particularly since 1918, the hold of the party over the individual member has been tighter. Though theoretically the member when elected is free to vote as and when he chooses, he knows that persistent independence will cost him party support, and almost certainly lose him his seat.

The Opposition in party government

Except in the case of a coalition the strongest party provides the Government; its chosen leader is Prime Minister, and its supporters are appointed to the offices great and small. The firm support of a strong party is essential to good government, and the party system helps to provide this.

Almost equally important is a strong Opposition: indeed so important is its function that since 1937 the Leader of the Opposition—Her Majesty's Opposition—has been paid a salary (now £2,000) to ensure that he gives his services fully to the state and the people as well as to his party. The Opposition sharpens Government policy by its criticism, and prevents abuses by its watchfulness. Open, candid and fearless opposition is an essential feature of parliamentary democratic government. It can modify and improve legislation, it can influence public opinion, it can protect minorities. By the proper performance of its duties, it prepares itself for the day when it will be called upon to take power.

The parliamentary register of electors

Every voter's name must be on the electoral roll or parliamentary register of electors, which is kept by the local government authorities, and can be seen in post offices and other public places. It is revised once a year. The same register is now used for parliamentary and for local elections. Property qualifications for all purposes have been abolished. All British subjects of twenty-one and over are entitled to vote unless they are certified lunatics, convicted persons serving terms of imprisonment of over a year, persons temporarily disqualified for offences against the electoral laws, members of the House of Lords, or Scottish peers who are not members of the House of Lords as Scottish representative peers.

Of the thirty-four million persons entitled to vote in October 1951, nearly twenty-nine million voted. This was 82·8 per cent, a high figure, but it will be seen that some five million did not vote, some through sickness or age or disablement, but many through failure to make use of their privilege.

The issue of writs on a dissolution

In 1911, a law was passed which limited the length of any Parliament to five years. The Prime Minister may ask the sovereign to dissolve Parliament, either when it nears the end of its term, or before then if he considers political circumstances warrant it. After the dissolution, writs are issued by the Crown Office to the sheriffs and mayors who are the returning officers in the different constituencies.

They are worded in the following terms:

Elizabeth by the Grace of God of the United Kingdom of Great Britain and Ireland, Queen, Defender of the Faith to the Sheriff (or Mayor) of the County (or Borough) of .... greeting.

Whereas by the advice of our Council we have ordered a Parliament to be holden at Westminster on the .... day of .... next, We command you that notice of the time and place of election being first duly given, you do cause election to be made according to law of a member to serve in Parliament for the said county (or division of the said county, or said borough) and that you do cause the name of such member when so elected whether he be present or absent, to be certified to us, in our Chancery, without delay.

As soon as the writs have been issued the local associations of the various parties begin to work with redoubled energies. In most cases the candidates will already have been selected before the dissolution of Parliament. The chief parties, the Conservatives and the Socialists, put forward candidates in almost every constituency, the Liberals

47

contest a considerable number, the Communists choose a few candidates for constituencies where they feel they have some hope of success.

Qualifications for a member of Parliament

The qualifications required for a member of Parliament are somewhat similar to those required for a voter. A member must be twenty-one years of age, but there is no need for him or her to be on the voters' register in the constituency for which he or she sits. Priests of the Church of England and the Roman Catholic Church are not eligible, nor are the holders of a long list of offices of profit under the Crown. Peers with a seat in the House of Lords cannot be members of the House of Commons nor may the small band of Scottish peers who are not members of the House of Lords. Other disqualifications from membership of the House of Commons are insanity, bankruptcy, corrupt practices at elections, and conviction for treason or felony.

Nomination day

The next stage is nomination day which, in a general election, is the same for all constituencies. On this day all candidates must produce to the Returning Officer a nomination paper signed by a proposer, seconder, and eight other voters of the constituency and a deposit of £150, which he will lose if he does not obtain one-eighth of the votes polled in the constituency. Most candidates produce many nomination papers, but it is not necessary for them to produce more than one. The £150 deposit is insisted upon to cut down the number of candidates who have no chance of success. If only one candidate presents himself he is declared elected unopposed. If the election is contested, as it almost always is, the poll is held nine days after nomination day.

The election campaign

The amount of money that a candidate may spend in election expenses is rigidly controlled. His agent must keep an exact account of all expenses incurred, and must see that the electoral laws are kept.

48

Each candidate may send out post free his election address with his photograph, details of his career, a statement of his policy and details of the meetings he will hold. It is probable that the candidate has been 'nursing' the constituency for some long time, and, if he is a party candidate, he has the valuable help of the local party organisation and also of the national headquarters of the party in conducting his campaign. If he is an important candidate, or if his constituency is a 'marginal' one, that is one where a few votes may turn the scale, he will have the help of some of the party leaders, who will come down to speak for him in an attempt to tip the scale in his favour. The candidate must speak as often as he can and appear in as many places as possible. He and his supporters must canvass the voters. He must be prepared to answer all kinds of questions, some of which have nothing to do with the election or his party; he must learn how to put up with, and if possible silence, interrupters or hecklers. He must always be cheerful and polite, however annoying the circumstances may be. His chief business, and that of his workers, is to see that all his supporters use their vote. Most people will have made up their minds for whom they will vote before the election begins, but a few, possibly a vital few, will be won over by the candidate's eloquence or policy.

Polling day

The voting, or polling, takes place in convenient places, usually schools, in different parts of the constituency. In charge of each polling station is an official responsible for the proper conduct of affairs. A policeman is also present to guard against unlawful acts, though his services are seldom, if ever, needed. The voter gives his name and address to the official in charge, who cancels his name on the register and gives him his voting paper. The voter then goes to a booth, puts a cross against the name of the candidate he favours, and drops his voting paper into a locked ballot box. The hours of polling are usually from 8 a.m. to 8 p.m., but powers exist for them to be extended with the candidates' consent, viz. 7 a.m. to 9 p.m. After polling has ended, the ballot boxes are sealed and taken to the Town

C

Hall or some similar centre, where they are opened in the presence of the Returning Officer. The votes are counted in the presence of representatives of the party candidates, after which the papers are collected and sealed in packages, which after an interval of one year are destroyed. Thus no one knows for whom any particular elector has voted, although it would be possible, on an order of the High Court only, for this to be discovered by an examination of the serial numbers of voting papers and counterfoils. Such an order would only be made when a case involving allegations of corrupt practices was before the Court.

When the counting is completed and the Returning Officer and the candidates are satisfied that the tally of votes is correct, the Returning Officer publicly declares the result, the candidates make short speeches, and the losers formally congratulate the victor. Except in a few constituencies, where communications are difficult, the result is declared in less than twenty-four hours after polling has ceased, and by that time the country knows which party has been successful.

By-elections

What has been said so far describes what happens in a general election. When a vacancy takes place through death or through a member's giving up his seat, there is a by-election in that constituency. In such a case, as in a general election, the Crown Office issues the writ, the nominations are made and the voters go to the poll. Such by-elections often attract much attention and bring many prominent politicians to support the candidates, for the result is considered to show the feeling of the electorate towards the Government. The loss of several important by-elections causes serious concern in a party and may even lead to a general election.

Corrupt and illegal practices in elections

The Ballot Act 1872 went a long way towards the clearing away of malpractices in elections, but it was found that the law required further strengthening. This was done in the Corrupt and Illegal Practices Act 1883, which increased the penalties for corrupt and illegal practices, so that they included hard labour and fines up to £200. It was made an offence for any person to treat voters, i.e. to provide any meat, drink or entertainment. Undue influence was closely defined. A candidate found guilty of treating or undue influence or any corrupt practice was excluded from Parliament for seven years, and prohibited for ever from representing the constituency in which the offence occurred. If the offence were committed through his agent he was disqualified from the constituency for seven years. In addition regulations were laid down with regard to expenses. A candidate was to appoint an agent and defray all expenses through him. He was restricted to £100 personal expenses, and the agent's expenses were closely restricted.

Subsequent legislation has modified and further defined corrupt and illegal practices. The latest provisions are included in the Representation of the People Act 1949. This Act requires the appointment of an agent and the notification of his name and address to the Returning Officer. The personal expenses of a candidate are still limited to £100. All other expenses not authorised by the agent are prohibited. The total of these is limited to £450 + 2d. for each elector on the roll in county constituencies, and £450 + 1½d. an elector in borough constituencies. Each candidate is allowed to send one communication post free. The agent is required to make a return of all expenses within thirty-five days of the declaration of the result of the election. Among the restrictions are limitations on the provision of motor vehicles for the conveyance of voters to the polls. The Act says that a person shall be guilty of corrupt practice, (i) if he is guilty of bribery, (ii) if he is guilty of treating, and, (iii) if he is guilty of undue influence, and further defines these offences.

The candidate is responsible, so far as the holding of his seat is concerned, for all the acts and misdeeds of his agent, committed in his capacity of agent. It is seldom that any one wilfully indulges in corrupt practices, but there are many ways in which an unwary agent may be drawn into practices and expenses which may be challenged by a defeated candidate.

Duties of a member of Parliament

When once elected, the new member must not only be a loyal member of his party but also the servant of his constituency as a whole. He must watch over the interests of the local authorities within its boundaries; he must take up questions raised by any of its inhabitants, whether they are his supporters or opponents; he must perform cheerfully and patiently many social duties. He must spend as much time in it as his parliamentary duties allow.

As a member of Parliament, he receives a salary of £1,000 a year. He may claim travelling expenses between London, home and constituency on parliamentary duties. He may also claim a sessional allowance in respect of expenses wholly, exclusively and necessarily incurred in the performance of his duties as a member, payable at the rate of £2 for every day on which the House meets (other than a Friday). This, however, does not apply to a minister. All this is small recompense for the duties he has to perform, for the meetings of the House of Commons and its committees allow him little time to carry on his own business or profession, if he has one, and the expenses he must incur are heavy. Many members, who have no private income or business or profession, are assisted by trade unions or supplement their salary by journalistic or similar work.

Membership of the House of Commons carries with it serious duties. It must not be entered upon lightly and it may not be lightly given up. For this reason a member of Parliament cannot resign his seat. As he cannot hold it at the same time as a salaried office under the Crown, except that of a minister, a member who wishes to vacate his seat applies for the office of Steward or Bailiff of Her Majesty's Chiltern Hundreds, or of the Manor of Northstead. These are offices of profit under the Crown, the acceptance of which causes a member to vacate his seat. He resigns his stewardship immediately on appointment. This seems a roundabout way of resigning, but it discourages resignations in the heat of the moment, or on trivial grounds. Because membership of the House demands a good deal of sacrifice as well as bringing much honour, it is highly esteemed, and there have been few in the last hundred years who have brought it into discredit.

CHAPTER V

THE HOUSE OF COMMONS, ITS CUSTOMS AND ITS PRIVILEGES

The Parliament House of the Commons

The official opening of the new House of Commons on 26 October 1950 recalled the disastrous happenings of the night of 10 May 1941 in the Second World War, when the former House was destroyed and the House of Lords damaged by aerial bombardment, and also the centuries of history in which the Commons' meeting place had had a profound influence, not only on their deliberations, but also on the evolution of the British form of government.

During the Middle Ages, of which the records are meagre, Parliament met wherever the King summoned it, maybe at Westminster or Windsor or Winchester. In the fifteenth century the Commons frequently met in the Chapter House of the Abbey of Westminster, which they then regarded as their home. In 1547, King Henry VIII gave the Chapel of the College of St Stephen, within the Royal Palace of Westminster, to the Commons as their Parliament House. The Chapel had seats arranged longitudinally facing one another, and these were retained, with the Speaker's Chair upon the steps where the altar once stood. The Lords, too, met within the Palace of Westminster, and Westminster Hall was used for the meetings of the Law Courts. Their palace being so used, the Kings went to live in nearby Whitehall or elsewhere. For a long time the interior of St Stephen's retained much of its ecclesiastical atmosphere, until Sir Christopher Wren transformed it by giving it a false ceiling, panelled walls and galleries resting on slender pillars. This was the

53

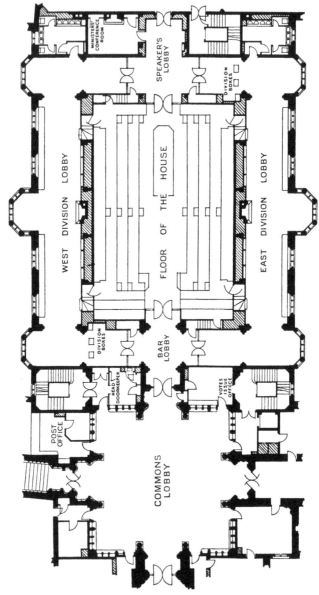

Fig. 1. Plan of the House of Commons and the adjoining rooms

54

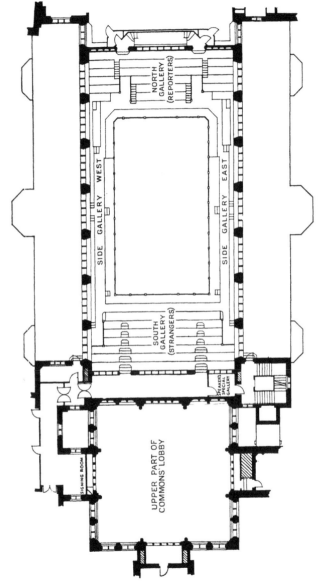

Fig. 2. Plan of the Galleries of the House of Commons

House that perished in the great fire of 16 October 1834, when the whole of the Palace of Westminster, with the exception of Westminster Hall, was destroyed.

In the following twenty years there gradually rose a vast new Palace of Westminster, designed in the Gothic style by Sir Charles Barry. It included a chamber for the House of Lords, a new House of Commons, and hundreds of rooms and miles of corridors, the whole being dominated by two great towers. It was still, and it is still a Royal Palace, and for this reason remains under the control of the Lord Great Chamberlain. The new House of Commons, which was finished in 1852, was not on the site of St Stephen's Chapel but at right angles to it and parallel to the river, the site of the former Chapel being occupied by St Stephen's Hall, which served as a way of approach from Westminster Hall to the new House. The rectangular plan of St Stephen's Chapel was retained, the new House being somewhat bigger, but still much too small to provide seats for all members. The close-packed rows of green upholstered benches facing one another, the compact mass of members on important occasions, gave an atmosphere of intimacy, and encouraged a conversational, unadorned style of speaking, with swift interventions and quick repartee. It also fostered the maintenance of the two-party system.

The House met in this building for nearly ninety years, until it was destroyed by enemy action. Immediately after its destruction, the Commons, under Sir Winston Churchill's influence, decided that the new House should preserve the essential features of the old. A Select Committee on Rebuilding, appointed in 1943 in the depths of war, decided to preserve the former dimensions, with seats for only 437 out of 615 members (increased to 630 by 1955). Of these 346 were on the floor of the House, and 91 in the side galleries. Thus the feeling of intimacy was maintained, though at the expense of comfort and convenience. The architect chosen was Sir Giles Gilbert Scott, whose design was in a modified Gothic which harmonised with the rest of the Palace of Westminster which had escaped destruction.

The plan of the floor of the House has been little changed: the

56

wide benches upholstered in traditional green face one another; the Speaker's chair recalls the design of the one destroyed. Above the chamber facilities for the Press and for strangers (i.e. visitors) have been much improved. Leading from the Lobby into the chamber is the Churchill Arch, constructed of burnt and damaged stones from the old House. In the new House, links with the Commonwealth and Empire are strong. The Speaker's chair was the gift of Australia and is fashioned in black beanwood; the Table of the House, in Canadian oak, was the gift of Canada; the despatch boxes were given by New Zealand; the Clerks' chairs by South Africa, the Serjeant-at-Arms' chair by Ceylon. The rest of the furniture and panelling of the House itself is in English oak. In the ministers' rooms and lobbies are gifts from every part of the Commonwealth and Empire.

For nine years the Commons sojourned elsewhere, first in the Church House and later in the chamber usually occupied by the Lords who met meanwhile in the Royal Robing Room. At length the Commons returned to the site of Barry's building and to a House of traditional form. For the official opening of the new House by His Majesty King George VI a great company assembled in Westminster Hall. It included the Queen and the royal family, members of both Houses, the judges and many distinguished visitors. Among the latter were twenty-nine Speakers, or bearers of the equivalent office, from legislatures in every part of the Commonwealth and Empire, testifying to the spread of the British parliamentary idea throughout the world.

The Speaker

The first duty of a newly elected House of Commons is the election of a Speaker, for until that is done it cannot conduct its business. At one time the Speaker was the sovereign's nominee, but since the time of Charles II the sovereign has ceased to express a preference for any one person, while still approving the Speaker's election. When a vacancy in the office of Speaker occurs, the parties in the House consult together. It is almost certain that the nominee of the largest party will be elected, but it is most important that he shall be acceptable to all parties. His proposer and seconder will be 'back-benchers', an indication that it is part of his duty to watch over the interests of private members and minorities. When once elected, the Speaker will probably continue in his office until death or retirement, irrespective of change of government, for it will take him some time to learn the many details which he must know. He must put party aside and exercise his office with patience, tact and impartiality. There is, therefore, no higher tribute to a member's integrity than election to the Speaker's Chair.

The election is carried out in a full sitting of the House, after agreement has been reached by the parties. During the formal proceedings, the candidate sits modestly on a back bench whence he is dragged by his proposer and seconder. He makes a token show of resistance, thus recalling the days when the Speaker as the intermediary between Commons and King often hazarded his freedom, and even his life. The importance of the office is recognised by the use, rent-free, of a residence within the Palace of Westminster, by the high precedence given to the Speaker in all ceremonial occasions, by a salary in keeping with his exalted office, and by the members' respect at all time. In order properly to discharge his office, the Speaker must make sacrifices. He must resign himself to taking no part in debates, and probably to never exercising the casting vote allowed him by custom. He must preside over the meetings of the House in full session, and must remain watchful throughout long and possibly tedious sittings when ordinary members may leave the House or doze on its benches. He has a Deputy who relieves him from time to time, but the House expects the Speaker to be in the Chair on all possible occasions. He leaves the House when it goes into Committee.

The Speaker has three main functions: to see that members behave in an orderly and seemly fashion; to keep them 'in order' in accordance with the customs and recognised procedure of the House; and to call upon members who wish to speak in debate. The working out of his functions has been one of the great contributions of Britain to the democratic method of government.

The Speaker's dignity is enhanced by his wig and fine gown. He needs no bell or gavel. When he stands, no other member may remain standing, and as no member may address the House in debate unless he is standing, it follows that when the Speaker stands the debate must be broken off. If a member fails to observe the normal procedure, the Speaker may order him to resume his seat. If he continues to disobey the Speaker's command, he can order him to withdraw from the House. If he is still recalcitrant the Speaker can name him, whereupon the minister in charge of the business before the House moves that the member be suspended. When this motion has been carried the offender must leave the House. If he refuses to go voluntarily, he is taken out, forcibly if necessary. The suspension lasts for five days for the first offence, twenty-one days for the second, and for the third until such time as the House decides it be terminated. In the case of grave offence the Speaker has the power to order the confinement of a member to the tower of Big Ben.

To keep members 'in order' according to customs, procedure and standing orders needs long experience and a deep understanding of the ways of the House as well as tact, judgment and knowledge of the members themselves. To get 'out of order' is not difficult. A member may forget that he must address Mr Speaker and not a party or an individual member. He may make use of an unparliamentary expression or wander from the point. He may refer to a member by name, instead of calling him the Hon. Member, or the Hon. and Gallant, or the Hon. and Learned, Member for such and such a constituency. Again, a member may mention the House of Lords directly instead of referring to it as 'another place'. Many of the rules and customs are of ancient origin and have a long history. All help to make the House of Commons as much a club as a legislature.

The third main function of the Speaker is to call on members to speak in the course of a debate, to decide who it is who 'catches the Speaker's eye'. A debate on a Government measure is opened by the minister in charge of the bill or the business in hand, and he is followed by the leading speaker for the Opposition. When an

59

important measure is before the House, Mr Speaker is informed by the Government and by the Opposition who their principal speakers will be. Other members wishing to speak sometimes inform the Speaker of their desire in advance. There are, of course, many members who wish to speak on an important measure who are denied the opportunity, for the Speaker has to weigh the time allotted to each party, and to give preference to those with special knowledge. He has also to bear in mind the time available for the debate.

At question time particularly, the Speaker's knowledge of the members and skill in control of the House are fully tested. He must know all the members by sight; he must decide who 'catches his eye'; he must judge when discussion on a particular question has gone on long enough; he must put his foot down firmly when in his judgment the time has come to call the next question.

There are other important duties that fall to the Speaker. He has to decide whether or not a bill is a money bill. He must watch over the interests of the House as a whole, and must see that the Government does not encroach too greatly upon the right of the Opposition and the private members to express themselves.

The Chairman of Committees, and the officers of the House

As has already been stated on page 58, the Speaker leaves the Chair when the House goes into Committee of the Whole House. The Chairman of Committees, or as he is also known the Chairman of Ways and Means, is elected by the House and is also Deputy Speaker. He in turn has a deputy, and these two alone can act as Deputy Speaker in the Speaker's absence. They too refrain from any part in politics after their election. The Chairman of Committees does not sit in the Speaker's Chair, but in a less imposing chair at the Table of the House, where the Clerk of the House sits when the House is under the Speaker's jurisdiction. The Chairman has the delicate task of maintaining impartiality when selecting which amendments to take in debate in the Committee of the Whole House.

The Speaker selects from among members of known integrity, impartiality and efficiency in the chair a panel of not less than ten members as 'temporary chairmen'. They can if required act as temporary chairmen of the House in Committee, and from them the chairmen of Standing Committees are appointed.

The Speaker is assisted in his duties by the Serjeant-at-Arms who sits, clad in court dress, at the opposite end of the House. He carries out the Speaker's instructions, and assists him in the preservation of order in the House and in the galleries. He is also the official guardian of the Mace, without which the House of Commons is not constituted as a House. It is part of his duties to see that the mace is properly placed. When the House of Commons is sitting as such the mace rests on brackets on the top of the table; when it is in committee, it rests on brackets beneath the table. The Serjeant-at-Arms makes the necessary adjustments, which may on occasion be frequent.

Of great importance also are the Clerk of the House, the Clerk Assistant and the Second Clerk Assistant, all of whom wear wigs and gowns when on duty in the House. The Clerk of the House is concerned with the business of the House as such, and is not present when the House is in committee. Then his seat, as has been mentioned above, is taken by the Chairman of Committees, the two other Clerks retaining their seats. The Clerk of the House is the adviser of the Speaker, and indeed of the members generally, on all matters of procedure. His advice is also much sought by parliamentarians of the Commonwealth and of the colonies, and even of foreign countries. He shares with the other Clerks the responsibility for recording the Minutes of the proceedings of the House as they appear in the Journals. There are the other Clerks with important and special duties, e.g. the Clerk of the Public Bill Office and the Clerk of the Private Bill Office. The Clerk of the House of Lords is known as the Clerk of the Parliaments.

The member and the customs of the House

Before a new member of the House of Commons can feel at home there, he has to learn the ways of the community he has entered, and to respect its rules and customs.

Some of the things the new member has to learn concern his

relations with his fellow-members. He must discover how to address them in the House. He must learn that certain expressions are 'unparliamentary' and will not be allowed by the Speaker. He must above all show proper respect for the Speaker. In short he must learn to conduct himself according to the established rules. He must also learn something of the procedure of the House in the conduct of its business. His experience in committee work outside Parliament will have taught him the elements of this. Everything proceeds by motions and resolutions. A member who wishes to move a motion must put it down by writing it and handing it to the Clerks at the Table of the House, who arrange for it to be printed in the Order Paper.

Some of the customs are not so easily learnt. For example, the member must always address the Speaker or Chairman of Committees standing and with head uncovered, except when raising a point of order during a division, when he must be seated and have his head covered. Again if a member is speaking from the floor of the House, i.e. the space between the Front Benches, he must not put a foot over the red line in the carpet on his own side, a rule originally introduced to prevent fighting in the House. The new member will quickly get used to customs which are commonplace in the procedure and are survivals from times long since past. One example is the shout 'Who goes home?' when the motion 'that this House do now adjourn' is carried. If there is a secret session, it will be initiated with the words 'Mr Speaker, I spy strangers', whereupon the Chamber and the public galleries are cleared of all who are not members of the House.

The new member will find that the House does not willingly endure the kind of rhetoric that is suitable for the platform or pulpit, though it will listen politely to his maiden or first speech, however bad it may be. He will learn to sit down and wait patiently when he is interrupted, and to keep his temper under pressure.

At the beginning of a new Parliament the members take the oath singly, sign the test roll and shake hands with the Speaker. It is customary for each member elected at a by-election to be introduced by two sponsors.

The oath prescribed by law is:

I swear by Almighty God that I will be faithful and bear true allegiance to Her Majesty Queen Elizabeth, her heirs and successors according to Law. So help me God.

Those who object to the form of the oath may make a corresponding affirmation.

The privileges of the House

The ancient privileges of the House are summed up in the Speaker's address at the opening of a new Parliament when, in the House of Lords accompanied by the 'faithful Commons', he asks royal approval of his appointment.

My Lords, I submit myself with all humility and gratitude to Her Majesty's gracious commands. It is now my duty, in the name and on behalf of the Commons of the United Kingdom, to lay claim by humble Petition to Her Majesty to all their ancient and undoubted rights and privileges; especially to freedom of speech in debate; to freedom from arrest; to free access to Her Majesty whenever occasion shall require; and that the most favourable construction shall be put upon all their proceedings. In regard to myself, I pray that if in the discharge of my duties I should inadvertently fall into any error, it may be computed to myself alone, and not to her Majesty's most faithful Commons. (Herbert Morrison, *Government and Parliament*, p.203.)

These 'ancient and undoubted privileges' were hard fought for in the reigns of Elizabeth I and the first two Stuarts. The very words recall Peter and Paul Wentworth, who dared to stand against the formidable Elizabeth, and Sir John Eliot, the courageous opponent of James I and Charles I, who died in the Tower and was pursued even after his death by the hatred of the monarch whom he resisted in the name of liberty. They conjure up the picture of Charles I entering the House and passing between rows of silent, standing members to the Speaker's Chair in his attempt to arrest the Five Members. We see the Speaker humbly kneeling before his sovereign, and saying, 'May it please your Majesty, I have neither eyes to see nor tongue to speak in this place, but as the House is pleased to direct me', and the King withdrawing frustrated to the cry 'Privilege, privilege'.

To-day the accent is no longer on privilege. The privilege of freedom of speech has been established by centuries of usage. While the member need not fear arbitrary arrest by the executive, he is no longer protected against arrest for indictable crimes or misdemeanours, except when within the precincts of the House. In the same way the right of peers to trial in the House of Lords for treason and felony has disappeared. Access to the Sovereign is easy on proper occasion, and the Queen refrains from public comment on proceedings in the House of Commons.

One of the most important committees of the House is the Committee of Privileges, which consists of ten members. Its function is to consider complaints of breach of the privilege of the House, which is something rather different from the privileges just mentioned. On the one hand there is a desire that the dignity, reputation, and proper working of the House shall be maintained and defended against breach of privilege; on the other hand there is no desire that the House's privileges should be exaggerated or extended, lest the democratic rights of the people should thereby be impaired.

Records and reports of proceedings in the House

The surviving records of Parliament before the Restoration in 1660 are scanty. The earliest entries in the 'Rolls of Parliament' relate to the Parliament of 1278, but there is no continuity, the chief source of information being the manuscript Journals of the Houses. Some of the most historic of these may be seen in the Members' Library—the volume from which the page bearing the Common's protestation was torn by James I; another of 1642 with an incomplete entry regarding the Five Members; a third with an erased entry regarding Cromwell's dissolution of the Long Parliament. In 1681 the House of Commons authorised the printing of the daily votes and proceedings, which has continued ever since, but in general until far into the eighteenth century the Commons regarded their deliberations as secret, and endeavoured to prevent any reporting of them. They carried their claim to privilege to such excessive lengths that in 1771 they committed the Lord Mayor of London, Alderman Brass Crosby, to the Tower for breach of privilege in a matter arising from the publication of debates. Since 1771, although the Commons' privilege was then upheld by the Court of Common Pleas, debates have been freely reported, but for a long time obstacles were put in the way of reporters. There was no proper accommodation for them, and until 1875 they were liable to be evicted with other strangers if one member 'spied' them. The first regular attempt to record debates was made in Cobbett's *Parliamentary History*. This was succeeded in 1803 by Cobbett's *Parliamentary Debates* which were taken over in 1812 by Thomas C. Hansard, Cobbett's name finally disappearing in 1822. The printing of the debates was maintained as a private venture till 1908, though with a subsidy from public money from 1855. Since 1909, each House has had its own staff of reporters, and official reports. In 1944 the old name Hansard was restored to the published debates, of which each member of Lords and Commons is entitled to receive a copy.

In addition to the official reporters, there are many press, or Gallery, reporters for whom, as for the representatives of the British Broadcasting Corporation, special seats are reserved in the galleries as well as special rooms in the precincts. There are also the Lobby, or political, correspondents who have the right of entry into the Members' Lobby, where they have direct contact with ministers and members. The interest of the public in parliamentary proceedings has been fostered by the Hansard Society. Only in times of emergency or when secrecy is thought to be essential are 'strangers spied', and the galleries cleared. Then there is only an official version of the debate published by the Speaker.

Several important cases since that of Brass Crosby have been fought about the publication of reports of parliamentary debates. One was *Stockdale* v. *Hansard* in which the plaintiff successfully sued Hansard, printer to the House of Commons, for libel contained in parliamentary papers. As a result, an Act of Parliament was passed by which a certificate from either the Lord Chancellor or the Speaker, that the publication was under the authority of either House, is a stay to all proceedings. And the case *Wason* v. *Walter* (the editor of *The Times*) established that the publications of words uttered in a parliamentary debate even if defamatory, and the comments on them, were not actionable if done *bona fide* in the public interest.

CHAPTER VI

THE HOUSE OF COMMONS—TIMETABLE, THE PASSING OF A LAW AND THE ELEMENTS OF PROCEDURE

A parliamentary session, week and day

Five years was adopted in the Parliament Act 1911 as the full length of a parliament's life as a compromise between the seven years then in force and the three years of the period from the Triennial Act of 1694 to the passing of the Septennial Act in 1716. The life of Parliament is divided into sessions lasting roughly a year. There is no statutory requirement that Parliament shall meet each year, but annual supply grants, the need to raise annual taxation (e.g. income tax), and the passing of the Army and Air Force (Annual) Act make this essential.

It is customary for the Queen, in person, to open each new session in late October or early November, and to read her Speech. This is composed by the Queen's Ministers, and sets out what the Government hopes to accomplish during the session. The Commons are summoned by the Queen's Messenger, Black Rod, to the House of Lords to hear the Speech; they listen to it standing at the 'bar' of the House. After the Speech, they return to their own House and begin a debate on the motion thanking Her Majesty for her most gracious

Speech. The Opposition takes this opportunity to attack the Government's programme. If the Government were defeated in the debate, it would resign. When this debate is over, Parliament settles down to its regular programme. It adjourns for the Christmas recess, and meets again in January. It then continues its work, with short recesses for Easter and Whitsun, until late July, or early August, when it is prorogued or adjourns for the long summer recess, which lasts until October or November. It is sometimes suggested that Parliament should meet for longer periods, but it must not be forgotten that the recesses are not times of rest for the ministers, who are often faced with big arrears of work in their departments. It is always possible in case of emergency for Parliament to be recalled at short notice.

In each week during the time the House of Commons is in session, it meets for a full day on Monday, Tuesday, Wednesday and Thursday, and for a shorter day on Friday. On the first four days it begins its sittings at half-past two, when the Speaker's procession solemnly enters the House. Prayers are then read by the Speaker's Chaplain, the Speaker standing at the Table and the members in their places.

During a short time after prayers and before question time, there is a period of some five or ten minutes during which a number of items may be taken, such as the Queen's answers to addresses, motions for new writs when a member has died or resigned, the presentation of public petitions and unopposed private business. The ancient right to present petitions to 'the Honourable the Commons of Great Britain and Northern Ireland in Parliament assembled' continues to exist, but public petitions to-day are of little significance. They must follow a prescribed form and comply with strict rules, and the petitioners must find a member to present the document. A member may present the petition by rising in his place and stating from whom it comes, the number of signatories, and the nature of the complaint, and concluding by reading the 'prayer' of the petition. No debate can take place. The Speaker directs that the petition be brought to the Table, and it then stands referred to the Committee on Public Petitions. Unopposed private business is composed of private bills to which no objection is raised. Should a private bill be opposed it must be brought forward on a fixed day at 7 p.m., when the business before the House will be interrupted and the bill taken.

Then follows question-time, which lasts a little less than an hour. During this time members put to ministers questions which they have 'put down' in advance by handing or sending them to the Clerks. A minister must have at least two days' notice of a question, so that the answer may be properly prepared. Most of the questions are answered in writing, but a member may, by marking his question with a star, insist on an oral answer. No minister can afford to take a question lightly, for he knows that a seemingly harmless enquiry may lead to an unexpected volume of criticism. When the minister has answered the question, the Speaker may allow one or two supplementary questions. If the member still find the answers given unsatisfactory, he can give notice that he will raise the matter again on the adjournment (see p. 81). As a great number of questions are put down, and the time allotted to answering them is short, they have to be carried through very quickly. Those 'starred' questions which have not been answered orally are answered in writing, unless the member still insists on an oral answer, in which case he must put the question down again. Questions form a very important part of the House of Commons' day, for by them members can bring before the House all kinds of matters of public importance. They give private members, and through them the general public, a control over the executive. If a member is particularly dissatisfied, he may move that the House adjourn under Standing Order No.9 to discuss 'a definite matter of urgent public importance', but it is only very occasionally that the Speaker will allow such a motion to be put.

After question-time there is another short period when a number of things may be done: 'private notice' questions may be taken—these may allow a long ministerial statement; there may be a statement regarding forthcoming business of the House; there may be a new member to be introduced, or a matter of personal explanation, or a question of privilege. Or there may be a motion for the adjournment of the House—of which more will be said later.

When question-time and the short period mentioned above are over, the Speaker calls on the Clerk of the House for the Orders of the Day, the name given to the agenda. The House now turns to the next part of its business, the debating and the passing of laws. This normally lasts till 10 p.m., when the motion 'that this House do now adjourn' gives members the opportunity of bringing forward on the adjournment minor matters, including grievances arising from unsatisfactory answers at question-time. At 10.30 p.m., the Speaker rises and announces, 'This House now stands adjourned.'

When urgent business makes it necessary, the Government can move the suspension of the Standing Order that the House adjourn at 10.30 p.m., and with its majority can carry the motion, in spite of the objections of the Opposition. The business under discussion then continues, and a long all-night sitting may result. Such sittings are less frequent than they were in the late nineteenth century, and they are naturally unpopular with members. They impose a severe strain on party discipline, and call for the utmost vigilance of the party Whips, especially the Government Whips, who must see that a 'quorum' is being maintained.

There are important matters that are 'exempted business' to which the rule (or Standing Order) does not apply, e.g. the Finance Bill and the Consolidated Fund Bills, and motions to approve or annul statutory instruments.

The timetable for a normal full day might therefore be:

2.30–2.35 p.m.	The Speaker's prayers
2.35–2.40 p.m.	Private business
2.40–3.30 p.m.	Question time
3.30–3.45 p.m.	Private notice questions etc.
3.45–10 p.m.	The Orders of the Day
(7.0– p.m.	Possible interruption to take a Private Bill)
10–10.30 p.m.	Debate on the adjournment

It remains to say something of the procedure on Fridays. Unless urgent pressure necessitates the taking of Fridays for Government business, this is private members' day. The House meets at 11 a.m.

and rises at 4.30 p.m. This arrangement is made to give members time to get home or to their constituencies for the week-end. Twenty Fridays are allotted for private members' bills or motions. The privilege of introducing such a bill or motion is obtained by ballot. Further mention of these is made on page 72. Thus Fridays, though producing little in the way of legislation, afford some of the five hundred 'back benchers' of all parties another opportunity of ventilating grievances, and of showing that they are not merely unimportant ciphers, voting at the party command.

The making of the laws

Among the most important of Parliament's functions are the making of laws, the voting of money, control and criticism of the executive, and the ventilating of grievances. Of these the most important is the making of laws, for from it are derived all Parliament's other functions. Parliament alone can make law or give power to other bodies to make law. Even the law derived from the decisions of the judges—case-law—is but the interpretation of statutes made by Parliament, or of rules made by Parliament or under its authority, and can be changed by act of Parliament.

With the making of statute law the sovereign, the House of Lords and the House of Commons are all concerned, though the part played by the House of Commons is predominant in the most important bills, and in all finance measures, which must originate there.

There are four main classes of parliamentary bills:

Public bills (other than finance bills)

Public bills (finance or money bills)

Public bills (Private members' bills)

and Private bills.

Of these public bills are those which, if passed, affect the whole community. The first two classes are sponsored and introduced by the Government, the third class is introduced by private members who have been lucky in the ballot for time on a Friday (see p. 72). The fourth class, private bills, deals with the special interests of a local authority, company or private person. In practice all measures that take up a substantial part of the time of the House of Commons are sponsored by the Government.

Public bills

Public bills other than finance bills. Before a public bill is brought before Parliament it must be agreed in principle by the Government. It must then be drafted. This is done by specialists in the Parliamentary Counsels' Office in consultation with the Government department concerned. The work is highly technical, and the staff of this office is heavily overworked. In due course, the minister responsible gives notice that the bill will be introduced, and on the appointed day comes the First Reading, which is purely formal. When called upon by the Speaker, the Minister in charge rises and bows, and the Clerk reads out the title. There is no discussion; a day is appointed for the Second Reading, and the Journal of the House records that the bill has had its First Reading. It is then printed in full, and copies are distributed to the members so that they can study it before the Second Reading. During the Second Reading a debate takes place on the principles of the bill, and a division may be forced. When the motion 'That the bill be read a second time' has been passed, it goes to committee where its details are examined, but before this is done, whenever a bill involves the spending of public money, a Financial Resolution is necessary authorising the expenditure. This resolution is passed in the Committee of the Whole House which considers financial matters. At the committee stage controversial bills and all bills of the highest importance are referred to the Committee of the Whole House which is presided over by the Chairman of Committees (see p. 60). The majority of bills are referred to one or other of the Standing Committees (see p. 77). When the Committee has done its work the Report stage is reached. The minister in charge of the bill may accept the suggestions of the Committee and frame appropriate amendments. The hard work having been done, the Third Reading usually takes little time. The principles of the bill are no longer open to discussion, and only verbal amendments, i.e. amendments of phrasing etc., are taken.

The majority of bills originate in the House of Commons, but any bill, except a money bill, may originate in the House of Lords. The stages in the House of Lords are similar to those outlined for the House of Commons. When a bill has been passed in one House and is sent to the other, it must go through similar stages in the other House. The committee stage in the Lords is usually carried through in a Committee of the Whole House. One House may suggest amendments to a bill originated in the other; these may be accepted or rejected, or a compromise solution may be found. When and if the House of Lords refuses to pass a bill already passed by the Commons, the provisions of the Parliament Act of 1911 and 1949 may be invoked, and the bill go to the Queen for signature, but the Lords' opposition is seldom carried so far.

The Royal Assent is given in the House of Lords by Lords Commissioners who hold a commission from Her Majesty authorising them to act for her. The Royal Assent is usually given to batches of bills at the end of a session, but in emergency is given at once. When the Royal Assent is given the Speaker is summoned, and with other members of the Commons stands at the bar of the House of Lords.

Finance bills. A finance or money bill is in a special class, owing to the limitations set on the power of the Lords by custom and by the Parliament Act of 1911. Any bill is a money bill if it is certified as such by the Speaker. When it has passed the Commons, it is sent to the Lords. If it is not passed there within a month it may be presented for the sovereign's assent forthwith. Further details of the procedure will be found in chapter x.

Private members' bills. Private members' bills are classed as public bills because in the most unlikely event of their being passed they affect the public at large. The private member who has been successful in the ballot and who wishes to introduce a bill must draft it himself or obtain the services of an expert. He may obtain a place for the First Reading on the Order Paper for a Friday, or he may introduce it under what is known as the ten-minute rule at the end of question time. If the House agrees it goes forward to a Second Reading. But there most private members' bills end. For most measures involve expenditure of public money in some way, and financial resolutions can only be introduced by the Government. Occasionally the Government may make room in the timetable for a private member's bill, or may adopt it. But in general the private member, having had his fling, accepts the inevitable fate of his bill.

Private bills

Private bills come before Parliament in great numbers. Their usual purpose is to obtain permission to interfere in some way with the property rights of private individuals or public bodies. The promoters of such bills are usually public authorities or companies. The bills are drafted by a specialised group of lawyers known as parliamentary agents. Many private bills originate in the House of Lords. The promoters, having obtained leave to introduce the bill, hand it to the Private Bills Office of the House of Commons or to the Clerk of the Parliaments in the Lords. Notice of the bill has to be given to all parties interested or affected. Most private bills are agreed to in private and accepted without debate, but if one is opposed it goes to a Private Bills' Committee of four members in the case of the House of Commons, or of five in the House of Lords. Procedure in these committees is judicial. The promoters and the opponents argue their cases through counsel. If the committee disapproves of the bill it fails; if it approves its views are accepted by Parliament. Even when a private bill is unopposed it must still be carefully examined by a committee to see that no new principle of law is being established by it.

Private Bill procedure has been superseded in many instances by Provisional Order Bills which confirm provisional orders made by a Government department. The local authority or company approach a Government department for permission to carry out some work, the department conducts an enquiry, issues an order and presents the Provisional Order Bill to Parliament. This is usually unopposed, and the method is quicker, surer, and cheaper than a private bill, and it is likely to become more and more used.

Delegated legislation

Such is the volume of legislation required in these days, that Parliament cannot find time to do all the detailed work involved. Delegation is therefore necessary. The idea is not new. The right to legislate in detailed matters, within the limits prescribed, has long been given by private act to companies and authorities, whose by-laws are enforceable in the courts. Somewhat similar powers of issuing detailed orders and regulations are given to government departments and to the great corporations like the Gas, Electricity and Transport authorities, and the British Broadcasting Corporation. The resulting regulations often have considerable effects upon the citizen. The alarm expressed in legal circles led to the setting up of a strong committee to investigate ministers' powers. The Statutory Instruments Act 1946 has attempted to bring about some order and uniformity in procedure with regard to such legislation. In general the Order must be laid on the Table of the House for forty sitting days, during which period a member may move a prayer to annul it. If no objection is raised, it becomes law. What appears an exceptional delegation of powers was made by Parliament to the Assembly of the Church of England under the Enabling Act of 1919. By this, the Assembly may pass any measures it wishes concerning the Church of England. These measures are presented to Parliament, and examined by the Ecclesiastical Committee. If they are then sanctioned by resolution of each House, they are submitted for the Royal Assent. The most important measure that has come before Parliament in this way was the Prayer Book Measure of 1928, which the House of Commons rejected.

As delegated legislation can be and often is of great importance, and may vitally affect the liberty of the subject, it is essential that Parliament should exercise vigilance and control. This is true in war time as well as in peace time. An example of an Act conferring exceptional powers in peace time is the Emergency Powers Act of 1920, which enables the executive to legislate by orders in council to safeguard the supply of food and essential services. The Government

74

must lay the order before Parliament within seven days; it lapses automatically if it is not renewed after seven days. These powers were invoked on 31 May 1955, during the strike called by the Associated Society of Locomotive Engineers and Firemen.

The Order Paper

The Order Paper, or Vote, is issued on every day on which Parliament is in session, except Monday—the paper for that day being issued on Saturday. It consists of the minutes of the previous day given in a brief and formal manner, a list of reports and documents that have been placed on the Table of the House, a list of private bills due for or under consideration, and Notices of Motion and Orders of the Day, the official programme or agenda for the day. The items must be taken in the order they appear, but the House seldom covers all the 'orders' on the paper. Two items, Supply—Committee and Ways and Means—Committee, usually appear, and it is customary for items above these on the Order Paper to be taken, and those below to be deferred. The remaining sheets of the Order Paper consist of notices of questions, motions and amendments handed in the previous day, and papers and minutes of Standing and other Committees.

Precedent and Standing Orders

One of the chief difficulties of Parliament, and particularly of the House of Commons, at the present time is to avoid inefficiency through being completely immersed in business, especially government business. Although custom and precedent determine the manner in which much of what Parliament does is accomplished, there is a strong determination to prevent archaic usages from blocking progress. The force of precedent is revealed by the influence of Erskine May's treatise on the Law, Privilege, Proceedings and Usage of Parliament. This huge work of 1,000 pages has grown out of a book first published in 1844. Erskine May, who spent a lifetime in the service of Parliament and was Clerk of the House from 1871 to 1886, saw it through nine editions before his death in 1886. Since then it has been revised and added to by successive Clerks; the fifteenth edition

75

was edited by Lord Campion, Clerk of the House from 1937 to 1948. Standing Orders as well as customs, precedents and Speaker's rulings are found in this volume. One of the features of parliamentary procedure has been the readiness with which the House agrees to a change in Standing Orders when it is thought desirable. Standing Orders relative to public business number 112, and relative to private business over 200. They are published by the Stationery Office, and any changes in them find their way into the next edition of Erskine May. The reading and digesting of Standing Orders is one of the first tasks of the conscientious member.

Debates and committees

Much of the business of the Commons is conducted in the House, but important functions are also performed by the Committees of the Whole House and by Standing and Select Committees. The main business in the House is conducted in debates on a definite motion or resolution. Any important motion or resolution is moved by a leading Government or Opposition speaker—motions moved by a member of the Government or by a member of the Privy Council need no seconder. The member in whose name the motion stands may make a formal gesture 'I beg to move' when the motion is an Order of the Day, or he may make a speech. Standing Orders impose no time limit on speeches, but in fact limitations are imposed by the patience or impatience of members, and more effectively by the timetable drawn up, often by agreement between the party Whips. In a formal debate in the House, no member may speak twice, except the intro-ducer of the motion or another member of his party, who has the opportunity of replying to criticisms at the end of the debate. Committee procedure is less formal. Members may speak more than once, but long set speeches are frowned on.

The Whole House as a committee, sitting under the Chairman of Committees, considers bills of major importance, Supply, Ways and Means, and money resolutions. The Committee of Supply considers details of the expenses of the public services, but in the course of its debates, for which twenty-six days are set aside in each session, the conduct of the Government and of particular ministers can be re-viewed and criticised. The Committee of Ways and Means discusses and passes the resolutions on which the Finance Bill is based and authorises payments from the Consolidated Fund. The House resolves itself into the Committee of the Whole House when the Order of the Day, e.g. Ways and Means—Committee is read out, and the Chairman takes his place at the Table in the seat normally occupied by the Clerk of the House, the mace having been placed beneath the table. The committee ends when a motion 'That the Chairman do report progress, and ask leave to sit again' has been passed. Thereupon the Chairman leaves the chair, the mace is re-placed and the Speaker resumes the Chair. The appointed day for the resumption of the committee is announced, and the House resumes its business.

Standing Committees, usually five or six in number, do valuable work on bills, other than those of the first importance, after they have passed their second reading. The Standing Committees, except the Standing Committee on Scottish Bills, usually consist of twenty members nominated by the Committee of Selection more or less in the proportion of the parties in the House, with twenty to thirty other members with special knowledge of the subject of the bill added. The Chairmen of the Standing Committees are appointed from the Speaker's Panel. The Scottish Committee consists of all the Scottish members. The normal quorum for Standing Committees is fifteen.

There are also sessional Select Committees, e.g. the Public Accounts Committee, the Committee of Selection, and Select Com-mittees set up *ad hoc*, i.e. for a special purpose, to carry out en-quiries which require the hearing of evidence and necessitate the 'power to send for persons, papers and records'.

Committees, apart from the large Scottish Committee and of course Committees of the Whole House, meet on the 'Committee Floor' in the mornings, and their meetings impose a severe strain on the patience and assiduity of the members.

Mention may also be made of the private bill groups, committees of four nominated by the Committee of Selection to consider private bills, and the occasional Joint Committees with the Lords which are really joint Select Committees.

Party differences tend to be less obvious in committee, where the atmosphere is informal and friendly. A genuine desire to produce a workable measure often overcomes the wish to make party points. It is the aim of every Chairman when he reports back to the House to have accomplished something really worth while.

The Closure, the Guillotine and the Kangaroo

Many of the Standing Orders of the House owe their origin to the hectic days of the last quarter of the nineteenth century, when the Irish Nationalists adopted a course of concerted obstruction of public business in an attempt to force Parliament to grant Home Rule. The most famous occasion was in 1881, when the House of Commons was kept in session from 4 p.m. on a Monday afternoon until 9.30 a.m. on the following Wednesday. The automatic interruption of business at 10 p.m., and the Speaker's rising at 10.30 p.m., to announce that 'This House now stands adjourned' prevents this kind of filibustering, although of course Standing Orders can always be suspended by motion of the House.

In order to bring debates within bounds, further methods have been adopted. One is the Closure, introduced in 1881. The method is the moving of the motion 'That the question be now put.' The Speaker has to use tact and discretion in accepting such a motion, and has to gauge the feeling of the House, but if it is put and a hundred members support it, then the main question in debate must be put and the debate thus terminated. Corollaries of this are the Guillotine and the Kangaroo. The guillotine is 'closure by compartments' in accordance with a programme drawn up by the Government, and enforced in spite of the objections of the Opposition to an interference with the freedom of debate.

The following is an example:

Transport Bill (Allocation of Time) 24 November 1952. The Leader of the House, The Lord Privy Seal (Mr Harry Crookshank) moved (at 4.1 p.m.)

78

'That the following provisions shall apply to the remaining Proceedings on the Transport Bill.

1. The Proceedings in Committee shall be completed in seven allotted days.

2. The Proceedings on Consideration shall be completed in two allotted days.

3. The Proceedings on Third Reading shall be completed in one allotted day and shall be brought to a conclusion at half-past ten on that day.

4. The Business Committee shall report their recommendation to the House—

(a) as to Proceedings in Committee not later than Monday 1 December.

(b) as to Proceedings on Consideration not later than the fourth day on which the House sits in 1953.

5. No motion shall be made to postpone any clause, Schedule, new Clause or new Schedule, but the Recommendations of the Business Committee may include alterations in the order in which the Clauses, new Clauses, Schedules are to be taken in Committee.'

Then follow eleven clauses to ensure the progress of the bill in committee and after. The subsequent debate on the Allocation of Time Motion occupies 120 columns of Hansard and lasted till 10.40, when the House finally divided on the main question: Ayes 301; Noes 275.

This procedure can be adopted at the committee stage of a bill in a Standing Committee (on a motion passed in the House itself) as well as in the Committee of the Whole House. The Kangaroo is the means by which the Speaker or the Chairman of a Committee has power to select for discussion only those amendments which he thinks representative of important sections of opinion.

Divisions

When the question is put in the House or in the Committee of the Whole House, the Speaker or Chairman listens to the cries of 'Aye' or 'No' and decides which are the more powerful. If his opinion is challenged, as it will be on all important matters, electric bells are rung through the corridors and adjacent rooms to summon members to a division. After about five minutes, the Speaker cries, 'Lock the doors.' The 'Ayes' then pass through the lobby to the right, and the 'Noes' through that to the left. The members are counted by tellers, two for each lobby, who report to the Speaker or Chairman the result of the division. The business of continually passing through the division lobbies takes up a great deal of time when an important measure is being discussed, and taxes the patience and diligence of the member. But he knows that he is under the eye of his party Whips who take careful note of his presence or absence, and call him to account if he is negligent in his duties.

If a member wishes to raise a point of order during a division, when most members are on their feet, he must do so sitting and with his head covered. This custom causes some difficulty as nowadays few members wear hats.

The Quorum

The 'Quorum' or minimum number of members who must be present during a debate is forty, including the Speaker. The Speaker must satisfy himself that a quorum is present when he takes the Chair, but his responsibility for observing numbers ends there. The number actually present in the House during an uninteresting debate or a tedious speech is often less than forty. The Speaker does not note this unless a member draws his attention 'to the fact that less than forty members are present'. If this is done, he orders strangers to withdraw. The electric bells are rung, and at the end of two minutes the Speaker begins to count. Usually sufficient members emerge to make up the necessary quorum. If they do not, the House stands adjourned till the next sitting day. By custom, the House does not notice the lack of a 'quorum' during the dinner-hour (8.15 p.m. to 9.15 p.m.) or before 4 p.m. on Mondays to Thursdays, and 1 p.m. on Fridays. The Speaker himself does not notice the lack of a quorum within a reasonable time after a count has been taken. It is also customary for him to be lenient about the quorum during private members' time on Fridays.

The quorum required in the Committee of the Whole House is also forty. If the Chairman, on a count being asked for, finds that less than forty members are present, the House resumes, the facts are reported to the Speaker, and, if a quorum is not found, the House is adjourned.

The Adjournment

Motions to adjourn in the House of Commons do not comply with the ordinary rules of debate, which require that there must be a proposal before the House to which members can speak, and that speeches must be to the point. Motions to adjourn are of four kinds. Firstly the normal daily motion 'That this House do now adjourn'; this is moved at 10 p.m., the 'hour of interruption', in accordance with Standing Orders. There follows half an hour, during which a member may (with the Speaker's permission) discuss any subject which does not involve legislation, or may raise again a question to which in his opinion an unsatisfactory answer has been given at question time. Secondly there is the motion to adjourn moved by a member of the Government immediately after question-time before any item on the order paper is taken. This, if agreed, gives an opportunity for a debate on a matter of special importance. Thirdly there is a motion, moved at the same time, for the adjournment of the House to consider 'a definite matter of urgent public importance'. To make out a *prima facie* case for the acceptance of such a motion a member must have the support of at least forty members. If he has more than ten supporters but less than forty, the Speaker may put the matter of acceptance to the vote, but in general the Speaker, knowing well the business already before the House, will only accept such a motion if he is clear that the 'public importance' is really urgent. If the motion is accepted it is taken at 7 p.m., other business being interrupted. The fourth kind of 'motion to adjourn' is the dilatory motion introduced to hold up proceedings in the course of the debate in the House or in committee. The Speaker (or Chairman) may refuse such a motion if he considers it an abuse of the rules of the House, or he may put it without debate, or he may allow a debate strictly relevant to the desirability of the adjournment.

When a debate occurs on a 'motion to adjourn' moved by a

member of the Government, usually the Chief Whip, after questions, the minute will read 'Adjournment—motion made and question put "That this House do now adjourn"' and the result of the division will be given. The subject of the debate, which may be of great importance, is not mentioned, nor is there any decision reached which is binding on the Government.

The Whips

The activities of Whips are mysterious to those outside Parliament, but very real to members. The Government Chief Whip is one of the chief counsellors of the Prime Minister, and, with the Leader of the House, arranges the programme of business. He acquaints the Prime Minister with the state of opinion within his party, and may be called upon to advise him on ministerial appointments and on the distribution of honours. He has frequent contacts with the Opposition Chief Whip, who with him constitutes 'the usual channels' through which Government and Opposition negotiate with regard to the use of the time of the House. By this means the Chief Whip is able to discover what degree of opposition to government measures is likely.

Both Government and Opposition appoint deputy and other Whips, whose duties are particularly to maintain contact with individual members and to see that they are regular in their attendance, especially at divisions. The usual practice is for each junior Whip to be responsible for a group of members.

The Government Chief Whip is Parliamentary Secretary to the Treasury, and, like his deputy and a number of the assistant Whips, is paid a salary in respect of the office he holds. The Opposition Whips have no such advantage and receive only their salaries as members of Parliament. In the eighteenth century the Chief Whip was known as the Patronage Secretary, but nowadays he does not dispense patronage in the wide sense understood in the days of Walpole and the 'King's Friends'.

The discussions between the Chief Whips of the Government and Opposition party or parties is a good example of the British method in politics. Such discussions are said to take place behind the Speaker's Chair. However hostile the parties may be in the House and in debates, personal regard and friendship between political opponents is possible. Cordial relations between the Chief Whips are particularly important, since it is in the interest of all that, whenever possible, the programme of the day shall be mutually agreed, including the hour for concluding a debate. To this end, the Opposition Chief Whip receives advance notice of the business the Government proposes to take during the following week. Any requests from the Opposition to the Leader of the House are referred for discussion through 'the usual channels' and after some bargaining a programme is often agreed.

In days of small majorities, the Whips have a difficult time in assuring themselves that there will be a maximum attendance on all important occasions. They have to persuade rather than coerce members. And they also have to convey to the Chief Whip the genuine grievances of back benchers. Some of their difficulties are reduced by members on opposite sides 'pairing', i.e. cancelling out one another's votes through absence, but this is discouraged for the most important measures. As mentioned on page 82, it is the task of a Whip, usually the Chief Whip, to move the Adjournment to provide the opportunities for an important debate.

A whip of another but of a complementary kind is the documentary whip. This is an outline of the chief business of the following week and is usually posted to members by the party Whips on Fridays. It gives the members instructions in polite terms as to what is expected of them. The relative importance of the items is gauged by the number of times they are underlined. A member who is in repeated opposition to his party may be deprived of the whip or may decline any longer to receive it, or may even apply to receive the whip of another party. The issue of whips may appear an infringement of the independence of the member, but it must be remembered that members are frequently not present for the whole of a debate, and may rely on the written whip for information.

The following is an example of a Conservative Party whip covering the last two days of a week:

ON THURSDAY 20 MARCH, the House will meet at 2.30 p.m.
Report stage of the Budget Resolutions
No Debate is in order, but several Divisions will take place immediately after questions.

Your attendance at 3.15 p.m. prompt is essential.

═══
═══

═══

Committee stages of:
Export Guarantees Bills;
Cinematograph Films Production (Special Loans) Bill, Miners' Welfare Bill; Report and 3rd Reading.

Your attendance is particularly requested after the Budget

═══

Resolutions are passed, unless you have obtained a pair.

═══

At 7 p.m. By direction of the Chairman of Ways and Means:
West Hartlepool Bill; 2nd Reading

ON FRIDAY 21 MARCH the House will meet at 11 a.m.
Private Members' Motions
1. Organisation of Distribution (Mr H. Hughes).
2. Blitzed Towns (Mr Morley).
3. Use of machinery and double shifts (Mr Foll).

Your attendance is requested

PATRICK BUCHAN-HEPBURN.

CHAPTER VII

THE HOUSE OF LORDS

Membership

The House of Lords, alone of the second chambers of the world, has retained its hereditary character. The qualification for membership, with few additions, remains as it was in the days before the Tudors. Originally, it was the right to receive an individual writ of summons to Parliament which established the hereditary nature of a peerage, but in the fourteenth century peerages were created by royal letters patent, and holders of these new peerages, like the old feudal nobility, received writs of summons. The Wars of the Roses in the fifteenth century so reduced the old nobility that only thirty-six lay peers were summoned by Henry VII to his first Parliament. The membership of the House of Lords was further reduced in the reign of Henry VIII by the dissolution of the monasteries, which removed the great abbots from the House of Lords. Even at the end of Elizabeth I's reign only sixty peers were entitled to writs of summons. Thus the vast majority of present-day peerages date from the seventeenth century and after.

The House of Lords to-day includes the royal princes, dukes, marquesses, earls, barons, peers representative of the Scottish and Irish nobility, archbishops, bishops and law-lords. Hereditary peers with seats in Parliament number about 850. There are sixteen peers representing the ancient Scottish nobility and elected afresh for each Parliament in accordance with the terms of the Act of Union of 1707, since which no new Scottish peerages have been created. The Act of Union with Ireland 1801 brought in twenty-eight Irish peers elected for life. No new Irish peers have been created since 1898, and there have been no elections since the creation of the Irish Free State in 1922. There are now only five Irish representative peers and in time the representation will die out. Irish peers who are not elected to the House of Lords may, if elected as M.P.s, sit in the House of Commons,

but Scottish non-representative peers may not. The ecclesiastical representation, the remnant of what was once the separate House,
or Estate, of the Clergy, consists of the Archbishops of Canterbury
and York, the Bishops of London, Durham, and Winchester, and the
twenty-one other bishops sitting in order of seniority. Whereas, in
the Middle Ages, the ecclesiastical members of the House of Lords
were usually in a majority, they are now, as is clear from the above
figures, only a small minority. The nine law-lords are the only life-
peers. They are appointed to strengthen the House of Lords in its
capacity as the final Court of Appeal, their creation having been first
sanctioned by the Appellate Jurisdiction Act of 1876. Though there
are a number of peeresses in their own right, i.e. holders of titles
which for some special reason may descend through the female as
well as the male line, no women are summoned to sit in the House of
Lords.

It must be made clear that not everyone who is called Lord is the
holder of a peerage. The courtesy title of Lord is given in some cases
to the son of a living peer, but it does not entitle him to a writ of
summons, and in law he remains a commoner. This fact has had a
profound effect on English history, for it has prevented the growth of
a big caste of nobility, which in France in the days before the French
Revolution amounted to thousands.

Judicial functions

The House of Lords has retained from the Middle Ages certain
judicial functions which the House of Commons does not possess. It
is the final Court of Appeal from the English law courts. These
judicial functions lapsed for a considerable period, but have been
fully revived since the Judicature Act of 1873 and Appellate Jurisdiction Act of 1876. It was to strengthen the House of Lords in the
performance of these important duties that the Lords of Appeal in
Ordinary or Law-Lords were created as a special class of non-
hereditary and salaried peers. When the House of Lords sits as the
final Court of Appeal, only the Lord Chancellor and former Lord
Chancellors, other peers who have held high judicial office, and the

salaried Lords of Appeal take part in the proceedings, though there is no law that prevents other members from being present. As the House of Lords hears appeals from Scotland as well as from England, Wales and Northern Ireland, it must include peers skilled in Scots law. Two other judicial functions formerly exercised by the Lords have ceased, e.g. the impeachment of an individual before the House of Lords by the House of Commons for 'high crimes and mis-demeanours' of a political nature, a form of trial which has not been used since 1806, and the trial of peers for treason and felony, which was abolished by the Criminal Justice Act of 1948. A third function, the right of deciding peerage claims, is now exercised by the Committee of Privileges of the House of Lords.

The judicial functions of the House of Lords are technically exercised in an ordinary sitting of the House, but they take place in the morning, and the Lord Chancellor when presiding over the House as a Court does not sit on the Woolsack. Another difference is that the sittings of the House in its judicial capacity can continue after Parliament has been dissolved. The judgments are delivered by the Lords who are acting as judges in the form of speeches to the House, and the House gives its decision by majority vote.

Legislative functions

The legislative functions and procedure of the House of Lords are similar to those of the House of Commons. Legislation on any matter except finance can originate in the House of Lords, and as in the Commons a bill there must pass through its first, second and third readings. As the Lords' time is not occupied to any extent with the discussion of finance matters, its sittings are shorter than those of the Commons, and there is much less formality about the proceedings. Government business is only given priority when the programme becomes congested.

The Lord Chancellor, sitting upon the Woolsack, presides over the House of Lords, except when it is in committee. Unlike the Speaker of the House of Commons, the Lord Chancellor is an important political member of the Government. He is also the leading member of the country's judicial system. The Lord Chancellor, unlike the Speaker, takes part in debates. When he does so, he moves aside from the Woolsack and speaks as a peer. The Lord Chancellor, unlike the Speaker, may exercise his right to vote, but he has no casting vote. On a few occasions in history, the Lord Chancellor has not been a peer, and then he had no vote in the House of Lords. The Woolsack on which the Lord Chancellor sits is a large red leather-covered cushion, which tradition says is a reminder of the days when wool was the chief wealth and source of revenue of the country.

Although any public bill, except a financial measure, may be introduced in the House of Lords, in practice, owing to the modern predominance of the House of Commons, all bills of the first importance are introduced into the Commons. This results in much congestion in the Commons, and a dearth of work in the Lords.

Limitation of powers

The restrictions on the power of the Lords in dealing with financial matters have been traced back to 1407 in the reign of Henry IV, but the strict limitation can be traced only to the reign of Charles II, when in the year 1671 the Commons resolved 'that in all aids given to the King by the Commons, the rate or tax ought not to be altered by the Lords'. This principle was accepted by the Lords, but disputes have taken place between the Houses as to what constitutes a finance measure or money bill. These differences became acute in 1860 when the Lords did not agree that a bill to repeal the paper duty was a money bill, and again in a much more acute form in 1909 when the Lords rejected the Finance Bill on the grounds that the principles it introduced went far beyond the limits of finance. The full claims of the Commons, that the Lords should not originate any legislative proposal imposing a charge on the people or interfere with any legislative proposals originating in the Commons by altering the amount of a charge or its method of collection, have never been accepted by the Lords. It is clear that a strict adherence to such claims would prevent the Lords from carrying out any effective work at all, since there is scarcely any Act passed by Parliament that does

88

not involve the expenditure of public money. On most occasions there has been give-and-take between the two Houses. The Lords do valuable work in the initiation of private bills, and in the careful examination of the clauses of bills sent up by the House of Commons. Many of their amendments are accepted by the Commons, provided that the underlying principles of the Act are not affected. The long experience of some of the peers, especially in overseas administration, is often valuable. On the whole, therefore, the relations between the Houses are friendly and there is much useful co-operation.

There have, however, been historic clashes, the most noteworthy of which took place in 1832 and 1909. On the former occasion, the House of Lords rejected the Reform Bill, and only passed it when the Government of the day made it clear that it would advise the King, William IV, to create sufficient peers to get the measure through. On the latter, the House of Lords rejected the Finance Bill of 1909, which proposed taxation of land values and increased income tax, and which was held to have a social as well as a fiscal objective. The threat to create peers was again heard but was not carried into effect. The Finance Bill of 1909 was only one of several important measures which had been passed by the House of Commons with its Liberal majority, and which had been rejected by the Lords, who thus seemed to be reopening the question of supremacy of the Commons in matters of finance, as well as questioning the mandate given to them by the electors. The Liberals twice appealed to the country in the general elections of January and December 1910 before taking strong action against the Lords. A more recent clash occurred in 1948, when the Lords refused to pass the Labour Government's bill to nationalise the iron and steel industries. The 1909 and 1948 clashes led to Acts that have substantially reduced the power of the House of Lords.

The Parliament Acts of 1911 and 1949

The main provisions of the Parliament Act of 1911 were:

1. If the House of Lords withheld its assent to a money bill for more than a month, it might be presented for the King's assent, and become law without the Lords' concurrence. A 'money bill' was

defined as any bill certified to be such by the Speaker after consulting two specially appointed members of the House of Commons.

2. If a bill, other than a money bill, was passed by the Commons in three successive sessions, it might, after the third rejection, be presented for the sovereign's assent, and would then become law.

3. The maximum length of a Parliament's life was reduced from seven to five years.

Since 1911, the Speaker has exercised his power of certifying bills as money bills with the impartiality traditional in holders of his office, and the Lords have seldom pressed their objection to a measure up to the point of rejecting it after it has thrice passed the Commons.

The accession to office in 1945 of a Labour Government, for the first time possessed of a secure majority in the House of Commons, but with only a handful of supporters in the Lords, brought about a new situation. The Lords frequently exercised their right of amendment of important measures. Many of their debates reached a high standard, and their suggestions often showed restraint and wisdom. The Commons, with equal judgment, often incorporated the suggestions of the Upper House in the final version of an Act. But a serious and irreconcilable difference of opinion at length occurred. The Lords were steadfast in their opposition to the Iron and Steel Nationalisation Bill, partly because of its principle and partly because they held that the Labour Government should not press so controversial a measure without a clear mandate from the people, which could only be obtained by holding another general election. To this the Labour Government were not prepared to agree and, after failing to devise a measure that had the support of all parties, it passed through the Commons the Parliament Act of 1949, which reduced the period for which the Lords could delay a measure passed by the Commons from two sessions to one session. In this way, they ensured that the Iron and Steel Bill would become law before the end of that Parliament.

The future of the House of Lords

The future of the House of Lords has been discussed on many occasions during the last fifty years. The problem of reform is two-fold; it concerns composition and powers. It is obvious that the composition of the House at present is a relic from bygone days, when the aristocracy and the landowners controlled the Government, and the mass of the people had no vote. It is equally obvious that something ought to be done to bring it more into line with modern social and political developments. But it is clear that, if this is done and the structure of the House is substantially changed, its functions must also be reformed, for few first-rate statesmen would voluntarily choose to be exiled to an assembly shorn of all real power and of most of its influence.

The two problems then interlock. Let us first consider the composition of the House to-day. Over eight hundred and fifty peers have the right to sit but except on state occasions such as the opening of Parliament by the sovereign in the House of Lords, when the peers attend in their robes and their ladies are resplendent in the galleries, few of them attend their House. Only about a hundred are regularly seen in its precincts. The regular attenders are for the most part those who can make a real contribution to the counsels of the nation, former ministers, former Viceroys and Governors-General of the Dominions, men ennobled for singular service to the community, together with peers whose family tradition leads them to take part in politics and those who have been given titles to provide the Labour cause with supporters in the Lords. These men between them bring to their deliberations much experience and wisdom. On most occasions they show restraint even when faced with measures distasteful to them. Their debates and amendments often set example of statesmanship to the Commons. But they are not dependent upon popular election, nor are they answerable to the general public for their conduct of affairs. Their powers are circumscribed by the Parliament Acts of 1911 and 1949 and by the control of the Government over legislation.

It is fairly generally agreed that the abolition of the second chamber is not desirable, for even in its present form it relieves the House of Commons by initiating and discussing fully a great deal of minor legislation and bý revising effectively many of the bills sent up to it. The House of Lords, though lacking the elective character consonant with modern democracy, performs its legal functions effectively and acts as a brake upon hasty legislation. Its reform is long overdue, but it is doubtful whether there is any body of opinion which seriously supports the extension of its powers. The Conservative Government of 1952 expressed its desire for an all-party agreement upon reform. It remains to be seen whether any measure can be produced that puts forward an acceptable proposal for a second chamber constituted in some more up-to-date manner than the present House of Lords. More than forty years ago the preamble to the Parliament Act stated, 'It is intended to substitute for the House of Lords as it at present exists a second chamber constituted on a popular instead of a hereditary basis.' The problem how to accomplish this has not yet been solved.

CHAPTER VIII

THE PRIME MINISTER AND THE CABINET

Historical development

The system whereby the executive government is carried on by a Prime Minister, his cabinet and other ministers not in the cabinet, who in their turn are dependent on Parliament, has been evolved not by definite plan or in accordance with a theory of government, but through governmental needs.

The ministers of the Tudors were personal servants of the sovereign; the ministers of the Stuarts were chosen according to the monarch's whim; even in the reigns of William and Mary and Anne, when the parties were taking shape and some of the monarch's powers were restricted by the legislation of the Revolution Settlement, the sovereign still selected ministers where he or she liked. Although this freedom of appointment and dismissal of ministers was retained by the early Hanoverian kings, the constitutional trend helped Parliament to strengthen its control over these ministers. The Hanoverians came to the throne in 1714 with a parliamentary title given them by the Act of Settlement of 1701 and they came to a political situation affected by the growing supremacy of Parliament in the constitution. The King's ministers now found that, unless they could command a working majority in Parliament, they could not carry on his government, and this fact indirectly influenced the King's choice. Walpole clearly expressed this dependence on Parliament in 1739 when he said in debate:

I have lived long enough in this world, Sir, to know that the safety of a minister lies in his having the approbation of this House. Former ministers, Sir, neglected it, and therefore they fell; I have always made it my first study to obtain it and therefore I hope to stand.

The early eighteenth century also saw the definite emergence of the cabinet council, the ancestor of the cabinet as we know it to-day. After 1688, the Privy Council had become increasingly unsuitable as the Crown's advisory body on policy: it was large and unwieldy and reflected too many different political opinions, and therefore did not accord with the growing tendency of the Crown to choose its advisers from one political party only. Consequently a smaller, more informal body, known as the cabinet council, came into existence. Presided over by the sovereign, it included the chief minister and the great officers of state. Its further development was influenced by the mere chance that the first Hanoverian king could speak little or no English and was not interested in English politics. By 1718 George I ceased to preside over it, and thereafter the cabinet council became a meeting of ministers only. It was not long before this cabinet of ministers became further divided into a full outer body and a much smaller inner directing cabinet, composed of the half-dozen or so ministers at the head of the important departments of state.

At this point came the man who was able to exploit its opportunities—Robert Walpole, who was the King's chief minister from 1721 to 1742.

It was Walpole [wrote Hearn] who first administered the Government in accordance with his own views of our political requirements. It was Walpole who first conducted the business of the country in the House of Commons. It was Walpole who in the conduct of that business first insisted upon the support of his measures by all servants of the Crown who had seats in Parliament. It was under Walpole that the House of Commons became the dominant power in the State, and rose in ability and influence as well as in actual power above the House of Lords. And it was Walpole who set the example of quitting his office while he still retained the undiminished affection of his King for the avowed reason that he had ceased to possess the confidence of the House of Commons.

Sir John Marriott, who quotes these words adds, 'We have in this passage an admirably succinct summary of the essential principles on which Cabinet Government depends.' Accident had brought about the absence of the sovereign from the council; Walpole's mastery of Parliament enabled him with confidence to expect its support; his temperament required the obedience of those whom he chose to be his colleagues, and his personality led to the general recognition that he was their head.

The office of Prime Minister

The office of Prime Minister was in Walpole's time, and for two hundred years after, an unofficial post. Walpole himself objected to the designation Prime Minister and the term remained repugnant to Englishmen for a century or more. The post has remained unsalaried to this day and was unrecognised by law until the passage of the Ministers of the Crown Act in 1937. Even to-day the Prime Minister receives his salary of £10,000 a year as First Lord of the Treasury.

Through the years of Whig domination in the eighteenth century the office was taking shape, and during the long tenure of the Prime Ministership by the younger Pitt from 1783 to 1801 its position was fully established. No sovereign after George III attempted to choose his ministers except from the predominant party in the House of

Commons. From that time forward, the position of the Prime Minister is clear. He chooses his cabinet and ministers; he presides over the cabinet; he is normally the leader of the strongest party in the state; he is the confidential adviser of the sovereign, and the means of communication between the sovereign and the cabinet and Parliament. As has been seen in chapter II (p. 24) the sovereign retains vestiges of the monarch's former powers of selection, as for instance when it seems that it was left to King George V to make a choice between Lord Curzon and Mr Baldwin in 1923, but in fact must act in accordance with the traditions of her office which require her to accept as Prime Minister the acknowledged leader of the predominant party in the House of Commons.

Though there is no constitutional law that prevents a member of the House of Lords from being Prime Minister, it is certain that future holders of the office will sit in the House of Commons, for on all important matters the Prime Minister must lead the Government in that House, even though he has delegated to another the title of Leader of the House. The last peer to be Prime Minister was Lord Salisbury, who finally resigned office in July 1902.

Since the days of Walpole the Prime Minister's residence in London has been 10 Downing Street. Most cabinet meetings are also held there. By the bequest of Lord Lee of Fareham, the Prime Minister also has at his disposal a country house, Chequers, in Buckinghamshire, where he can relax and where he can also entertain important guests in a fitting manner at week-ends, an adequate staff being maintained at the charge of the state.

Sir Robert Peel, who has been called 'the model for all Prime Ministers', said in 1845,

I defy the Minister of this country to perform properly the duties of his office; to read all he ought to read, including the whole foreign correspondence; to keep up the constant communication with the Queen and the Prince; to superintend the grant of honours and the disposal of civil and ecclesiastical patronage; to write with his own hand to every person of note who chooses to write to him; to be prepared for every debate including the most trumpery concerns; to

95

THE PRIME MINISTER

do all these indispensable things and also sit in the House of Commons eight hours a day for one hundred and eighteen days.

Many of the duties required of Peel are no longer expected of the Prime Minister, but the complexity of modern affairs makes the burden of office almost intolerable for all but those of iron constitution and serene temperament.

The Prime Minister and his cabinet

Though the Prime Minister appoints the cabinet, and its members are his personal nominees, he is not entirely free in his choice. He must, unless he wishes to cause acute disaffection, pay attention to the wishes and ambitions of his most powerful party colleagues, especially those who have previously held high office. In the rare event of a coalition, the Prime Minister's choice is even more strongly dictated by requirements of party balance. Those whom he appoints must resign their offices if he dies or resigns, for his successor will make his own appointments, subject to the same limitations.

The Prime Minister has at his disposal much of the patronage that previously was the sovereign's. Twice yearly at the New Year and on the Queen's official birthday he makes recommendations for titles and honours. He has the right to be consulted about all high appointments in the service of the Crown and in the hierarchy of the Church of England; indeed to many of these posts he virtually has the right of nomination.

The power and influence exercised by the Prime Minister depend in part upon his personality. As chairman of the cabinet meetings, he can have a decisive influence upon all matters of importance, or he can leave decisions of the highest importance to his senior colleagues and give them his support in the cabinet. He can if he wishes allow matters to be thrashed out in the cabinet and cast his vote like any other member. The harmony and usefulness of cabinet meetings will depend greatly upon his skill as a chairman. He may step in and take matters out of the hands of the head of a department, as Neville Chamberlain did at the time of Munich, and as Lloyd George did at the Peace Conferences of 1919–20. He may hold another office as well

96

as that of Prime Minister, as Lord Salisbury and Ramsay MacDonald did when they took the office of Foreign Secretary, or Gladstone when he was also Chancellor of the Exchequer, or Winston Churchill who during the War, and for a short time in 1951–2, was Minister of Defence. This holding of dual office is unlikely in the long run to increase efficiency or make for harmony.

Only a weak and complaisant Prime Minister would be content to be first among equals. Under modern conditions such a man would not hold the office, for it is on his personality and popularity that his party largely depends in fighting an election. He must have urbanity and firmness, unremitting industry and devotion to his office, and the ability to relax when the opportunity occurs. He must be prepared to advise and yet allow his ministers wide discretion, especially in matters of detail. He must be able to represent and speak for the country as well as to gain credit for his party. He must tolerate the opinions of others, but not hesitate to call for the resignation of a minister who by independent action threatens to bring down the Government. On occasion he must anticipate the decisions of the cabinet, and he must have the judgment to know the feeling of its members in advance. He must guide his colleagues without being a dictator.

As in recent times there has been an increasing tendency for meetings of head of governments to be held, the Prime Minister must have the personality, dignity and powers of decision that enable him to hold his own in such company, and the persuasiveness and tact successfully to commend to a parliamentary democracy decisions thus taken.

Membership of the cabinet

The cabinet, which is the directing committee of the Government, has become a better defined body during the last forty years. In the reign of William IV it was described as 'Such of His Majesty's confidential advisers as are of the Privy Council'. Though this definition is no longer valid, it is true that members of the cabinet are sworn as members of the Privy Council, and that no other oath than that of a privy councillor is required of them. Until the War of 1914–18, the cabinet was an unofficial committee with no secretariat, the only note of its proceedings being the memorandum submitted by the Prime Minister to the sovereign. Sir Maurice Hankey, afterwards Lord Hankey, became Secretary of the War Cabinet in 1916 and continued as Secretary of the Cabinet until his retirement in 1938. From 1938 there has been a fully organised secretariat, headed by the Secretary of the Cabinet.

The cabinet is a committee of experienced members of the dominant party in the House of Commons. Its membership and size is determined by the choice and decision of the Prime Minister, who is to some extent guided by party as well as personal consideration. For most of the twentieth century, until recently, it has numbered between twenty and twenty-two members. This has proved too big for informal discussions. Mr Attlee, therefore, reduced the number to seventeen members in his 1945–51 Government and Mr Winston Churchill in his 1951 Government presided over a cabinet of fifteen ministers. The exigencies of the two great wars led to the formation of a small inner ring of ministers specially charged with the direction of the war effort.

Certain ministers are invariably members of the Cabinet—the Lord Chancellor, the Chancellor of the Exchequer, the Foreign Secretary and the Home Secretary, and the holders of the ancient offices of Lord President of the Council and Lord Privy Seal which, being sinecures in themselves, are usually held by important ministers who, being free from departmental worries, are able to preside over important committees or undertake special tasks. The creation of the Ministry of Defence has led to the inclusion of its head in the cabinet and the exclusion of the First Lord of the Admiralty, the Secretary of State for War and the Secretary of State for Air, who previously were almost always included. The Secretaries of State for the Colonies, for Commonwealth affairs and for Scotland are likely to find places.

There has recently been an advance in importance of the Ministry of Education, the Ministry of Housing and Local Government, the

Board of Trade, the Ministry of Agriculture and Fisheries, and the Ministries of Labour and Health, which provide opportunities for able and ambitious politicians to make their mark or mar their reputations. In the Conservative Government formed in 1951, there was a marked increase in the number of co-ordinating ministers, responsible for the general principles of policy and the oversight of a number of ministries, and representing them in the Cabinet, but the experiment was quickly abandoned.

By the Ministers of the Crown Act 1937, ministers in the cabinet and those designated as of cabinet rank but outside the cabinet are paid the same salary. Exceptions are the First Lord of the Treasury (who is also Prime Minister) and the Lord Chancellor, whose salaries are £10,000 a year each, and the Law Officers. The uniform salary for all important ministers helps to mitigate the disappointment and discontent that arise from non-inclusion in the cabinet.

The composition of the Conservative ministry of May 1955 is shown in the Appendix to this chapter on page 103.

Cabinet business and procedure

The main functions of the cabinet, as set out in the Report of the Machinery of Government Committee 1918, are the determination of the policy to be submitted to Parliament, the supreme control of the executive in accordance with the policy prescribed by Parliament, and the co-ordination of the work of the departments of state. Walter Bagehot wrote, 'The efficient secret of the English Constitution may be described as the close union and nearly complete fusion of the executive and legislative powers.' It will be seen that the report of the 1918 Committee emphasises this fusion.

The cabinet usually meets twice a week for two hours during the time Parliament is in session. Its usual place of meeting is the cabinet room at 10 Downing Street. While the cabinet under the chairmanship of the Prime Minister discusses and accepts responsibility for all general policy, it does not at its meetings require or expect a minister to deal with matters of detail, though it is clearly his duty to consult the cabinet on all matters of major importance.

The extent to which all members of the cabinet participate in discussions and secrets varies from government to government. Thus the terms of the Budget, the most important government measure in the year, are not circulated in detail to the cabinet, but are disclosed orally by the Chancellor of the Exchequer shortly before his statement in the House, except where fresh taxation involving some new principle is included. There has been a tendency towards the direction of policy by an inner ring, and the prior discussion of important matters by cabinet committees composed of all interested ministers.

The essence of cabinet procedure is its informality. The amount of business has greatly increased, but the time taken in discussion of individual items has been decreased by the practice of prior consultation and decision, and by the issue in advance of detailed information and statistics. If the long agenda is to be concluded, speeches must be made only by those vitally concerned, and must be kept short. Proper study of papers in advance is essential. Even with full and free consultation in the cabinet, policy will be dominated by a few members of personality and experience, or possibly by the Prime Minister alone if he is of sufficient stature. Normally the policy ultimately endorsed by the cabinet is the result of compromise. This is not always an easy matter, when disagreement with the final decision may lead to resignations and even to the downfall of the Government.

Cabinet committees

An important development in cabinet organisation during the period since the First World War has been the evolution of a system of cabinet committees. Mr Lloyd George made use of a number of committees to assist his small war cabinet. The system was revived in the Second World War and was extensively used by Mr Churchill, who had the Defence (Operations) Committee and Defence (Supply) Committee under his own chairmanship, and a powerful committee under the Lord President of the Council, which he described as 'almost a parallel cabinet concerned with home affairs'. There were also a Civil Defence Committee, a Reconstruction Committee and others as the need arose. Mr Attlee, as Prime Minister in the Labour Government of 1945–51, had a number of standing committees of the cabinet, among the most important being the Defence Committee, which included the Foreign Secretary, the Chancellor of the Exchequer, the Minister of Labour and National Service and the Minister of Supply, as well as the Minister of Defence and the three Service Ministers, and was presided over by the Prime Minister himself, and the Lord President's Committee, which was a kind of General Purposes Committee. There were also a number of other committees to deal with routine and special matters.

The Lord President of the Council and the Lord Privy Seal, once holders of sinecures, now seem often to have most important duties in connexion with cabinet committees (see Herbert Morrison, *Government and Parliament*, pp. 16–27).

Collective responsibility

Collective responsibility is another essential feature of cabinet government. A minister who is not prepared to defend cabinet policy as ultimately decided must resign. There is particular difficulty in coalition governments like the National Government under Ramsay MacDonald, 1931–5, when on one occasion an agreement to differ within the cabinet was made public. The key principle is collective loyalty, even when it has been necessary for an important decision to be taken without the cabinet's being consulted.

Secrecy of cabinet proceedings

The disclosure of the proceedings and discussion within the cabinet is forbidden under the Official Secrets Act as well as by the moral obligation of the Privy Council oath. If a minister on resignation wishes to make a personal explanation involving the mention of cabinet discussions, he must obtain the Queen's permission, since cabinet conclusions are theoretically advices to the sovereign. Since 1916, formal cabinet minutes have been kept by the Secretary but these are never published. Sometimes an agreed statement is issued to the Press. Much of what we know about cabinet procedure and discussions is derived from statements made in the biographies and autobiographies of statesmen, but these are mostly based on memories, for cabinet ministers on resignation are required to return all their papers.

The Cabinet Secretariat

Since the regularisation of the Cabinet Secretariat in 1938, its functions have been clearly defined: to circulate memoranda; to compile the agenda; to summon the cabinet and take down and circulate its conclusions and those of its committees; to prepare the reports of cabinet committees; and to keep cabinet papers and conclusions. The need for accurate statistics and the demands of economic planning have necessitated the development of the Central Statistical Office as a branch of the Cabinet Office. The final agenda papers name the ministers outside the cabinet who are invited to be present during the discussion of specific items. Undoubtedly the full establishment of a Cabinet Secretariat has made for increased efficiency.

The Privy Council

Although the Privy Council has lost the all-important position it held in the sixteenth and seventeenth centuries as the chief instrument by which the King's government was carried on, and has been superseded by the cabinet, it still exists and has a number of functions.

There are to-day some 300 Privy Councillors who are styled 'Right Honourable'. Those sworn of the Privy Council include all cabinet ministers and Dominion Prime Ministers as confidential advisers of the Crown, holders of certain great offices such as the Archbishops of Canterbury and York, the Lord Chief Justice, the Lords of Appeal in Ordinary, the Lords Justices of Appeal, and others eminent in political life or in the service of the Crown. Ex-cabinet ministers retain their membership of the Council, a fact which partly explains the large number of Privy Councillors. The minister responsible for the Privy Council is the Lord President of the Council.

The full Privy Council meets only on important occasions such as the acclamation of a new sovereign. Otherwise the Privy Council meetings are attended by a few ministers and officials for formal acts of state such as the admission of a minister to office or for the transaction of such business as the issue of proclamations and the submission of Orders in Council to the Queen, after whose assent the Order is authenticated by the signature of the Clerk of the Privy Council.

There still exist a number of standing committees of the Privy Council; the most important is the Judicial Committee (see chapter XI). Down to the mid-nineteenth century or later various matters of government that have since become the responsibility of specially constituted departments were dealt with by committees of the Privy Council: the origins of the present-day Board of Trade, Ministry of Education, and Ministry of Health are to be found in such committees. The standing committees of the Privy Council that exist to-day, besides the Judicial Committee, are concerned with the Channel Islands, the Universities of Oxford and Cambridge, the Scottish Universities, the grant of charters to municipal corporations, and the baronetage.

Appendix. The Conservative Ministry, May 1955.

Prime Minister: The Rt Hon. Sir Anthony Eden, K.G., M.P.

Ministers in the Cabinet: 18

The Prime Minister and the First Lord of the Treasury (£10,000); Lord President of the Council; Chancellor of the Exchequer; Secretary of State for Foreign Affairs; Lord Chancellor (£10,000); Chancellor of the Duchy of Lancaster; Lord Privy Seal (Leader of the House of Commons); Secretary of State for Home Affairs and Minister for Welsh Affairs; Secretary of State for Scotland; Secretary of State for Commonwealth Relations; Secretary of State for the Colonies; Minister of Labour and National Service; Minister of Defence; Minister of Housing and Local Government; President of the Board of Trade; Minister of Agriculture, Fisheries and Food; Minister of Pensions and National Insurance; Minister of Education.

Ministers not in the cabinet: 18

First Lord of the Admiralty; Secretary of State for War; Secretary of State for Air; Minister of Fuel and Power; Minister of Health;

Minister of Transport and Civil Aviation; Minister of Supply; Minister of Works; Postmaster-General; Minister without Portfolio; Paymaster-General (£2,000); Minister of State for Foreign Affairs (£3,000); Minister of State, Board of Trade (£3,000); Minister of State, Scottish Office (£3,000).

Law Officers

Attorney-General (£10,000); Lord Advocate; Solicitor-General (£7,000); Solicitor-General (Scotland) (£3,000).

The salaries are £5,000 except where they are stated.

CHAPTER IX

THE DEPARTMENTS OF STATE AND THE CIVIL SERVICE

The cabinet, entrusted as it is with the duty of carrying on the Queen's government, must decide along what broad lines it proposes to govern and what fresh legislation for the purpose it will submit to Parliament for approval. It must also ensure that the permanent executive or Civil Service in applying the measures approved by Parliament does not exceed the powers granted it by legislation. It is the responsibility of the ministers, or political heads of the departments to see that the adminstration is carried on within legal bounds. It is the purpose of the chapter to describe in outline the functions of the ministers and the working of the departments under their direction.

The minister

The minister divides his time between the political duties of Parliament and his constituency, and the administrative tasks of his department. In the latter he is assisted, if he is in charge of an important department, by a parliamentary under-secretary, and parliamentary private secretaries—all members of his political party—and also a permanent under-secretary, a civil servant, and an appropriate staff of civil servants of all ranks. The calls on his time and energy are so many that he greatly relies on the help and advice of the senior civil servants, without which he would be unable adequately to present his department's policy, actions and interests to the cabinet and Parliament. Generally the minister does not do more than lay down the broad outlines of policy, and from time to time, and after he has had the fullest information and advice, make rulings on important points. It is his business to know the reactions of Parliament and the public, and to make his party's and his department's policies and needs agree as closely as possible.

The minister is responsible to Parliament for the actions of the officials of his department in all cases when they have carried out direct orders from him or have acted in accordance with the policy he has laid down, or have made a mistake which does not involve an important issue of policy. When his officials have acted wrongly or inefficiently he is not obliged to endorse their actions, but he remains 'constitutionally responsible to Parliament for the fact that something has gone wrong'. So considerable is the skill and caution of senior civil servants in their conduct of business that it is comparatively rare for ministers to be embarrassed by such situations as the last mentioned.

The departments of state

The machinery of government in Great Britain is organised in departments which number about 100; they work on a functional basis as their names indicate, e.g. Board of Trade, Ministry of Health, Ministry of Education and so on. Their size and importance vary considerably and about twenty-five of them are important enough to have as their political heads ministers who are in the cabinet or who are of cabinet rank. One hundred and fifty years ago there were not more than a dozen government departments of any consequence. Their numbers have grown because of the ever-increasing responsibilities which the state has undertaken during the last eighty years or so. The need to administer social legislation relating to public health, education, factory acts, the demands of two world wars and the need to organize methodically the country's economic resources, have all led to the creation of new departments. The 'Welfare State' of the post-war era automatically led to an increased Civil Service because of the detailed and complicated provisions affecting millions of citizens in such matters as health and insurance: these could not be carried out without new departments.

Below are given the more important departments and for convenience sake they are grouped together where their functions are related or complementary.

CENTRAL GOVERNMENTAL DEPARTMENTS

The Treasury
Board of Inland Revenue
Board of Customs and Excise
The Home Office
Scottish Office (for Scotland only)
Lord Chancellor's Office (administrative side)

FOREIGN, COMMONWEALTH AND IMPERIAL RELATIONS

Foreign Office
Commonwealth Relations Office
Colonial Office

DEFENCE

Ministry of Defence
Admiralty
War Office
Air Ministry
Ministry of Supply

ECONOMIC

Board of Trade
Post Office
Ministry of Fuel and Power
Ministry of Agriculture, Fisheries and Food
Ministry of Transport and Civil Aviation

SOCIAL SERVICES

Ministry of Education
Ministry of Health
Ministry of Labour and National Service
Ministry of Pensions and National Insurance
Ministry of Housing and Local Government

COMMON SERVICE DEPARTMENTS
Ministry of Works
H.M. Stationery Office
Central Office of Information.

This grouping is in many ways arbitrary. The Treasury for instance exercises a general financial supervision over all departments and over the Civil Service; the Home Office has many functions which could be included under social services; the Post Office is sometimes described as a revenue-producing department.

To illustrate the work of the departments, the functions of two of the most important, the Treasury and the Home Office, are outlined in the following sections. It should be noted that the internal organisation of a department of state may change from time to time. It may lose some of its functions to another department or new branches may be created to put into effect the provisions of laws recently passed by Parliament. Departments may be amalgamated, as the Ministries of Agriculture and Fisheries and of Food have been; they may be abolished, like the Ministry of Aircraft Production.

The Treasury

The senior political head of the Treasury is the First Lord, who is also Prime Minister. Executive control of the department is, however, exercised by the Chancellor of the Exchequer, who is Second Lord of the Treasury, and by his second in command, the Financial Secretary to the Treasury. As a department the Treasury is small in size, but in it is concentrated much of the talent of the Civil Service. It holds a 'key' position, not only in relation to the activities and staffs of the other departments, but also in the wider field of economic planning and direction of the nation's finance at home and abroad.

Its economic planning is done chiefly in conjunction with the Central Statistical Office, which is a branch of the Cabinet Office. Such planning involves a survey of the whole of the national resources, especially raw materials, labour supply and productive capacity. A network of committees made up of representatives of the departments interested and under Treasury chairmen deals with important matters of overseas finance such as the balance of payments with the rest of the world, the state of the gold reserves and exchange control policy.

In domestic finance the Treasury makes the final calculations on which the Chancellor of the Exchequer bases his Budget. It also deals with the raising and repayment of loans, and issues instructions to the Bank of England. The financial activities of the other departments come under its review: the Treasury sees that the sums of money authorised by Parliament under the various votes are not exceeded by any department. The annual estimates of each department are scrutinised by the Treasury, to prevent waste or overlapping expenditure.

The staffing or establishment of each department is also an important concern of the Treasury: it is significant that the head of the Civil Service is the Permanent Secretary of the Treasury. Departments must get Treasury approval for increases of staff. The Treasury decides policy regarding recruitment and makes regulations for the grading, pay, discipline, leave, promotion and pensions of the Civil Service. Its Training and Education division co-ordinates, and advises on, training, and gives 'refresher' courses for those already in the service. There is also an Organisation and Methods division, which aims at applying scientific organisation and labour-saving methods in the Civil Service, to increase efficiency and reduce costs.

The Home Office

The Home Office, in charge of the Secretary of State for Home Affairs, is one of the most important of the departments. It is responsible in the widest sense for the maintenance within the realm of that law and order which is essential for the life of the community. It has also many detailed responsibilities, relating to the safety and welfare of the citizens, under the provisions of the social legislation of the last hundred and twenty years.

The diagram opposite shows the full extent of the work of the Home Office, of which only some details are mentioned below.

To maintain law and order there must be an efficient police force; to enforce punishment imposed by the courts on those convicted of criminal offences a prison system is needed. The Home Secretary is directly interested in police matters. (See chapter XII.) The administration of prisons and treatment of prisoners is the responsibility of the Prison Commission, acting in accordance with general policy laid down by the Home Office. When offenders are placed on probation instead of being sent to prison they are dealt with by a probation service directed by the Home Office.

Other services intimately connected with the maintenance of order and safety in peace or war are the Civil Defence and Fire Services. The former, as its name implies, is concerned with the services necessary for the protection of the civilian population in time of war, particularly against aerial bombardment. The Fire Services are closely connected with civil defence in addition to their everyday job of fire fighting.

The admission of aliens and control of immigration are matters which affect public security. The Home Office decides what aliens may be admitted·for residence and work within Great Britain. Undesirable aliens can be deported, i.e. expelled by order of the Home Secretary. Aliens after a sufficient period of residence may apply for naturalisation, i.e. British citizenship; the Home Office will decide whether to grant or refuse this privilege.

Where the lives of the citizens may be harmed by dangerous weapons or materials, the Home Office, under various Acts of Parliament, makes safety regulations for their control, e.g. firearms, dangerous drugs, poisons, explosives, petroleum.

The Home Office has a large children's branch, which is concerned with the welfare of children. It administers the extensive legislation on this subject and gives its instructions to the local authorities and voluntary societies who do the detailed executive work in the following cases: juvenile offenders, care of children who need protection, orphans, adoption, cruelty to children, employment of children and young persons.

The Home Secretary has the exacting task of advising the Queen in the exercise of her royal prerogative of mercy, which is the exercise of discretion by the Crown to dispense with or to modify punishment inflicted on those who have been convicted of offences of a public character. This has included the recommendations of reprieves for prisoners under sentence of death, the sentences being commuted (i.e. changed) to life imprisonment. In other cases there may be commutation of sentence, or the grant of pardon.

If petitions are made to the Queen by her subjects, they will go by way of the Home Office. Her Majesty's Government uses the Home Office as its channel of communication with the governments of Northern Ireland, the Isle of Man, the Channel Islands, and with the Church of England. Since 1951 the Home Secretary has also been Minister for Welsh Affairs. It should be noted that in Scotland practically all the diverse functions of the Home Office are carried out by the Scottish Home Department, which is part of the Scottish Office under the Secretary of State for Scotland.

The Civil Service

It has been noted that the political head of a department decides what the objects of its policy are to be. It is the business of the Civil Service to advise the minister how those objects can be attained, and to devise the administrative methods by which they can be put into effect. The civil servant must be prepared to carry out the policy prescribed whatever the party in power may be. The permanent under-secretary and others of the higher civil servants in contact with the minister undoubtedly have opportunities of influencing policy, particularly by pointing out the results of former experience, but the responsibility for the policy decided upon rests with the minister, who lacks the security of tenure which the civil servant enjoys.

A civil servant has been defined as 'a servant of the Crown (not being the holder of a political or judicial office) who is employed in a civil capacity and whose remuneration is wholly paid out of moneys provided by Parliament'. This is a wide definition and includes the following:

(i) The administrative, executive and clerical classes.

(ii) Customs and excise officers; inspectors of taxes; the departmental classes of the Ministry of Labour and National Service and some other departments.

(iii) Professional, scientific and technical staff, i.e. doctors, architects, lawyers, scientists and engineers working in their professional, or in an expert advisory, capacity.

(iv) Post Office officials (minor and manipulative grades)—a numerous class of some 200,000.

(v) An industrial Civil Service made up of the 400,000 employees in arsenals, dockyards, shipyards, ordnance factories and aircraft factories.

(vi) A maintenance element of messengers, cleaners, office keepers and porters.

The details that follow concern the first of the groups given above.

The evolution of the Civil Service

Down to the beginning of the nineteenth century the executive staffs of the relatively few departments then existing were not particularly numerous or efficient. Their appointment depended on patronage exercised by some minister of the Crown or other politically influential person, and while there were occasional examples of able civil servants under this system there were many who were inefficient or corrupt. The growth of governmental activities, the spread of education, and the increase of population in the nineteenth century called for a Civil Service of higher quality than that provided by patronage and nomination. The Northcote-Trevelyan report of 1854 brought about extensive reform. After the setting up in 1855 of the Civil Service Commission, an independent body, examinations for candidates nominated by the departments were begun, and appointment by political patronage was severely limited. Open competitive examinations were first effectively adopted after the Order in Council of 1870 which stipulates that they should be held for all branches of the Civil Service. The principle of competitive examinations was firmly established and this remains the rule to-day for appointment to what are known as the 'Treasury

Grades', viz. the administrative class, the executive class, and clerical class. The standard of examination for each grade is related to the various levels of education: that of the administrative class corresponds with that required for a high University honours degree: the executive standard corresponds to the Advanced level of the General Certificate of Education, and that of the clerical grade is about the standard of the Ordinary level of the General Certificate of Education, or the old School Certificate.

The work of the grades

The administrative class is small in numbers, being less than one per cent. of that part of the Civil Service we are considering. But it carries heavy responsibilities and those who belong to it, if they are to reach the rank of assistant secretary and above, must be of high intelligence. They must have the ability to see all sides of a question, the power of expressing themselves clearly on paper and in conference, and sufficient flexibility of mind to deal with widely varying problems. Among the exacting tasks of the senior ranks of this grade are collaboration with parliamentary counsel in the preparation of new legislation which will eventually be laid before Parliament, a task which requires the most exact care and consideration; the briefing and advising of ministers for the conduct of their parliamentary business; discussions with such bodies as the Federation of British Industries; the thrashing out of problems with local government authorities, the shaping of administrative policy for their department, i.e. what principles will be applied in the various circumstances likely to arise so that the department's objectives may be attained. And as application of principles will lead to decisions which will form precedents to be acted on subsequently, policy must be carefully based on sound lines from the beginning.

The work of the executive class has widened since 1947. Formerly its duties were somewhat limited, e.g. routine application of administrative policy or the performance of standardised accountancy, contract, supply, and audit duties. The senior executive officers now deal with some of the work previously done by the administrative class and judgment, initiative and resource are required of them. But their responsibilities fall short of higher policy making and co-ordination of policy with other branches.

The executive class number some ten per cent. of the non-industrial Civil Service. They are important because of their knowledge of office practice, the precedents that must be followed, and the proper way in which business should be transacted. Occupying a middle position, they are a vital link in the chain of work above and below them.

The clerical class is large in numbers and includes higher clerical officers, clerical officers and clerical assistants (women). Their duties are those found in all organisations where 'paper' work predominates, e.g. filing correspondence, drafting routine letters, interviewing members of the public.

The code of conduct

The reputation and effectiveness of the British Civil Service have been greatly assisted by a code of conduct which has grown up over the past eighty years or so. Much of this code is custom, while the rest is laid down in Treasury minutes and departmental regulations. Its chief aim is to ensure political impartiality and financial integrity.

With regard to political impartiality, we may start with a contrast. In many countries, even in democratic ones such as U.S.A., political considerations frequently influence Civil Service appointments. In the extreme cases in some totalitarian states, all appointments are made on a political basis: party membership is an essential qualification for appointment.

The British tradition is different. It requires that its Civil Service must be politically neutral. This is based on a common-sense argument that the best results for democratic government will only be achieved by an impartial and objective consideration, without any political bias, of the facts on which decisions will be taken. As a result the British Civil Service has been able to serve all governments, whatever their political complexion, with exemplary loyalty.

From this a requirement of political neutrality follows: the general rule is that civil servants who become candidates for parliamentary election must resign their appointment. In 1948, the Masterman Committee was set up by the then Labour Government to examine the existing limitations on the political activities of civil servants in both national and local politics. Although, in the case of industrial civil servants and Post Office grades, it recommended some re-laxation of the rule requiring resignation on standing as a candidate for parliamentary election, it emphatically endorsed the prohibition of such candidature in the case of the administrative, clerical, pro-fessional, technical and scientific classes.

Financial integrity is the second pillar of the code. Civil servants in the course of official business may acquire information which they might apply for their own financial gain. They also handle govern-ment contracts worth large sums and consequently may be offered bribes to gain their favour. What is expected of them is best given in the words of a Board of Enquiry in 1928 which investigated the con-duct of three civil servants involved in speculative foreign exchange transactions:

A civil servant is not to subordinate his duty to his private interest; but neither is he to put himself in a position where his duty and his interests conflict. He is not to make use of his official position to further these interests; but neither is he so to order his private affairs as to allow the suspicion to arise that a trust has been abused or a confidence betrayed . . . His position clearly imposes on him restric-tions in matters of commerce and business from which the ordinary citizen is free . . . The public expects from civil servants a standard of integrity not only inflexible but fastidious, and has not been dis-appointed in the past.

Pay and conditions

Councils to determine pay and conditions of service for the Civil Service were set up in 1919, and to a considerable extent have dealt successfully with the relations between the state as an employer and the civil servant as an employee. It was Mr J. H. Whitley, Speaker of the House of Commons, who in 1917 presided over a committee set up to consider relations between employers and employed. This led to joint councils of employers and employed, on a basis of equal representation, to settle wage claims and improve working conditions in major industries. After some delay the Government accepted the idea for the Civil Service. This was a notable advance, for hitherto the numerous staff associations of civil servants had found it difficult to further their claims for better pay and conditions owing to the unreceptive attitude of the Treasury.

Whitley Councils are of two kinds: firstly the National Whitley Council, which considers matters affecting the Civil Service as a whole, such as working hours; secondly the departmental councils which deal with matters arising internally in each department, e.g. promotion. In all councils there is an 'official' side and a 'staff' side. In the National Council the 'official' side is composed mostly of senior civil servants usually of under-secretary rank together with some Members of Parliament: the 'staff' side contains representatives of the various staff associations together with civil servants from the departments.

The declared aim of Whitley Councils is to 'secure the greatest measure of co-operation between the state, in its capacity as employer, and the general body of civil servants in matters affecting the Civil Service, with a view to increased efficiency in public service combined with the well-being of those employed; to provide machinery for the ventilation of grievances; and generally to bring together, with a view to free discussion of many diverse and complex problems, the experience and different points of view of representatives of the many grades and classes constituting the administrative, clerical and manipulative Civil Service of the country'. In practice the aim is to settle disputes by the attainment of complete accord, without voting. Where agreement or compromise cannot be reached, the matter is referred to the Civil Service Arbitration Tribunal, whose decision is binding on both sides.

CHAPTER X

FINANCE AND GOVERNMENT

The scope of public finance

During the twentieth century in Great Britain, as in other countries, the older idea that the functions of the state were limited to defence against external enemies and to internal protection of the lives and property of its citizens, has been replaced by a much wider and more positive conception of what the state may properly and usefully do. It now seeks to achieve the social and economic aims of the Welfare State, and in Great Britain, since 1945, governments, whether Conservative or Labour, have in turn developed and extended the social services necessary to attain this Welfare State. Among these services are education, housing, health, public assistance, old age pensions, social insurance, children's allowances and certain maternity services. At the same time the Government maintains heavy expenditure on the defence services of the Navy, Army and Air Force, and, together, these defence and social services involve an annual expenditure running into thousands of million pounds. The state therefore must have an efficient system of finance, in order to estimate correctly how much money is involved, and to provide for raising the sum required by taxation or loans, and there must also be control to ensure that it has been correctly spent. It must also do all in its power to maintain the general economic health of the nation by stimulating productivity at home, maintaining its gold and dollar reserves, and keeping steady its balance of trade with the rest of the world. It is on this continuance of economic health that the provision of defence services, and the maintenance of our standard of living and the social services at their present level, depend.

After the Revolution of 1688, it was established that levying of money by the Crown without the consent of Parliament was illegal, and in this matter Parliament came to mean the House of Commons only.

By the eighteenth century the Commons secured the right of deciding for what purposes the money voted should be spent. In 1860 the House of Lords, in theory still claiming financial powers, rejected the paper duties; the Commons henceforth adopted the practice of the single Finance Bill, in which all the taxes for the year were included, and no further trouble from the Lords was experienced until their rejection of the Finance Bill of 1909. Consequently, in order to assert the financial supremacy of the House of Commons, the Parliament Act of 1911 was passed. By this the financial powers of the Lords were extinguished, apart from the nominal delay of up to one month which they could impose (see p. 89).

General principles

The finance of government in Great Britain is based on the following general principles:

(1) For all expenditure and levying of taxes a motion of the Government and the assent of Parliament are necessary.

(2) Money voted may be spent only on the purpose for which it has been voted. By this means the financial control of the legislature over the executive is preserved.

(3) A single fund, the Consolidated Fund, is maintained into which all receipts are paid, and out of which all payments are ultimately made.

(4) The national accounting period is the year running from 1 April to 31 March; for this period, income and expenditure are estimated in advance. Each year for which a balance between revenue and expenditure is aimed at is financially separate and self-contained.

Expenditure

Expenditure authorised by Parliament falls under two main heads:

(1) The current expenditure of the various departments, e.g. the War Office, Admiralty, Ministry of Health, etc. These are known as Supply Services and are debated and authorised by Parliament every year; they are subdivided into Defence Services and Civil Expenditure.

117

(2) The Consolidated Fund Services, which include such payments as the annual interest on the National Debt, the Queen's Civil List, annuities to certain members of the Royal Family, and the salaries of the judges and of the Comptroller and Auditor-General. This expenditure, once authorised by Parliament, continues year by year, until the Act concerned lapses or is repealed. It is not, like the Supply Services' expenditure, the subject of annual parliamentary debate. Quite clearly the special constitutional position of the sovereign and independence of the judiciary could not be preserved if the Civil List and judges' salaries were debated and criticised in detail each year by Parliament.

The estimates

The financial year begins on 1 April, but for some six months previously the preparation of estimates is proceeding. During this time, the departments have informal discussions with the Treasury about their financial needs for the coming year. In October, they receive a formal request from the Treasury for the submission of their estimates by about 1 December. When received by the Treasury, the estimates of the civil departments, which are given in detail, undergo criticism and detailed amendment by the Treasury. Those of the defence departments (Admiralty, War Office and Air Ministry) are subjected to close scrutiny within the department concerned, and are given in less detail. If the estimate *en bloc* of a defence department is thought by the Treasury to be excessive, a decision about it will have to be obtained at cabinet level by the Chancellor of the Exchequer.

When approval by the Treasury has been given, and the estimates have been signed by the minister who will present them to the House of Commons, they are printed and presented to Parliament. They comprise four volumes: one each for the three defence departments and one for all civil departments together. Within each estimate the unit is the Vote. The Vote is divided into three parts: the head which states the service or purpose for which the estimate is required; the total amount of money required for that service; and a further division into sub-heads, showing the amount of money estimated to be spent on, or received under, each sub-head.

The Committee of Supply

The Committee of Supply considers with great care the estimates which are presented to it by the ministers responsible. During debate, amendments can be moved to reduce, but not to increase, the Vote. Moving a reduction is a method whereby Her Majesty's Opposition can show their disapproval of the Government's policy. The Committee finally votes the sum proposed in the estimate, or refuses it or reduces it. Twenty-six days every session are allotted to Supply, and to the legislation giving final authority to Votes of Supply, and these must come between February and the end of July, by which time the estimates must be passed. British parliamentary practice gives the Opposition the right to be consulted over the choice of the estimates for discussion on any one day. The time allotted in the Committee of Supply is insufficient to bring all proposed expenditure under review, and at the end of the twenty-six days much that has been left unexamined is voted without debate. Critics have pointed out that this procedure needs reforming, since a disproportionate amount of time is spent in Committee of Supply on a few selected estimates and on the Report stage of Supply resolutions to the House, while much expenditure is passed without comment.

The Committee of Ways and Means

The Committee of Ways and Means is chiefly concerned with putting money into the Consolidated Fund. It is in this Committee therefore that the Chancellor of the Exchequer makes his Budget proposals.

When the Committee of Supply has authorised a programme of national expenditure, the Committee of Ways and Means provides the money for it. It does this by authorising the issue from the Consolidated Fund of the sums voted in Committee of Supply: if it does not give this authorisation, no money can be spent.

REVENUE

This is how the Government collects each £ of Revenue

Taxes on Income and Capital 10/2

TAXES ON PERSONAL INCOMES
Income Tax and Surtax, including tax on dividends and interest (£1317 million)

5/7

TAX PAID BY COMPANIES
Income Tax, Profits Tax, and Excess Profits Levy (£901 million)

3/10

DEATH DUTIES (£185 million)

9d.

Taxes on Spending 8/11

TOBACCO (£660 million)

2/10

ALCOHOL (£388 million)

1/8

ENTERTAINMENTS AND BETTING (£70 million)

4d.

PURCHASE TAX (£368 million)

1/7

OIL AND MOTOR DUTIES
Oil, including petrol (£320 million)
Motor (£80 million)

1/8

OTHER Stamp Duties, Import Duties (except on Alcohol, Tobacco, Oil), etc. (£197 million)

10d.

Non-Tax Revenue 11d

Broadcast Licences, Receipts from loans and Government trading, and other miscellaneous revenue (£224 million)

 11d.

Total £4710 million   **£1. 0s. 0d.**

EXPENDITURE

This is how the Government spends each £ it collects

Defence and National Debt 9/3

6/7   DEFENCE (£1557 million)

NATIONAL DEBT
Interest on War Loans, National Savings Certificates, etc. (£636 million)

2/8

Social Services, Subsidies, etc. 7/8

2/-   HEALTH (£462 million)

1/5   EDUCATION (£343 million)

PERSONAL PAYMENTS
Family Allowances, War Pensions, National Assistance, Government contribution to Insurance Fund (£414 million). Excludes benefits and pensions paid out of personal insurance contributions

1/9

AGRICULTURAL AND FOOD SUBSIDIES (£311 million)

1/4

ASSISTANCE TO LOCAL AUTHORITIES Housing, Police, Roads, etc. (£265 million)

1/2

Other Services and Surplus, 3/1

GENERAL SERVICES
Commonwealth and Foreign, Tax Collection, Broadcasting, Employment Exchanges (£574 million)

2/5

SURPLUS
Helps to finance the Government's loans to Local Authorities and other capital expenditure (£148 million)

8d.

£1. 0s. 0d.   Total £4710 million

Fig. 4. The Nation's Budget, 1955-1956

120

The Budget

The Budget is the Chancellor of the Exchequer's review of the national finances; he usually introduces it in April of each year. It is customary for him in his Budget speech first to survey the finance of the year which has just ended, to show whether it has ended with a financial surplus or deficit, and to indicate what changes have taken place in the composition of the National Debt. Next he considers the financial prospects and needs of the current year. He gives estimates of the money to be expended for the Consolidated Fund Services and for Supply as voted by Parliament. He estimates whether or not these sums can be met from revenue at existing tax rates, or whether increased taxation will be necessary: sometimes a reduction in taxation is possible if the Chancellor sees a large surplus in prospect. Then follows his detailed taxation proposals, which increase or remit taxes, or keep them as before, according to the needs of the current financial year; sometimes old taxes are dropped and new ones introduced. These proposals are contained in the tax resolutions which the Ways and Means Committee debate and pass or reject. These resolutions are finally embodied in the Finance Act, which must be passed by the end of July, and which gives statutory authority for the imposition of the Chancellor's taxation proposals. As it is necessary that the taxes proposed shall be imposed forthwith, a resolution is passed on Budget Night, allowing their immediate collection. Should the tax be rejected or reduced subsequently, any excess paid would be refunded. Complementary to the Finance Act is the Appropriation Act, which is also based on Ways and Means resolutions: it authorises the issue of sums out of the Consolidated Fund to cover the grants made in Committee of Supply. It also appropriates the sum granted for each Vote of the estimates to the service of that Vote and that Vote alone, so as to prevent any improper application of public money by the department concerned.

Collection of revenue

The greater part of the national revenue comes from taxation; other less important sources are fees received from services rendered, e.g. the Post Office, income from Crown lands and state investments. Lastly, the state can borrow on its credit, if it is necessary to bridge any gap in revenue not covered by the yields from the sources given above.

Taxation is of two kinds, direct and indirect. Direct taxes such as income-tax, surtax, and estate duty, charged on the estates of deceased persons, are assessed and collected by the Board of Inland Revenue. Indirect taxes are charged and collected by the Board of Customs and Excise. These taxes are of two kinds: (1) Customs' duties levied on all dutiable goods entering the country: the duty is as a rule so much per cent. *ad valorem*, i.e. 'on the worth' of the imported product; (2) Excise duties, which are levied inside the country on certain commodities such as beer and spirits, or purchase-tax on certain goods sold internally.

The revenue departments seek to collect these taxes and duties as fully as possible, with as little evasion by the tax-payer as possible, and as economically as possible: what they gather is paid into the Consolidated Fund.

Payments from the Consolidated Fund

The Comptroller and Auditor-General sees that payments from the Consolidated Fund conform to statutory authority. He is an important official; his position is an independent one, resembling that of a judge: he is appointed by letters patent and is removable from his office only by the Queen on a joint address of both Houses of Parliament. His functions are to control the issue of money from the Consolidated Fund, and to examine and audit all the accounts of the issues made during the year for Consolidated Fund and Supply Services.

To obtain the release of money from the Consolidated Fund the Treasury makes a demand to the Comptroller and Auditor-General for either Consolidated Fund or Supply Services. The Comptroller and Auditor-General then approves the necessary issue if he is satisfied that there is authority for it under the relevant Act. On his order the money for supply services is transferred by the Bank of England to the Paymaster-General's account. The Revenue Departments make their own payments. In the case of Consolidated Fund Services, payments are made by the Treasury, or by the Bank of England on its behalf.

Control of public expenditure

In Great Britain the cabinet, the House of Commons, the Treasury, and the Comptroller and Auditor-General are concerned with the various aspects of control of public expenditure. The Government has a pre-eminent position in the matter. In financial matters it has unquestioned initiative: it alone, on behalf of the Crown, can initiate proposals involving expenditure, and these proposals, when introduced in Committee of Supply, are regarded as a matter of confidence by the Government; if defeated on them it will resign. The Government's proposals for expenditure directly depend on its policy and the financial climate at the time: it may wish to expand or to maintain or to contract the activities of the various branches of government, and proposals for expenditure will be affected accordingly.

Control by the House of Commons is effected through the procedure described for the Committees of Supply and Ways and Means. Though party discipline operates strongly during supply debates as far as the Government supporters are concerned, the Opposition always finds plenty to criticise in the Government's expenditure proposals; in Ways and Means debates on taxation proposals, there is likely to be criticism from both the Opposition and Government supporters. When discussion has finished, Parliament must give (or withhold) its approval of the Finance and Appropriation Acts. After the money has been granted and spent, the House has the right to see, from the appropriation accounts submitted by the departments, that the money has been spent as Parliament directed. This parliamentary control is exercised by the Public Accounts Committee appointed under Standing Orders at the beginning of each session. Its fifteen members represent all parties and its job is to examine the 'accounts showing the appropriation of the sums granted by Parliament to meet public expenditure'. It studies the reports of the Comptroller and Auditor-General, examines accounts, calls for personal explanations from officials concerned, and makes its report to Parliament. Parliamentary control is limited by the use of the closure procedure and the restriction of time of supply debates, with the consequence that many of the estimates are never debated; and also by the fact that the estimates are long and complicated documents, the understanding of which require both time and financial knowledge.

The general importance of the Treasury has already been mentioned (see p. 118). It exercises control over expenditure through its advice on cabinet expenditure, and its close touch with departmental policies. With much expert knowledge and ability at its disposal, the Treasury has a full and balanced picture of the financial situation of the country. Besides co-ordinating expenditure and preventing overlap between departments, the Treasury disciplines them as well, administering reproofs when irregularities have been reported by the Public Accounts Committee.

Lastly there is the control of the Comptroller and Auditor-General, who in the auditing functions of his office has to examine the accounts of the moneys issued for Consolidated Fund and Supply Services, and such other accounts as the Treasury may require. His report to Parliament covers the technical correctness of the accounts, and includes an examination of the appropriation accounts of each department. Points of irregularity raised by him are considered by the Public Accounts Committee. He may also, in his report, criticise expenditure which appears unnecessarily extravagant, inconsistent or wasteful.

CHAPTER XI

THE COURTS OF LAW, THE JUDGES AND THE MAGISTRATES

The origins of English law

Law and justice, and the protection they are designed to give, are the foundations of society. The existence of law presupposes the existence of a community of men and women, who are agreed on certain fundamental rules without which no society can exist. In primitive societies, custom provides the rules or law, and rough and ready justice is dispensed by the King or chief, who also imposes penalties and affords his subjects protection. The more civilised and the more complex the society, the more complicated the law becomes. It is then necessary that the law should be written and regular courts of law set up. At the same time legal sanctions (i.e. penalties) must be determined so that the law may be obeyed, and the legal system may work. Laws are not necessarily concerned with morality; they are the practical rules by which a community lives.

The basis of English law is the common law, which had its origins in the customs of the Germanic tribes, who settled in England 1,500 years ago. Many of these customs have never been incorporated in statutes, but they are accepted as law. They have been treasured by lawyers and judges as the basis of English society. These customs and the judgments based on them constitute the body of common law to-day.

Before the development of Parliament as a law-making body, the King himself was the source of law. The law he made was of two kinds, the ordinance, which was often of temporary application, and the assize, which was submitted to the Great Council and was permanent. With the growth of Parliament, another source of law developed. By Tudor times all important laws were passed as statutes by Parliament, the King's power of legislation by proclamation being limited to matters which did not affect the life and property of his subjects. The supremacy of the law over King, as over subjects, was asserted in Magna Carta and in many subsequent documents. 'The King of England cannot at his pleasure make any alterations in the law of the land,' said Fortescue, Chief Justice in the reign of Henry VI. The laws he was thinking of were those governing the fundamental liberties of Englishmen, derived from ancient custom and common law.

With the growth of the courts of common law, increased import-ance was attached to the decisions of judges. These together formed a body of 'case-law' which served to fill in the gaps in common and statute law.

Thus English law springs from four main sources, the common law, Parliament-made statute law, judge-made or case-law and king-made law or proclamations, or in modern times orders in council. English law is continually growing and changing. No attempt has been made to codify it as Roman law was codified, and as Napoleon, drawing his ideas from Roman law, codified the laws of France. In law, as in our constitution, we have avoided stating principles, and have evolved a practical system.

The early courts of law

The courts of law are less ancient than the common law. They developed like Parliament from the King's Court or Council, the Curia Regis. The great administrator Henry II, who reigned from 1154 to 1189, laid the foundations for them. He found, as rivals of the King's Court, the courts of the feudal lords, where the cases of tenants were heard, and the Shire Courts presided over by the sheriff, who was the King's chief officer in the shire, and who attended to the King's interests in local matters, particularly taxation and justice, but who very often grew too independent of his royal master.

Henry II was determined to win for the King's Court as much authority as possible. As most of the disputes in those days concerned land, Henry II decided that no free man could be called into question regarding the possession of his land, unless his opponent obtained a writ of right from the King. He also determined to extend the area of the King's justice by sending judges to try offences against the King's peace. These were called Justices in Eyre (or on tour) and the courts they held were called assizes. He established the principle that serious offences by one man against another were the King's matter, as they were offences against his peace. The assizes system continues to this day, and by means of his new system Henry II attracted much business away from the lords' courts into his own.

The next great law-giver and reformer was Edward I, in whose reign the King's Court was divided into three separate divisions, the Court of the King's Bench, the Court of Common Pleas and the Court of Exchequer—the first hearing cases in which the King was interested, the second cases between his subjects, and the third cases involving the King's revenue. The King's chief officer in legal and other matters of state was the Chancellor, who issued the King's writs. The Chancellor was always an ecclesiastic and as such was 'keeper of the king's conscience'. 'The King's conscience' was offended when he saw his subjects suffering from the deficiencies of the common law, which did not provide a remedy for every issue that might arise. The Chancellor therefore remedied these shortcomings of the common law by giving judgment according to equitable principle or equity i.e. that which is naturally fair and right. Equity drew its inspiration from the moral law upheld by the Church, and from the canon law of the Church, which was based on the legal maxims of Roman law. In time, the courts of common law saw in the equity jurisdiction of the Chancellor's Court a rival which was taking away much of their work and prestige. Other rivals of the common law courts in the Middle Ages were the courts of the Church, which had jurisdiction not only over all clerics but also over laymen in such matters as their morals, wills and marriages.

Under the later Yorkist and Tudor Kings a number of courts originating from the King's Council appeared; the most important were the Court of Star Chamber, the Court of Requests and the Court of High Commission. They were essential aids to the new monarchy in its task of establishing law and order. They did much

THE COURTS OF LAW

good work in the sixteenth century, but in the seventeenth became unpopular and somewhat tyrannical. The Long Parliament abolished them in 1641, and they were not brought back at the Restoration in 1660. The only surviving descendent of the prerogative courts is the Judicial Committee of the Privy Council.

The attempt of the common law courts in the reign of James I to overthrow the Court of Chancery failed; and the system of equity was greatly strengthened by the work of eminent Lord Chancellors in the second half of the seventeenth century. A dual system resulted in which the common law courts administered the law based partly on ancient custom and partly on statutes passed by Parliament, and the Court of Chancery decided cases by equity. This rivalry between the two systems continued until the Judicature Act of 1873, when the administration of common law and equity was fused; this act has been repealed and replaced by the Supreme Court of Judicature (Consolidation) Act of 1925. Now judges of the High Court are bound to recognise equitable rights and can grant equitable remedies: law and equity are administered together on an equal footing, but where the rules of one conflict with the other, the rules of equity prevail.

The judges

Her Majesty's judges enjoy a high reputation and prestige not only at home, but also far beyond Britain. Their ability and impartiality are unquestioned. By their training, experience, and temperament they have acquired a 'judicial mind'. By the terms of the Act of Settlement (1701) they hold office during good behaviour—'quamdiu se bene gesserint'—as the Latin formula has it. They can only be removed from their office on an address to the Queen by both Houses of Parliament. Their salaries are paid directly from the Consolidated Fund, and are not the subject of an annual vote by Parliament. They are not required to give opinions on matters involving political issues, as they are above and outside politics. In general they dispense justice publicly, though there are some special kinds of cases that are held *in camera*.

High Court judges are appointed by the Queen, acting on the

advice of the Prime Minister and Lord Chancellor. Similarly the Prime Minister nominates for appointment the Lords of Appeal, who sit in the House of Lords, the Lord Chief Justice and the Master of the Rolls. The Lord Chancellor appoints County Court judges. The Lord Chancellor, as has been explained elsewhere, holds a political as well as a judicial appointment, but the high traditions of his office ensure that he will act in his judicial capacity with the same impartiality that actuates his colleagues in their work.

Judges are paid according to their rank. Their salaries are adequate but not comparable with the sums earned by barristers of high skill and repute. Yet barristers with large practices are frequently appointed to the Bench, perhaps because of the prestige, honour and dignity of the office, perhaps because in the exercise of their appointments they will make as well as dispense law.

Appointments to high judicial office are seldom made before the age of fifty. A man whose ambition is to be a judge must first make good as a barrister. It is not possible in England, as it is in France, to choose to make a career either as a lawyer or as a judge, nor has there ever been any suggestion of election to judgeships as in the United States.

Barristers and solicitors

A brief word must be said about barristers and solicitors, the two categories into which English lawyers are divided. It is difficult to give a precise picture of the scope and limits of the functions of the two professions. Barristers have the right to plead in any court; solicitors can only plead in Petty Sessions and County Courts. Approach to a barrister to plead a case must be made through a solicitor. Solicitors are the general practitioners of the legal profession, giving general advice on many questions, whereas barristers give advice on legal matters when approached by solicitors, and undertake advocacy in the courts. To become a barrister it is necessary to be a member of an Inn of Court and to keep twelve terms and pass the examinations of the Council of Legal Education. A barrister may not form a partnership or advertise. It therefore takes time and individual ability for him to get together a practice. A barrister of ten years' standing may apply to the Lord Chancellor for a patent appointing him a Queen's Counsel. This is called 'taking silk'.

A solicitor is an officer of the High Court. The Law Society, to whom the courts delegate the duty of watching over the conduct of solicitors, may in case of misconduct strike a solicitor off the roll, which is kept by the Master of the Rolls. A young man intending to be a solicitor, must, generally speaking, serve as an articled clerk for five years, and must pass the Law Society's examinations. Having qualified, he finds it easier to support himself immediately than a barrister, but he will never make the high fees that a fashionable barrister can command.

It may be noted that the law officers of the Crown, the Attorney-General and the Solicitor-General, are always barristers. Their appointments are political, but they take charge of the legal business of the Government and may conduct important prosecutions. The Attorney-General is usually held to have the right to be considered for the office of Lord Chief Justice if it falls vacant while he holds office.

Juries

Juries were introduced into England by the Normans. In its earliest form a jury was a means used by the Norman kings to find out facts. Selected persons of each district came before the King's officers and replied to certain questions on oath. Later, in the reign of Henry II, in criminal matters the 'jury of presentment' was used: this was made up of twelve 'lawful men' of each hundred who 'presented' or reported the crimes of which they knew or had heard. This became subsequently the Grand Jury, which survived till 1933, and which decided whether there was a *prima facie* case against the accused. The work begun by the Grand Jury was continued by the Petty Jury, which developed in the later Middle Ages and which was the forerunner of the modern jury; the Petty Jury decided the guilt or innocence of their fellow-countrymen on trial. Originally the juries were selected because they knew something of the matter in dispute.

Now the jury is selected for its impartiality and lack of connexion with the accused.

To-day juries are used in criminal cases tried in the higher courts, and in certain civil cases. They never sit in the Chancery Division or Admiralty Court, and very seldom in the County Courts. The duty of the jury is to decide questions of fact; it is the judge's duty to decide questions of law, but he must explain to the jury any legal principles they must take into account when considering the facts. Jury service is obligatory upon £30 ratepayers in towns and £20 ratepayers outside towns, with the exception of certain classes—peers, members of Parliament, judges, barristers, clergymen, officers of Her Majesty's Forces, and doctors for example. The names of persons liable for jury service are marked with a J in the electoral registration lists. The qualification for jury service excludes so many from the duty that only one in twenty qualify in towns and very few in the country, so that it is difficult to describe trial by jury as trial by equals. Any one who is summoned for jury service must attend; failure to do so, unless a satisfactory medical certificate is produced, may lead to imprisonment. As each case comes before the Assize Court or Quarter Sessions, the names of the twelve persons summoned to serve are called. The accused may challenge any or all of the jury for a definite cause, and may even challenge up to seven without showing a cause. When the judge has finished his summing up, the jury retire to consider their verdict, which in England must be 'Guilty' or 'Not Guilty' and must be unanimous. If a jury cannot reach such a decision, the judge must discharge it and empanel a new one, and the case must be tried again. Jury service is a serious, unpopular, inconvenient and at times expensive duty for those who are liable to serve. It may sometimes seem a cumbrous and inefficient method of reaching a decision, but most judges and counsel would testify to the common sense and fairness of a British jury. It has also afforded some protection for the citizen against the use of unfair means in obtaining evidence; it has also had its influence against the imposition of cruel and excessive punishments, and it gives a comparatively few citizens a close insight into the working of the law. The Juries Acts of 1949 and 1954 introduced an important new principle, as they made possible payments to jurors for expenses and loss of earnings.

Criminal and civil cases

Criminal law has as its intention the protection of the community and the punishment of the wrongdoer. Criminal proceedings are taken in the name of the Queen—the Queen (Regina) against the person accused. The chief classes of criminal offences are treasons, felonies and misdemeanours. Trials for treasons, which are crimes against the sovereign's person or the state, are rare, the most famous of modern times being those of Sir Roger Casement, during the First World War, and of William Joyce, after the Second World War. The distinction between a felony and a misdemeanour used to be important, because a person convicted of a felony forfeited his property. A more important modern distinction is between indictable and non-indictable offences. The former, the more serious felonies and misdemeanours, are those that require a written indictment or accusation, and they are tried in one of the higher criminal courts, before a judge, sitting with a jury. The less serious non-indictable offences may be dealt with by a magistrate, or magistrates, sitting without a jury and giving an immediate or summary decision.

The purpose of the civil law is to protect and redress the wrongs of the individual citizen, as distinct from the community as a whole. The cases brought are between one citizen and another, or between one company or corporation and another, or between a company or corporation and an individual citizen. They concern contracts, debts, partnerships, wills, property and the wide class of 'torts' or civil injuries by which the rights of a private citizen are infringed—such things as slander, libel, trespass, breach of promise or negligence. Not all civil actions are brought in an unfriendly spirit; for example many cases are brought in the Chancery Division to obtain a settlement on some uncertain or obscure point of interpretation of the clauses of a will or a deed of trust. The Queen cannot through her officers stop or interfere with a civil case, nor can she grant a pardon for a civil wrong.

The courts of law to-day

The system of law courts to-day rests on the provisions of the Acts of 1873 and 1925 already mentioned and the Appellate Jurisdiction Act of 1876.

The highest court is the High Court of Parliament exercising its powers through the House of Lords. The procedure in the House of Lords when acting as the final Court of Appeal has already been outlined on pages 86-7. Appeals to the House of Lords in criminal cases can only be made on the *fiat* or authority of the Attorney-General, and this is only granted if in the opinion of the Attorney-General the case raises a point of great public importance. In civil cases, there is no limitation on the right of appeal to the House of Lords, save that an appeal can only be brought by leave of the Court of Appeal or alternatively of the Appeal Committee of the House of Lords. Most of the cases that come on appeal to the House of Lords are civil. The House of Lords at present has no power to order a retrial in a criminal case, but there is a strong body of opinion in favour of its being allowed to do so.

By the Act of 1873, a new Court of Appeal was formed to take over the appellate jurisdiction previously exercised by the Privy Council, except in those matters reserved for its Judicial Committee which are mentioned on page 138. The judges of the Court of Appeal are the highest legal dignitaries, the Lord Chancellor, the Lord Chief Justice, the Master of the Rolls and the President of the Probate, Divorce and Admiralty Division together with eight Lords Justices of Appeal. The Lord Chancellor, as has already been mentioned, presides over the House of Lords when it sits as the Supreme Court of Appeal. He is also the nominal head of the Chancery Division. The Lord Chief Justice presides over the Court of the Queen's Bench; the Master of the Rolls is the chief judge of the Court of Appeal; the President of the Probate, Divorce and Admiralty Division is the chief judge of that division, the functions of which will be briefly described later. The Court of Appeal sits in divisions of two or three Lords Justices and gives its decisions by a majority of the members.

The High Court of Justice is composed of the Queen's Bench, the Chancery, and the Probate, Divorce and Admiralty Divisions. The Queen's Bench Division deals with common law matters, civil and criminal, and also includes within its scope the work formerly done by the ancient Common Pleas and Exchequer Courts. The Chancery Division is concerned chiefly with equity work, the interpretation of wills and trusts, bankruptcy and company law, the affairs of infants, and revenue cases, e.g. appeals in income-tax cases. The Probate, Divorce, and Admiralty Division deals with matters that formerly came either before Church courts or before a court that dealt with matters relating to shipping. A witty writer, Sir Alan Herbert, has said that it deals with wrecks of wills, wrecks of marriages and wrecks of ships. The Admiralty Court administers a kind of international law based on Roman rather than common law.

In criminal cases the majority of 'indictable' charges are heard at Assizes or Quarter Sessions, or in London at the Central Criminal Court. Of these, the Assizes and Central Criminal Court, or 'Old Bailey' as it is usually called, can try any indictable offence, the Quarter Sessions are concerned with less serious cases. The Assizes, which are held at regular intervals at various towns of England and Wales, and the Central Criminal Court, are presided over by judges of the Queen's Bench. Occasionally an experienced barrister may be appointed as a 'Commissioner of Assize' when there is a shortage of judges, and in London the Recorder of London and the Common Serjeant sit as well as Queen's Bench judges.

Quarter Sessions, as their name implies, are held four times a year. In the counties, all justices of the peace for the county are entitled to sit on the Bench. They are presided over by an experienced lawyer, and they sit with a jury. In boroughs which have the right to hold Quarter Sessions of their own, a Recorder, a barrister acting as sole (paid) judge, takes the place of the magistrates. From Assizes and Quarter Sessions appeals in criminal cases mostly go to the Court of Criminal Appeal, but on occasions appeals from Quarter Sessions may be made to the Queen's Bench Division when a point of law is involved.

Justices of the peace, magistrates and magistrates' courts

There are no fewer than 940 courts of summary jurisdiction in which justice is dispensed. The majority of the magistrates of these courts are justices of the peace, who are unpaid and untrained in the law. They are 'such persons as are assigned by the Crown to the Commission of the Peace' and appointments are made by the Lord Chancellor on the recommendation of the Lord Lieutenant of a county. The work of the courts makes considerable demands upon the time of the magistrates, who are therefore often retired or of independent means. There is now an age limit of seventy-five, beyond which magistrates may not continue to exercise the office of justice of the peace in court without special permission.

In big cities, paid or stipendiary magistrates are appointed, and in London, police court magistrates do the work that elsewhere is performed by the Petty Sessions, i.e. a court in which at least two justices of the peace are sitting.

Petty Sessions

The vast majority of criminal cases are dealt with in Petty Sessions, where justices of the peace administer summary justice, and also act as investigators of the more serious indictable offences. As they are not trained lawyers they are advised on matters of law by the Justices' Clerk, who is usually a solicitor. There are many kinds of cases that may be tried at once by these magistrates' courts, e.g. minor motoring offences, damage to property, cruelty to animals. In most cases the accused chooses to be tried summarily; for some offences he may choose to be tried by jury at the Assizes or Quarter Sessions, where more serious penalties can be imposed if he is found guilty.

Where the accused is charged with one of the more serious indictable offences, e.g. murder or manslaughter, the magistrates in Petty Sessions carry out a preliminary examination, before committing the accused for trial at the Assizes. Those accused of other indictable offences may be sent for trial to either the Assizes or Quarter Sessions. Other kinds of cases dealt with by Petty Sessions are matrimonial

proceedings between husband and wife for separation or maintenance orders, bastardy cases and guardianship of infants. A special
division of the Bench, the Juvenile Court, deals with offenders under
seventeen. A Juvenile Court must sit on a different day or in a different room from the ordinary Petty Sessional Court, and must
exclude all persons from the court, except the Press and those
directly concerned with the case. The object is to keep the young
offender away from the atmosphere of crime, and to create a court
that will attempt to win back the young people to the ways of good
citizenship. The Press, as a general rule, does not give the names of
juvenile offenders in its account of proceedings.

Appeals can be made from Petty Sessions to Quarter Sessions, and
where a point of law is involved the justices may set out the facts (or
as it is said state a case) for the opinion of the Queens' Bench Division.
In guardianship cases, appeal may be made to the Chancery Division,
and in matrimonial cases, to the Divorce Division of the High Court.

The whole system of courts and the channels of appeal are summarised in the diagram below.

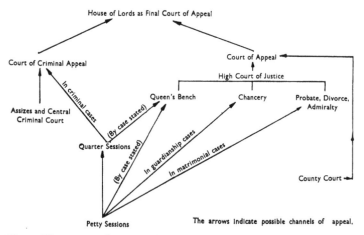

Fig. 5. The system of courts and channels of appeal. Cases may be sent for
trial from Petty Sessions to the Assizes or Quarter Sessions, as explained
on page 135

County Courts and Coroners' Courts

Standing somewhat apart from the plan of courts outlined so far are the County Courts and Coroners' Courts.

The County Courts in their modern form date from 1846, and have no connexion with the ancient Shire Courts which were presided over by the Sheriffs. The judge of a County Court must be a barrister of not less than seven years' standing. His jurisdiction is less important than that of a High Court judge; he almost invariably sits without a jury. There is no appeal from his decisions on questions of fact, except with leave, but there may be appeals on questions of law to the Court of Appeal. Many thousands of cases are settled in County Courts every year in a quiet and unspectacular fashion and with a minimum of expense. Recently, owing to the considerable increase in divorce work, many County Court judges have been appointed Divorce Commissioners with the powers of High Court judges, but it must be noted that they are not acting as County Court judges when sitting as Divorce Commissioners.

The Coroner's Court is an ancient survival dating back to Norman times. The coroner's business is to enquire into death from violence or sudden death, or where the cause of death is unknown and the doctor is unable to sign a death certificate. In certain cases, e.g. where death has resulted from a traffic or factory accident, cases of alleged murder, manslaughter or infanticide, he must sit with a jury of not more than eleven or less than seven persons. He examines witnesses and gathers information; in jury cases he sums the case up for the jury, who return their verdict. A second ancient function of the coroner is to hold an enquiry into the ownership of 'treasure-trove'—money, gold and silver which has been found hidden in the earth and whose ownership is in doubt. If the owner cannot be determined the 'treasure-trove' belongs to the Crown. In some areas, e.g. the City of London, the Coroner also has duties with regard to the investigation of cases of fire.

The Judicial Committee of the Privy Council

The jurisdiction of the Privy Council as a court of appeal for English colonies survived the abolition of the other prerogative jurisdictions carried out by the Long Parliament in 1641. The case of *Fryer* v. *Bernard* in 1724 established the principle that all appeals from the colonies should lie to the Privy Council. In 1833 an Act of Parliament defined the composition and jurisdiction of the Judicial Committee of the Privy Council, later amended by the Appellate Jurisdiction Acts of 1876 and 1887, and the Judicial Committee Amendment Act of 1895.

The Judicial Committee consists of the Lord Chancellor, the Lord President and Lords of Appeal in Ordinary, and other members of the Privy Council who have held high office, and up to five Dominion Chief Justices or Justices. It is the final court of appeal in ecclesiastical causes, admiralty prize cases within the United Kingdom, and civil and criminal appeals from the Isle of Man and the Channel Islands. Of the Commonwealth countries only Australia (under certain conditions) and New Zealand now retain appeal to the Judicial Committee.

Appeals to the Judicial Committee are either as of right or as of grace. In the former case the subject has the right of appeal, subject to any legal restrictions existing, without asking special leave of the Judicial Committee; in the latter case he can ask for special leave to appeal and this may be granted or refused by the Judicial Committee. The procedure of the Judicial Committee is to hear the allegations and proofs submitted, and then to advise the Queen in Council as to whether the appeal should be allowed or dismissed or the judgment varied. Effect is given to this advice by order in council. Finally, it should be noted that the Crown may refer to the Judicial Committee important issues that do not arise on appeal, e.g. in 1927 it considered Newfoundland's claim to a large part of Labrador.

Rivals of the law courts

Lord Hewart, in his book *The New Despotism*, called attention in a striking way to what he considered the grave danger to the citizen and the law arising from the powers given to Government departments to legislate under the clauses of Acts of Parliament, and to set up tribunals with judicial powers. Many examples of such tribunals could be mentioned, e.g. the special tribunals set up under the National Health Act, the Courts of Referees appointed to deal with industrial matters, the Milk Marketing Board, set up by the Ministry of Agriculture at the request of the farmers. Somewhat similar are the disciplinary powers exercised by the General Medical Council and the Law Society, whose decisions are seldom if ever questioned in the courts. There are advantages and disadvantages from the point of view of the citizen in the procedure of the tribunals. There is a lack of legal 'jargon'; there is less formality; the members of the tribunal are experts in the matters before them; decisions are reached more quickly and with less expense. On the other hand, the tribunal sits in private and needs to give no explanation of its decision. Furthermore, it may be that it is more susceptible to political pressure than a judicial court, and that the official may be at a greater advantage in such a tribunal than in a court where he could claim no special consideration by virtue of his office and duties. There was a famous dispute in the days of Charles I between the common lawyers and the King's prerogative courts which ended with the victory of the common lawyers and the abolition of the prerogative courts. Lord Hewart envisaged a similar, if less spectacular, dispute between the courts administering the common law and the administrative tribunals administering departmental regulations.

Scottish courts of law

This chapter has been concerned exclusively with the English courts of law. Scotland has a different system of law and different courts. Scots law differs considerably from that of England. In it there are few evidences of Celtic or tribal law; it is chiefly derived from the law of Rome, the canon law of the Church of Rome, feudal law and the English system. In civil cases the Sheriff Court corresponds in some respects with the County Court, but it has a wider jurisdiction, and there is no pecuniary limit set to the cases it may hear. The Court of Session has civil jurisdiction over the whole country, the judges, who number fifteen, being Senators of the College of Justice. Five of these sit as judges of First Instance in the Outer House, and the other ten in two divisions in the Inner House, which hears appeals. Appeal from the decisions of the Inner House lies to the House of Lords. In criminal cases, Justice of the Peace Courts and Police Courts deal with breaches of the peace and petty offences. From these there is appeal to the Quarter Sessions of the former courts, and to the High Court of Justiciary on points of law. Most of the work in criminal cases is done by the Sheriff Court, which can impose fines of up to £25 and sentences of up to three months' imprisonment by summary procedure, and up to two years' imprisonment by solemn procedure, i.e. when sitting with a jury, which is of fifteen not of twelve as in England. The High Court of Justiciary, the highest criminal court, consists of fifteen Senators, who are Lords Commissioners of Justiciary. They sit at Edinburgh and also go on circuit. Appeals against conviction by the High Court are heard by three or more judges of the High Court, and from their decision there is no appeal to the House of Lords.

The Lord Advocate is the law officer representing the Scottish legal system in the Government at Westminster.

CHAPTER XII

THE POLICE AND THE ARMED FORCES

THE POLICE

The English police tradition

The chief functions of the police force in Britain are the maintenance of law and order, the prevention of crime and the apprehension of criminals. The emphasis is on the preservation of order and the protection of the lives and property of the citizens. That the police exist to increase the powers of the executive, and as a convenient weapon under its direct control, is not part of the British tradition. It is this which marks the difference between Great Britain and what are sometimes called 'police' states, where in addition to normal police forces there are forces of special police with political functions. A further important feature is that the British police forces are civilian in character. This derives from the long tradition of police duties carried out locally by members of the community. The civilian nature of the British police is emphasised by the fact that they carry no arms, except a wooden truncheon to be used in self-defence.

Historical development

Permanent, regular and paid police forces in Great Britain are of comparatively recent growth. A few small forces, such as the Bow Street runners, attached to particular London magistrates' courts, were set up during the eighteenth century, but 1829, the year of Sir Robert Peel's Metropolitan Police Act, marks the real beginning of the police force of to-day. For the centuries prior to this date, each parish elected an unpaid constable, whose duty was to prevent breaches of the King's peace and to arrest criminal offenders and bring them before the justices of the peace. The great increase of population at the end of the eighteenth and beginning of the nineteenth century, and especially the rise of heavily populated towns, rendered these old police methods inadequate.

In 1829, Sir Robert Peel, then Home Secretary in the Duke of Wellington's Tory ministry, brought the Metropolitan Police Force into existence under the powers given by the Police Act of that year. The success of Peel's Metropolitan Police, in spite of much early opposition, led to the establishment of regularly enrolled and uniformed police forces elsewhere. In 1835 the reformed municipal boroughs of England and Wales were required by Act of Parliament to set up police forces. By an act of 1839 the counties of England and Wales could, if they wished, establish their own police forces. By the County and Borough Police Act of 1856, it became compulsory for such county police forces to be set up.

Police organisation in England and Wales

There is no single, national police force for the whole country. Instead there are in England and Wales between 120 and 130 separate police forces and a similar number of police authorities which control them administratively. At the centre, there is the Secretary of State for Home Affairs. He has a special responsibility for the Metropolitan Police, and exercises a general supervisory authority over the various police forces; he is particularly concerned with standards of efficiency and to this end can make regulations regarding conditions of service. He also receives the annual reports, made on the police forces (other than the Metropolitan Police) by Her Majesty's Inspectors of Constabulary.

County and county borough police forces

Each county (or in a few cases a union of neighbouring counties) maintains its force for policing its area. The police authority of the county is known as the Standing Joint Committee and is made up of an equal number of justices of the peace for the county and of representatives of the county council. This committee is concerned with the general policy relating to the maintenance and finance of their force, the details of size and ranks, and its buildings. Executive control and direction of the county force are in the hands of a Chief Constable appointed by the Standing Joint Committee. The Chief Constable of a county force has the power of appointing, promoting and dismissing members of the force, as well as disciplinary powers.

Most county boroughs, being counties for administrative purposes, have their own police force. The police authority is a committee of the county borough council known as the Watch Committee. Like the Standing Joint Committee in the county, the Watch Committee appoints a Chief Constable to direct its force, but on the other hand retains the powers of appointment, promotion, dismissal and discipline in its own hands.

In some areas, combined police forces have been formed by amalgamation, either on a voluntary basis or by compulsion exercised by the Home Secretary under powers given him by the Police Act of 1946. Examples are the counties of Breconshire, Montgomeryshire and Radnorshire, and the county of Chester and the city of Chester. The police authorities set up to control these combined forces are Joint Boards, on which the constituent authorities are represented.

The City of London Police Force

This is quite distinct from the Metropolitan Police. Its separate existence is largely explained by the ancient rights of self-government, including control of police, of the City of London, and the City's wealth and prestige. The police authority is the Court of Common Council of the City which delegates its powers to a Standing Police Committee. At the head of the City Police is a Commissioner.

The Metropolitan Police

This is by far the largest force in Great Britain, with an establishment of some 20,000 men. It polices an area with a radius of 15 miles from Charing Cross, which includes the whole of the County of London (except the city of London), the county of Middlesex, parts of the counties of Hertfordshire, Essex, Kent and Surrey, and the three county boroughs of West Ham, East Ham and Croydon. Unlike the other police forces of England and Wales the Metropolitan Police Force is not controlled by any local authority; it is directly under the Home Secretary, who is responsible for general policy relating to it. Parliament takes a particular interest in this force because of its size and its special relationship with the Home Secretary.

Constitutional importance of the British police tradition

The British police are the instruments of law, not of policy, that is, their executive task is primarily to secure observance of democratically made laws, not to enforce obedience to the mandates of a government. In achieving the observance of the laws the British police have shown that physical force need be little used if the good will and co-operation of the public can be secured. They have therefore cultivated good relations with the public, have emphasised their own civilian and unarmed character and have aimed at an impartial enforcement of the law. On the whole their aim has been achieved, and the public has realised the value of order and security maintained in this way.

THE ARMED FORCES

The armed forces of the Crown are the Royal Navy, the Army and the Royal Air Force. Our concern here is not with their organisation and operational use, but with the constitutional status of the forces themselves and of the officers and men who belong to them. History shows the danger to the democratic state if it leaves unregulated the position of its armed forces; there is then a temptation for the executive to usurp control of the armed forces, to use them to over-throw constitutional government and to set up dictatorship instead. Therefore the legislature must establish its control over the armed forces; it must also make provision for their internal discipline and determine the legal status of their officers and men.

Distrust of armed forces controlled by the sovereign, particularly of a standing army, was felt by British people as long ago as the seventeenth century. In the Petition of Right (1628), Parliament showed their distrust of armed forces by their demand that there should be no use made of martial (or military) law and that the troops should not be billeted in the houses of private citizens. Some years later, in 1642, the Long Parliament deprived Charles I of control of the militia, or local force, which was important in days when there was no standing army. The rule of the Commonwealth (1649-60), which to a considerable extent was military government by an army controlled by Cromwell and the senior officers, left bitter memories in the minds of Englishmen. Some authorities think this period was decisive in imprinting on the minds of Englishmen an enduring dis-trust of standing armies as the enemies of free government, and also in fostering the subsequent determination to bring about strong parliamentary control over the armed forces. The action of James II who, in his attempt to establish despotic rule, brought an army ten

144

thousand strong to overawe the City of London proved decisive in the matter. After his overthrow, the Declaration of Rights (1689) limited the royal prerogative by enacting that the Crown should not, in time of peace, keep a standing army without consent of Parliament. No such limitation was imposed in the case of the Navy, which it was felt could not endanger liberty in the same way as a standing army.

Command of the armed forces

A statute of 1661 declared that the supreme command of all forces by sea and land was an undoubted right of the sovereign. From 1661 onwards, the Crown delegated its powers of command over its land forces to variously named officers such as 'Captain-General' (e.g. Marlborough during the Spanish Succession War), or more usually 'Commander-in-Chief'. In 1904, an important change in the system of command was made when by letters patent the Army Council was constituted. This body had both civil and military members, and to it were transferred all the sovereign's prerogative powers of command and of administration of the Army, which formerly had been delegated to the Secretary of State and Commander-in-Chief. Similar bodies exist for the Royal Navy and Royal Air Force, viz. the Board of Admiralty and the Air Council.

Parliamentary control

The First Lord of the Admiralty, the Secretary of State for War and the Secretary of State for Air are all ministers of cabinet rank, but of recent years have not had seats in the cabinet, where their place has been taken by the Minister of Defence. They are the constitutional and responsible advisers of the Crown in all matters connected with their respective services. They are also responsible to Parliament for the conduct of affairs of each service by the particular body over which they preside, viz. the Board of Admiralty, the Army Council, and the Air Council. Parliamentary control is exercised by questions addressed to the minister concerned, and by criticism during the debates on the Navy, Army and Air Force estimates. The Opposition can also move, by way of censure on the Government's policy with regard to the Armed Forces, a token reduction of £100 in the vote of supply for any of the three services.

The discipline of the armed forces

The maintenance of good order and discipline in the armed forces in peace and war is accomplished, in the case of the Army and Royal Air Force, by a comprehensive code of military law contained in the Army and Air Force Act and also by regulations deriving their authority from this Act. Discipline in the Navy is provided for by the Navy Discipline Act of 1866 and subsequent amendments of this Act. While the members of the armed forces, both officers and men, are governed by these codes of law in peace and war, at home and abroad, they are still subject to the ordinary law of the land, and for offences against it may, in certain circumstances, be tried by a civil court and not by a court-martial. Thus the principle is established that members of the armed forces do not gain immunity from the ordinary law of the land by their membership of these forces, or because they are already subject to naval, military or air force law. Furthermore, the armed forces are deemed to take the law of England with them wherever they may go abroad, and their members may be tried by a court-martial for civil offences they commit there, unless there has been an agreement, between Her Majesty's Government and the government of the country concerned, that such offences should be tried by the courts of that country.

The Mutiny Acts, 1689 and 1878

The need for powers to enforce discipline in a standing army led indirectly to an increase of parliamentary control. This was brought about by the Mutiny Act of 1689. Its primary purpose was to legalise the existence of a standing army and the enforcement of military law by court-martial with appropriate punishments for mutiny, sedition and desertion, but for no other military offences. As this Act remained in force for a limited period of up to a year at a time, the Crown had to seek its annual re-enactment by Parliament because otherwise it would be unable legally to enforce discipline in its land forces within the kingdom. The yearly renewal of the Act gave both Houses of Parliament opportunity to criticise matters connected with the Army.

The Articles of War

The Mutiny Act of 1689 was limited in its operation to three offences against military discipline: mutiny, sedition and desertion. It also applied only to soldiers within the kingdom in time of peace. The Crown therefore had to provide means of dealing with the many other offences against military discipline committed by troops in time of war outside the kingdom either in its own dominions or elsewhere. It did this by the Articles of War, which were issued by the prerogative authority of the Crown and enforced by courts-martial similarly authorised. This prerogative basis was altered by the Mutiny Act of 1718, when Parliament gave statutory authority to the Crown to make Articles of War, and set up courts-martial for their enforcement in time of peace for all troops within the Crown's dominions. In 1803, an Act extended these powers to troops operating outside the dominions of the Crown, who hitherto had been disciplined by Articles of War issued under the prerogative.

The Army Act, 1881

Down to 1879 discipline in the Army had been enforced by the Mutiny Act and the Articles of War. Between 1879 and 1881 they were combined together and enacted as the Army Act of 1881. This Act specified in detail the offences against discipline and laid down the powers and procedure of courts-martial which could try them. It also provided for certain administrative matters such as enlistment, terms of service, billeting of troops on civilians and requisitioning of vehicles. It should be noted that, in the case of billeting and requisitioning of vehicles, private citizens are affected, and are liable to penalties under the Act for non-compliance.

For the Army Act has now been substituted 'The Army and Air Force (Annual) Act'. The preamble, or opening paragraph, of this Act repeats what was first stated in the Mutiny Act of 1689, viz. that it is illegal to raise or maintain an army in time of peace without consent of Parliament, thus reasserting the doctrine of parliamentary control.

Duties in aid of the civil power

The armed forces may be called out to aid the civil power when there are public disturbances (which may include unlawful assemblies, routs, riots or insurrections) beyond the power of control of the magistrates and police. The members of the armed forces are then carrying out the common law duty, which applies to all citizens, of suppressing, by all the means in their power, breaches of the Queen's peace. Custom, rather than any Act of Parliament, has placed this duty on the armed forces. The use of troops to aid the civil power is as a rule only granted by the military commander on requisition by a magistrate or chief constable. The commander of troops sent to aid the civil power is in a delicate position which calls for exercise of great judgment. He will, as a rule, be held responsible if he allows an unnecessary amount of force to be used by his troops in quelling the disturbance, and he will also be culpable if he and his troops remain so inactive that the disturbance gets entirely out of hand, and loss of life and damage to property ensue.

CHAPTER XIII

LOCAL GOVERNMENT I. ITS DEVELOPMENT AND PRESENT-DAY ORGANISATION

The development of local government before the nineteenth century

Local government in its present form was developed in the nineteenth and twentieth centuries, for it was not until after the passage of the great parliamentary Reform Act of 1832 that any attempt was made to reform or organise local government. In the eighteenth century, there were only survivals from medieval and Elizabethan times. Among them were the Lords Lieutenant of the counties, the sheriffs and the coroners, whose offices continue to the present day and about whom more is said on page 160. But the chief responsibility in the rural areas rested upon the justices of the peace and the parishes, and in the towns with the borough councils. The justices of the peace acquired their title in the fourteenth century. In the fifteenth and sixteenth centuries, they became the general agents of the Tudors in the maintenance of order in the countryside, and they worked in close co-operation with responsible people in the parishes —parish vestries was the name given to their meetings. Their chief functions were the maintenance of law and order, the administration of the poor law and the repair of the highways, but the justices also had other duties, including wage regulation, the relations between masters and servants, the enforcement of laws about religion and the licensing of ale houses. They did their work with little supervision from the central government, and their practice varied greatly in different districts, though they had opportunities for discussion at their Quarter Sessions. The justices of the peace and the parishes were more concerned with keeping down the expenditure than with efficient services. Indeed, various other local authorities for special purposes were set up for the provision of better amenities, e.g. the turnpike trusts for the building and maintenance of trunk roads. But the importance of the justices of the peace remained, and until the passing of the County Councils Act in 1888 the only unifying authorities in local government were the justices of the peace sitting in Quarter Sessions. They have retained some of their former administrative duties to-day, for instance with regard to the licensing of inns, and, in partnership with the county council, as the responsible authority for police through the Standing Joint Committee.

The powers of the boroughs rested on their charters, which were granted by the monarch and which allowed them certain privileges, e.g. the right to have a mayor and corporation or council, the right to collect their own taxes and to hold markets. Many of the boroughs were very small, and the method of election of the mayor and corporation varied from place to place and often very few people were qualified to vote.

The beginning of reform

The first big measure of reform affecting local government was the Poor Law Amendment Act of 1834 which swept away the old Elizabethan system of relief by the parishes acting under the supervision of the justices of the peace and substituted administration of poor relief through unions of parishes, who were supervised by three Poor Law Commissioners appointed by the government, thus beginning central control. These unions were created without regard to existing poor law units and often overstepped the boundaries of shires, or, as they are now known, counties. They were under the immediate control of Boards of Guardians, of which the justices of the peace were ex-officio members. The same units, the unions, were used in 1836 when compulsory registration of births, deaths, and marriages was introduced. The Poor Law Board took the place of the Poor Law Commissioners in 1847, and the Board itself was absorbed into the Local Government Board in 1871. The Poor Law of 1834 remained on the statute book until the passage of the Local Government Act of 1929.

Next came a measure of the greatest importance in the history of local government—the Municipal Corporations Act of 1835, which established uniformly elected town councils in place of the ancient and often corrupt corporations of the boroughs, and which introduced a system of audit, an essential feature of the reform. The process of simplification was, however, not continued and, as new needs arose, new bodies were in many places created to meet them, e.g. burial boards, boards of health, lighting commissioners etc., all with powers to levy rates, with the result that local government became a 'chaos of areas, a chaos of franchises and a chaos of rates'.

The next significant measure was the Public Health Act of 1848. Serious outbreaks of cholera had impressed on Parliament and the public the need for vigorous action. The Public Health Act of 1848 set up a general Board of Health of three members which had powers to create local boards but which had no coercive powers. A further Royal Commission in 1869 urged the creation of a new department responsible for the services connected with public health, and in 1871 the Local Government Board was formed with this as one of its functions. In 1875 a new Public Health Act divided the country into urban and rural sanitary districts to improve local conditions and to combat infectious diseases. These districts were the basis for the urban and rural districts in the more general reform of local government in 1894. Reforms in housing were made at the same time, authorising for the first time slum-clearance schemes by local authorities.

The Local Government Acts of 1888 and 1894

The time had now come for radical change. By the Local Government, or County Councils, Act of 1888, county councils and county borough councils were established. The functions of the county councils were at first narrow, for they did little more than take over the local government functions of the justices of the peace in Quarter Sessions and provided for the establishment of Standing Joint Committees of county councillors and justices of the peace to deal with police matters in the counties. The same act separated the largest boroughs from the counties and made them county boroughs, which combined the functions of counties and boroughs. At the same time a new county of London was created.

The Local Government, or Parish Councils, Act of 1894 aimed at the improved organisation of the areas covered by the urban and rural sanitary districts, and the transfer to the new county districts created by the Act of the functions previously performed by various commissioners, highway boards, boards of health and other *ad hoc* bodies, which had in the course of time been established. As sub-divisions of the rural councils, civil parishes, which were not necessarily coincident with the long-established ecclesiastical parishes, were given minor powers.

Twentieth-century developments

There have been in the twentieth century many acts dealing with various aspects of local government. These have sometimes conferred and sometimes taken away powers, but the main outline of local government structure has remained as it was after the passage of the 1894 Act, even though the chief responsibility for the oversight of local government was first transferred from the Local Government Board to the Ministry of Health, and later from the Ministry of Health to the Ministry of Housing and Local Government. The Local Government Act of 1929 extended the powers of the bigger authorities at the expense of the smaller, and made other important changes, particularly with regard to rating. The centralising process has been continued in the last twenty-five years, and in consequence county councils and county boroughs have lost some functions to bodies controlled by the central government, and have gained others from boroughs and county districts. Extensive reorganisation and redrawing of local government boundaries has also been contemplated, with further moves towards the creation of 'regions', but for various reasons there has not yet been any action resulting from the report of the Boundary Commission which sat from 1946 to 1949.

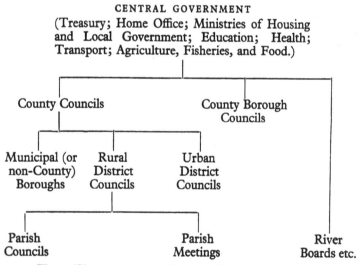

Fig. 6. The present organisation of Local Government.

Local authorities to-day

There are six types of local government authorities to-day: in England and Wales there are rural parish councils and meetings numbering about 11,000; rural district councils numbering 474; urban district councils, 562 in number; municipal, or non-county, borough councils numbering 318; county councils, of which there are 62, and county borough councils, of which there are 83. These carry out the general work of local administration. There are, in addition, a number of special, or *ad hoc*, bodies which exercise independent powers in the local government areas and on which the local authorities are represented. The local government of London requires a special scheme of administration which is explained later in this chapter.

Qualifications for local government electors and candidates

The qualifications for the vote for local government elections are in general similar to those for parliamentary elections. The electors are British subjects of either sex of the full age of twenty-one years, who have not by any reason been disqualified, and who are resident in the local government area or who have a non-resident qualification by occupying rateable land or property of a yearly value of not less than £10. Thus an elector may be entitled to vote in more than one local government area. He may, however, vote in only one ward or parish in any particular area in any one election.

Candidates for local elections must normally reside in the district where they seek election. The most important disqualification applying to candidates in local government elections in addition to those that apply in parliamentary elections is the holding of paid office directly from the authority to which election is sought. Any qualified person who can obtain a proposer and seconder and eight supporters to his nomination may stand; he need not produce a deposit, nor has he to pay any forfeit if he fails to poll a certain proportion of the votes.

The amount a candidate may spend in contesting an election is strictly limited, and there are penalties for corrupt and illegal practices. Polling is conducted under the same strict supervision as in parliamentary elections. There are differences in the actual conduct of local elections from parliamentary elections. For example if there are six vacancies in any one ward, or sub-division of a district or borough, an elector is able to vote for six candidates.

As has already been stated, most local elections are nowadays contested on a party basis. Support therefore is usually sought by candidates from the local branch of one of the parties, with the result that there is a steady decrease of independent candidates. The composition of the local council varies according to the nature and size of the area. The county council often has a high proportion of retired persons or persons of independent means, as the meetings of the council and of the committees are held during the day time, and members often have to travel considerable distances to the county headquarters. Even on county councils, however, men and women of all classes and occupations are to be found, including professional men and women, trade union officials, business executives, clerks, skilled and unskilled workers and housewives.

There is little enthusiasm about local elections. The poll is invariably lower than for parliamentary elections, and rarely reaches fifty per cent. of the electorate. In the counties particularly the poll is usually low, and there is a high proportion of uncontested seats. In spite of the lack of interest and glamour, local government work is of high importance and makes many demands upon council members. It provides a valuable training for those with political ambitions, and soon induces a sense of responsibility which is sometimes lacking in new members of local government councils.

The parish

The smallest units of local government are civil parishes in rural districts. In the smallest parishes, with a population of under three hundred, there is a parish meeting which all ratepayers may attend and which meets twice a year, one meeting being in March. In parishes with a population of more than three hundred, a parish council of from five to fifteen members is elected. Parish meetings, the only example of direct government in Britain, have very limited powers and parish councils are only slightly more powerful. They may provide amenities such as parks and recreation grounds, and also a water supply, street lighting, baths and cemeteries. As agents for the rural district council, they may perform further functions. Complaints may be made to the district councils, and, if no satisfaction can be got there, to the county council. Parishes are not compelled to appoint any officers. An unpaid clerk or treasurer may be appointed, or a paid clerk. In general the rural district council does the local governing, and the parish council makes its views known to the rural district council.

Rural and urban districts

The rural district is made up of parishes. The urban district, as its name implies, is an area of denser population; in it parishes have no local government powers. These county districts, which are subdivisions of the county in which they lie, have councillors elected for parishes or wards for three years; usually one-third of the councillors retires each year, but in urban districts, by permission of the county council, the whole council may be elected every third year. The chairman is elected by the council from among or from outside its members, and is a justice of the peace for his year of office. The functions of the councils of the county districts (urban districts, rural districts and municipal boroughs) interlock in a complex fashion with those of the county council. The county council exercises a general supervisory authority in matters of sanitation, and has special powers with regard to rural housing. Urban districts may have powers which make them indistinguishable except in civic dignity from boroughs. An urban or rural district appoints a number of officers, including a clerk, a treasurer, a surveyor, a medical officer of health and a sanitary inspector. And it levies rates, on its own behalf and for the county council.

The municipal borough

As has been indicated in the preceding paragraph, the powers of municipal boroughs (i.e. boroughs which are not county boroughs) differ little from those of urban districts, and they are part of the area of the county council for many purposes. The borough has a charter of incorporation. Its government is in the hands of the mayor, the aldermen and the councillors, who together form the corporation. One-third of the councillors retires each year, and half of the aldermen each third year, the aldermen being elected by their fellows on the council. The mayor is elected annually, and is a justice of the peace while he is in office. Occasionally someone outside the council is chosen as mayor as a special honour, or in case of some difficulty. An urban district that wishes to acquire the dignity of a borough must give notice to the county council and the Ministry of Housing and Local Government, and make a petition to the Queen. If, after enquiry by the minister, the petition is supported by the appropriate committee of the Privy Council, and if no objection is made locally, a charter may be granted by order in council.

The borough appoints officers similar to those of an urban district, and may in addition appoint a borough education officer if it is an 'excepted district', i.e. a district which retains a degree of independence in educational matters, which normally are within the province of the county council. There are still many very small boroughs maintaining their ancient dignity, and even exercising the privilege of appointing their own Recorder, who acts as sole magistrate at the Borough Quarter Sessions.

The county councils

The County Councils Act of 1888 retained most of the ancient shires as administrative councils, but subdivided some to form more than one administrative county, e.g. Yorkshire was divided into three Ridings, Sussex into East and West Sussex. London also was made an administrative county. The size of the administrative counties varies greatly from Rutland, with a population of about 20,000, to

Lancashire, with over 2,000,000. The demarcation, being based on historical causes, results in many anomalies and inconveniences. There are sixty-two administrative counties in England and Wales, and out of them eighty-three county boroughs have been carved. The separation of these county boroughs has often caused great difficulties in the administration of the counties, and for this reason the creation of a new county borough is vigorously opposed by the county council from whose territory it would be formed and no new county borough has been created since 1933.

The county council is elected every three years in April. It elects, and is presided over by, a chairman who is a justice of the peace while holding his office. Aldermen to the number of one-third of the councillors are elected by the council for six years. The county council must meet at least quarterly. Its meetings are held in the administrative capital of the county and, as many councillors have some distance to travel, meetings are held in day time. County councils do not levy rates directly, but, as precepting authorities, rely on the municipal boroughs and the urban and rural districts in their areas to collect the rates they demand of them.

County boroughs

A county borough combines the functions of a county council and a municipal borough. It is thus an all-purpose local authority. County boroughs are places of considerable importance, and, with one or two exceptions, of considerable population. In some instances a county borough may be dignified with the title of a city, in which case the mayor sometimes becomes a lord mayor. The Local Government Act of 1888 laid down 50,000 as the minimum population for a county borough. This figure was raised to 75,000 in 1926. The distribution of county boroughs is irregular. In the geographical county of Lancashire there are seventeen; in Kent with a population of 1,500,000 there is only one, and that is the ancient city of Canterbury with a population of about 30,000; in Middlesex, which is almost wholly urban and which has a population of 2,000,000, there is none.

London

London is an administrative county, and through historical causes and for reasons resulting from its paramount importance as well as from its great population and extent has a local government system differing from that of any other part of the country.

The Corporation of the City of London

First of all there is the City of London, whose government system is ancient and unique. The City is divided into twenty-six wards, which return councillors to the Court of Common Council, the electors being those with business or residential qualifications. In addition to over two hundred councillors, the Court of Common Council includes twenty-six aldermen who, with the Lord Mayor, form the Court of Aldermen. There is also the Court of Common Hall composed of Aldermen and the Liverymen of the City Companies, the descendants of the ancient guilds of craftsmen and merchants. The Court of Common Hall each year elects the sheriffs, and selects two aldermen, from whom the Court of Aldermen makes the final choice of the Lord Mayor. The Court of Common Council is the governing body of the City, and exercises powers similar to those of the councils of the metropolitan boroughs, with certain additions e.g. the city has its own police, and civil and criminal courts. The City of London, the financial centre of the United Kingdom, and still in some respects of the world, retains enormous prestige as well as much of its ancient privilege.

The London County Council

Before the passage of the County Councils Act of 1888 vestry, or parish, meetings conducted the affairs of the districts of the metropolis outside the city boundaries. There were also in the City and in the surrounding parishes many *ad hoc* bodies of improvement commissioners, etc. as elsewhere in the country. Some degree of central control was brought about by the setting up in 1855 of the Metropolitan Board of Works, on which each vestry was represented. The

County Councils Act established the county of London with a directly elected council, and in 1899 the vestries were replaced by twenty-eight metropolitan boroughs, with powers similar to, but not exactly corresponding with, those of the municipal boroughs.

The London County Council is elected every three years in April. It consists of 126 councillors and 21 aldermen elected for six years, half retiring each three years, and is organised on a basis of political parties. The Chairman of the Council was in 1935 granted the style of Right Honourable, a distinction he shares with the Lord Mayor of London.

The budget of the London County Council is as big as that of some European states. Its income is derived from rates, levied through the metropolitan boroughs and the City, government grants, and income from property and trading activities.

The responsibilities of the London County Council are immense—in education, housing, welfare, town planning and many other spheres. Unlike the counties and county boroughs it has no responsibility for police, for the Metropolitan Police alone among the police forces of the country is directly under ministerial control, that of the Home Secretary (see p. 143).

The metropolitan boroughs

The metropolitan boroughs share the local government of the county of London with the London County Council in much the same way as the municipal boroughs co-operate with the county councils. Each has its own councillors and aldermen, and its own mayor, who is a justice of the peace during his year of office. The metropolitan boroughs are the rating authorities, and are responsible for compiling the voting registers. Some have their own housing schemes. They have their own libraries and baths, and supplement the provision for parks and recreation grounds made by the London County Council.

'Ad hoc' authorities

There are numerous *ad hoc*, or special purpose, authorities

159

operating within the London County Council area. The Metropolitan
Police cover an area which extends beyond the L.C.C. area. The
Metropolitan Water Board also covers a much wider area than the
County of London. The Thames Conservancy Board, the Port of
London Authority, London Transport, and the various Gas and
Electricity Boards all perform functions which come, or formerly
came, within the scope of some local government authorities. In
common with other local authorities the London County Council has
representatives upon these bodies, but they do not control them or
their policy. The removal of these functions, and in some cases
sources of income, is a feature of twentieth-century centralisation and
nationalisation.

Scottish local government

Local government in Scotland, like that in England and Wales, has
been extensively reformed in the last thirty years. Owing to the
scattered population, there has been a greater concentration of powers
in the hands of the county councils, which are composed partly of
representatives elected by the burghs, or towns, and partly of
councillors chosen directly by the rural districts. The burghs are of
three kinds: royal, many with ancient charters dating from long
before the union with England; parliamentary, and police. The royal
and parliamentary burghs are usually independent of the county
councils except for education, of which only the most important royal
burghs have control. In general, as in England, the powers of the
county councils are being extended at the expense of the smaller
burghs, and the central government is taking over functions formerly
performed by local authorities.

Ancient offices surviving in local government

Among the ancient offices surviving in local government, as is
mentioned on page 148, are those of the Lord Lieutenant, sheriff and
coroner.

The Lord Lieutenant to-day is the Queen's personal representative
in the county. He is the chief of the county justices of the peace and

keeper of their records, and, with the assistance of an advisory committee, recommends to the Lord Chancellor persons for appointment as justices of the peace. His duties are chiefly ceremonial, and, as the Queen's personal representative, he takes precedence over all office holders in the county. He also has important duties in connexion with the Territorial Army and the cadet force. He appoints twenty Deputy Lieutenants from persons in the county who have rendered worthy service, and he selects a Vice-Lieutenant to act for him in his absence.

The sheriff of a county has few important administrative duties. He summons juries, carries out the judgments of the Assizes, and is responsible for the carrying out of death sentences. He attends on the Justices of Assize and is returning officer in parliamentary elections.

The coroner, who in medieval times was elected by the freemen's court of the shire, is appointed by the county or county borough council. His duties have been mentioned in chapter XI, page 137.

Composition and functions of the full council

One of the first duties of a new council is the election of a chairman. In the case of a borough or county borough the chairman is styled the Mayor or in some cases Lord Mayor. A mayor or chairman may be granted a reasonable sum to cover the whole, or part, of the expenses that fall upon him as holder of the office.

The aldermen of county councils, county borough and municipal borough councils do not in any sense form an upper house, but sit with and have the same voting rights as the elected councillors. They are almost invariably the most experienced members of the council, and provide a valuable element of continuity. Where the division of the council is on party lines, an attempt is made at the election of aldermen to preserve a similar distribution of parties.

The council itself is responsible for the setting up of its committees, the provision of the necessary finance, the general structure of the staff of the council, and the working of the administrative machine. Perhaps its most important duty is to receive the estimates placed before it by the chairman of the finance committee and, when the 'budget' has been approved, to fix the rate which will provide a large part of its income. It is through the financial estimates that the council exercises control over its committees.

Another function of the council is to make by-laws, which it is permitted to make on certain subjects within the terms of the charter or Act of Parliament from which it derives its authority. It is also part of its work to promote private bills in Parliament, when local schemes require such action.

The procedure in the council is governed by standing orders, which have regard to its statutory obligations and lay down rules for procedure and debate. The standing orders, which often conform to model standing orders drawn up by the Minister of Health in 1935, are accepted from year to year with whatever change is considered necessary, a two-thirds majority usually being necessary for an amendment. Firm rules of procedure are essential in view of the amount of business that has to be carried through in a short time by the full council, whereas procedure in committee can be far more free-and-easy.

The effects of the introduction of party politics into local government have been felt not only in the election of mayors and chairmen of council, but also in the composition of committees. An attempt is often made to see that the pattern of the more important committees conforms to that of the council as a whole. In practice it is often difficult to define a 'party line' which council members must follow. Independent action is much more common, especially among experienced members, than in the House of Commons.

Committees

Local authorities could not carry out their many different activities if all discussions had to be carried on in meetings of the full council. So that matters can be more fully and more informally discussed, councils appoint a number of committees. The appointment of some of these is required by statute, e.g. a county council must appoint committees for finance, education, small-holdings, diseases of animals, fire-brigades, health, housing, children's services and welfare, and must also nominate members to the Standing Joint Committee. Though other authorities are less rigidly bound by statutory requirements, necessity forces the committee system upon them. It is customary for every member of a council to be nominated to at least one committee—in all probability he will be called upon to serve on several. In this way many calls will be made upon his time, and he will have plenty of opportunities of showing his worth to the community he is serving.

At its first meeting, each committee appoints its chairman. Upon him a great deal of work and responsibility falls, for he has to make decisions between the meetings of his committee and, as he afterwards has to obtain its approval of these, he must be a person of tact and judgment. Each committee has power to appoint sub-committees to deal with specific aspects of its work, and to report back to the main committee. The chairmen of the various committees often form a kind of inner cabinet, whose advice is sought by the chairman of the council or mayor. One of the most important of the committees is the finance and general purposes committee, which has the task of reviewing the estimates and expenditure of the various departments, and of presenting the consolidated estimates to the council.

In big authorities, some of the committees have so complex and important a task that they become almost autonomous. An example is the Education Committee of a big county authority, which must itself make many decisions in carrying out the statutory functions which have been delegated to it by the county council. Such committees must of course submit their estimates to the county council for approval.

Each committee is usually authorised by the council to spend the amount specified in the estimates for the objects approved, the treasurer paying the accounts submitted to him. It should be noted that all capital expenditure must be approved by the full council, which alone can raise a loan.

The real limitation on the autonomy of the committees is the requirement that they shall submit a report to the council. Some reports are merely accounts of what has been done, e.g. extracts from committee minutes, others are in the form of recommendations for which the approval of the council is sought, the chairman of the committee submitting a motion that the report or recommendation be adopted and acted upon. Such a motion gives members a chance of defining policy by raising objections, referring back, or even rejecting the recommendations of the committee.

The functions of committees vary greatly from authority to authority, depending partly upon the extent to which the council delegates its power. The statutory committees are generally the largest, but the size of each committee is usually laid down in standing orders. The most important committees sometimes comprise the full council.

The length of time between meetings of county councils and their committees makes particularly heavy the responsibilities of chairmen of committees, who must have plenty of time to devote to the council's affairs and to keep in touch with its officers. The agenda for meetings is drawn up by the appropriate officer in consultation with the committee chairman and, as he has greater knowledge than other members of the matters under discussion, he can easily influence and direct the course of a debate.

Local government officers

As the scope of local government has been extended, so the need for full-time officers has increased. In the smallest authorities, it is still possible to find a part-time clerk or treasurer, but the number of these is diminishing. The increased mass of legislation and governmental regulations demand a technical knowledge which only a full-time and fully trained officer can have. This applies not only to the town clerk, or clerk of the council, and the treasurer, but also to other important officers such as the medical officer of health, the education officer, the surveyor, and the sanitary inspector. The officers are considered to be uninfluenced by those local interests which may affect the opinions and judgment of the elected representatives.

The importance of the local government service is becoming more fully recognised. By reason of its nature, organisation and recruitment on a national scale are not possible, although the charters negotiated with the local government authorities by the National Association of Local Government Officers have achieved some uniformity of salary scales. Thus no effective comparison can be made with the Civil Service. The chief technical adviser to the council may be, indeed almost certainly will be, the chief administrative officer of the department, so that division into grades like those of the Civil Service is impossible.

All councils must by law appoint a clerk—the town clerk in the case of a county borough or borough, the clerk of the council in the case of the county and other councils. Every county council must also appoint a treasurer, a medical officer, a chief education officer and a surveyor. All boroughs, urban and rural councils must appoint treasurers, medical officers of health, surveyors, and sanitary inspectors.

The town clerk or clerk of the council is usually a solicitor and is responsible for the general co-ordination of the work of the council. His authority varies with his personality and ability. He is the chairman's, or mayor's, right-hand man. He is at the service of chairmen of committees, and has a particularly heavy responsibility in times of transition, when a new council with many new members is taking over. His advice is of paramount importance in any local matters concerning the council, and he must see that it keeps within its legal powers. He keeps the official records of the authority.

The treasurer, especially of a big county or county borough, has heavy responsibilities. With the chairman of the finance committee he prepares the estimates for presentation to the council and suggests the rate to be levied. Receipts, payments, audits, the keeping of statistics, the raising of loans and the investment of council funds are within the compass of his appointment.

The medical officer of health must be a fully qualified doctor, and usually also holds the diploma of public health or a similar qualification. He is chiefly an administrator; within his jurisdiction are sanitary inspection, food sampling and analysis, the prevention of infectious diseases, maternity and child welfare services, the ambulance service, home nursing and the welfare of old people, and as school medical officer, the medical examination of school children.

The duties of the education officer are briefly explained on pages 170-2. In the county and county boroughs these are of paramount importance, concerning as they do, not only the council which employs him, but also the whole of the children of school age, the teachers and the numerous other employees of the committee.

The surveyor is usually a qualified surveyor or an engineer. He too has many and varied duties connected with roads, sewers, housing, the maintenance and repair of council property, and whatever else of a similar kind the council requires of him.

These are only the chief officers. There are others of importance, the number varying with the size and nature of the authority. The highest officers receive remuneration comparable with what they might receive in the Civil Service, but probably not commensurate with what they would receive for work of similar responsibility in commerce or industry. The remuneration of those not in the highest class is often not in keeping with either the dignity or the duties of the post. In consequence, in days of full employment, it is difficult to obtain recruits of the right calibre. It must not be forgotten that in addition to the general, clerical, administrative, professional and technical grades for which national scales have been negotiated, local authorities employ an even greater number of manual workers, whose wages are determined by trade union agreement.

CHAPTER XIV

LOCAL GOVERNMENT II. ITS SCOPE, FINANCE, AND RELATIONS WITH THE CENTRAL GOVERNMENT

The scope of local government

Local government affects the citizen in all phases of his life. The house in which he lives may have been built by the borough or district council; the road in which it stands is probably maintained by it; the sewage system is provided by it; the refuse is collected by it; the bus that takes him to work may be run by it; the school attended by his children is probably provided by a local authority.

Local authorities derive their powers from Acts of Parliament. Even the powers conferred on boroughs by charter are confirmed directly or indirectly in Acts of Parliament, for it is a first principle of the British form of democratic government that no one shall be taxed or have a rate levied upon him except on the authority of his elected representatives. The acts under which local authorities carry out their functions are of three kinds: general acts applying to all authorities in a particular class; adoptive or permissive acts, which a local authority may, if it wishes, apply; and local acts, obtained by a local authority for its own specific purposes.

Local government has grown to meet the changing needs and conditions of the day and of the community. It has never been completely reorganised nor have its relations with the central government ever been codified or redefined. In consequence there is a lack of uniformity, which has not been removed by the great reforming acts of the nineteenth and twentieth centuries.

So great is the variation in the powers of local authorities that it is impossible to make any general statement that will apply to all authorities of the same standing. The central government, through the enactment of adoptive acts, has intentionally allowed local authorities freedom of action to use or not to use certain powers, or in the case of county councils to delegate or not to delegate them to a county district or borough. Co-operation between adjacent authorities also varies. In some places joint committees of adjacent areas are common, especially for town and country planning, in others the authorities work in virtual isolation.

Some indication of the range of functions carried out by local government authorities, and the distribution of them between the various authorities, is given on pages 176-8.

Sanitation and public health

The necessity for the provision of safeguards of public health was largely responsible for the reforms of local government in the second half of the nineteenth century. These safeguards were partly preventive and partly curative. The preventive services largely remain with the local councils, the curative functions have in great part been taken out of their hands by the Ministry of Health.

The preventive or sanitary services include public baths, swimming baths and washhouses, the provision and inspection of drains and sewers, the collection and disposal of refuse, the cleansing of streets, the provision of public conveniences, the suppression of nuisances, the supervision of trades and industries which may cause offence by smoke pollution, objectionable smells, the contamination of streams or rivers, the inspection and disinfecting of verminous persons or filthy premises.

The inspection of food and drugs is another important duty that devolves upon local authorities. This includes the maintenance of proper standards of purity and quality, the supervision of conditions of manufacture, storage and sale, the investigation of food poisoning, the inspection of markets and slaughterhouses. A public analyst is appointed by a county or county borough to carry out tests of samples of foods, drugs, water, milk, etc. within its area.

The prevention of the spread of infectious diseases is another duty of the local authority. A list of diseases notifiable to the medical officer of health is compiled. Persons suffering from such diseases may be compulsorily removed to hospital, if satisfactory arrangements cannot be made for their isolation at home. Arrangements are also made for the disinfection where necessary of premises, clothing, bedding, etc. Local authorities are also required to make provision for the free vaccination of all children within six months of birth.

National and local government responsibilities are now interwoven, to provide a comprehensive cover in all matters of public health. Among the public health duties still resting upon the local councils are the establishment of maternity homes and ante-natal and post-

168

natal clinics, where advice, assistance and treatment may be obtained free of charge. Local authorities must assure themselves that there is available an adequate number of qualified midwives, employed either by themselves or by voluntary organisation, and they may provide a service of domestic help for expectant and nursing mothers. The supervision of foster-parents, who undertake the maintenance of children for reward, and of children who are destitute or in need of care and attention, is among the important responsibilities of local authorities. Among other services which the local authority may provide are day nurseries for the children below school age of mothers who go out to work, home nursing, domestic help for the sick, and a welfare service for the blind. The provision of ambulances, an important part of the public health system, devolves upon the county or county borough councils.

The central government, through the establishment in 1948 of regional boards, has undertaken the responsibility for hospitals, sanatoria and convalescent homes, and for many of the services formerly undertaken by local authorities in connexion with the poor law.

Housing and open spaces

The provision of housing and general supervision of housing conditions, town and country planning, parks and recreation grounds are complementary to the public health services. The haphazard, unplanned jerry-building of much of the nineteenth century led to overcrowding and slum conditions. The need for the intervention of local authorities was recognised in the Artisans' Dwellings Act of 1875, the first serious attempt to grapple with the problem of housing the working classes. The housing shortages that followed two world wars led to an extension of the housing provision by local authorities, who have received considerable assistance from government subsidies. New estates, indeed new towns, with shops, community centres, schools and parks have been developed as a result of the policy of the last thirty years, particularly of the post-1945 era. Slums have been cleared, war-damaged areas have been redeveloped, conditions of life have been transformed for hundreds of thousands. It has also been possible to assist intending purchasers of small houses for their own use by the advancement of loans on favourable terms. The supervising power of local authorities extends to the siting, erection and construction of private dwelling houses, which must conform to established standards and comply with the by-laws with regard to sanitary arrangements, water supply, fire precautions and ventilation. In recent years town and country planning has prevented the un-controlled development of sites which led in the nineteen-twenties to the disfigurement of much of the English countryside. In every development scheme due attention is paid to the provision of parks and recreation grounds as 'lungs' for the population. Round the big cities there are 'green belts'—areas in which building is restricted—so that there may be country within easy reach of the densely populated areas.

Education

One hundred years ago there was little elementary education, and it was provided by voluntary societies usually connected with the Established and Nonconformist Churches assisted by government grants. The rapid growth of population, the development of industry and the extensions of the franchise in 1867 and 1884 compelled legislative action. By the Education Act of 1870 school boards were set up to supplement the work of the voluntary bodies, and by later Acts elementary education was made compulsory and free and the leaving age was gradually raised to fifteen. In 1902 the 2,517 school boards were abolished and their duties transferred to 317 local authorities, who were empowered to provide secondary education, which in those days meant grammar school education. Important Acts which followed in 1918 and 1921 provided for further re-organisation. Numerous committees and commissions investigated the conditions and scope of the educational system and recommended fundamental changes. It was therefore possible for the Education Act of 1944 to be passed in the midst of war, so that far-reaching changes could be put into effect as soon as conditions allowed. A Ministry of Education took the place of the old Board of Education.

The responsibility for the whole system of primary, secondary and further education was placed upon the county and county borough councils, all of which had to produce and submit to the Minister of Education development plans for primary and secondary education, and schemes for further education (including art, technical and adult education) showing how they proposed to carry out their duties. They were required to appoint education committees and chief education officers and to provide the necessary machinery for efficient administration. Some decentralisation in the larger counties was found to be necessary. This was achieved by some degree of delegation to divisional executives. Some areas obtained somewhat greater powers as 'excepted districts'. But the final responsibility for education within their areas remains with the 146 county and county borough councils.

The 1944 Act made provision for assistance to the 'voluntary' or non-provided schools, whose buildings had been erected and were maintained by a religious body, usually the Church of England or the Roman Catholic Church, but whose running costs were met by the local education authority. In such schools denominational religious teaching has been retained whereas in all other schools religious instruction of an undenominational character must be given.

The duties of the education authority extend far beyond education, e.g. to school milk and school meals, to the provision of transport and boarding accommodation where necessary, the granting of clothing allowances, the supervision of the health of school children, the provision of a youth service and a youth employment service.

Parents are under a legal obligation to see that children of school age, i.e. from five to fifteen, attend school. It is the business of the responsible local authority to enforce attendance when necessary, and to provide the educational facilities required, including special schools for those children who are unable to benefit from the ordinary courses. Scholarships or exhibitions for university and further education, with adequate grants, enable all with the necessary ability, irrespective of parents' means, to pursue their education at a university, or in some form of technical education.

The retention and extension of the powers and responsibility of the county and county borough councils have preserved the variety and independence from central control which have been the leading characteristics of the English educational system. Syllabuses, curricula and textbooks are left to the discretion of the heads of schools, who have the benefit of the advice of Her Majesty's inspectors of schools and local inspectors. This enables schools to develop in the way required by the locality and allows individuality and experiment by the teaching profession.

Much that was envisaged in the 1944 Act remains to be done—for instance the establishment of county colleges for part-time education after school life—and the systematic development of technical and adult education. Local authorities are sometimes hampered in the carrying out of their schemes by local opinion, which is influenced by the high proportion of the rates absorbed by expenditure on education. This is one of the penalties paid for the retention of local control.

Highways

The responsibility for the repair and maintenance of highways and bridges is perhaps the oldest of all local duties. For centuries the citizen was liable to be called upon to perform unpaid labour to put the roads in order. To-day, the central government, through the Ministry of Transport, is responsible under the Trunk Roads Act 1946 for the upkeep of certain designated trunk roads; the Ministry usually nominates the county or county borough to act on its behalf. For the provision and maintenance of all other roads a local authority is responsible. Local roads and streets in boroughs and urban districts are usually the concern of the immediate local authority. Roads named as county roads and all roads in rural districts are the concern of the county councils. County borough councils are of course responsible for all roads within their boundaries except trunk roads. Most bridges are maintained by local authorities, though some are the property and responsibility of the British Transport Commission or of ancient trusts.

The poor

Poor relief was one of the first objects of local government, and it remained the chief activity of the parish vestries until the passage of the Poor Law Amendment Act of 1834. This Act remained on the statute book until 1929, when the functions of the Boards of Guardians which it established were transferred to the county councils. In 1948, the National Assistance Board assumed full responsibility for the care of the poor and aged, and since then the local authorities have only provided residential accommodation for those persons in need of care and attention for whom such accommodation is not otherwise available.

Fire services and civil defence

The needs of war led to the establishment of a central control of all fire brigades, some of which were only semi-official bodies, and the setting up of an elaborate civil defence organisation. The Fire Services Act of 1947 placed on county and county borough councils the responsibility for the maintenance of adequate and efficient fire prevention services. The civil defence organisation lapsed after the end of the Second World War for a short time, but in 1949 the Civil Defence Act imposed upon local authorities the duty of the organisation of civil defence—a difficult task owing to the apathy of the general public.

Public utilities

In the nineteenth and early twentieth century there was an emphasis on public supply services and trading undertakings in local government. The tendency in recent years, and particularly in the years after the Second World War, has been to remove more and more public utilities from local control. Electricity and gas undertakings were taken over by regional boards, established by national authorities in 1947 and 1948 respectively. Forms of transport, especially tramways in the London area formerly operated by local authorities, have been absorbed by London Transport.

There remain some utility or trading services which may be operated by local authorities: transport services, civic restaurants, theatres, markets, water supplies. The latter are particularly important, and often require the expenditure of much capital and the exercise of much skill and foresight. The need for some national water 'grid', which might involve the nationalisation of water services, is brought forcibly to the attention of the public every time there is a drought.

Finance

The sources of income of a local authority are rents from properties and houses and profits from municipal trading, loans, grants of various kinds from the central government, and rates raised locally.

Property and houses owned by the council bring rents to the council; there may be a water undertaking, markets, harbours, civic restaurants, or transport services that produce a revenue. The sphere of municipal trading has already been restricted by the transfer to central authorities of the gas and electricity undertakings, which were formerly sources of income to local authorities. It is doubtful whether rents of council houses ever cover outgoings on repairs and maintenance and loan charges. Indeed municipal trading in any form seems to find as little favour with many of the ratepayers as with the central government.

The second means by which local authorities finance their operations is by raising loans. These must be authorised by the Minister of Housing and Local Government. They may be raised on the credit of the local authority in the open market or through the Public Works Loans Board, which has often been able to lend money at lower than market rates. Such loans are only sanctioned for capital works the full cost of which it would be unreasonable to expect councils to meet out of current revenue, as they will benefit not only present but also future citizens. Loans for land purchases may be repaid over a period up to eighty years; for other purposes up to sixty years.

The Government, with parliamentary sanction, often encourages local authorities to provide better services than they could afford if they had to rely only on its own resources. By means of financial assistance of various kinds, it helps both those authorities who are favourably placed and particularly those whose resources are more meagre. There are grants for specific purposes on the basis of a percentage of expenditure, e.g. for fire and police services, for which the Government makes respectively a twenty-five per cent. and a fifty per cent. grant, for the construction and maintenance of roads and for certain health services. There are housing subsidies which are paid on a 'unit' basis, the subsidy on a house being the same whatever its cost or quality. There are also more complicated 'formula' grants, of which the main education grant is an example. 'Equalisation' grants are also made according to formula, the general idea being to give assistance to areas where conditions are abnormal, e.g. where the school population is above the national average, or where the rateable value is below the national average. County boroughs retain such grants for their own use. County councils have to share these grants with the county districts and municipal·boroughs. Through the system of grants and by control over loans, the central government exercises a powerful influence upon the policy and expenditure of local authorities, even though theoretically the latter could raise all the money they need from rates.

Rates

The balance of local government expenditure, between a third and a half, has to be met out of the rates. County borough councils are concerned almost entirely with their own requirements. Municipal boroughs and county urban and rural districts collect not only their own rates but also those demanded by the county council as a precepting authority. There may also be one or two other small rates demanded by other precepting authorities, e.g. for police.

Rates, which are really local taxes, are levied on immovable property, which may be land or premises, the rateable value being calculated on the rent at which the property might reasonably be expected to let. There are certain exceptions: since the Derating Act of 1929 agricultural land and agricultural buildings (not including farmhouses) have been exempted completely, and mines, workshops, factories, etc. have been assessed at a quarter of their value. Special arrangements are also made with regard to electricity and railway properties which are exempt from local rates, but for which a contribution is made from a national pool.

Before 1950 valuation for rating was carried out by local assessment committees. Since 1950 a complete revaluation, the first since 1934, has been carried out by the Inland Revenue Commissioners, to whom the duty was transferred by the Local Government Act 1948. The valuation of houses is based on letting value in 1939, and of other property of the rents commanded to-day. The new valuation, which has brought about great changes in the rateable values of the various authorities, came into force in 1956.

The rateable value, and with it the product of a penny rate, varies greatly from area to area. In spite of the obvious drawbacks of the imposition of a flat rate in the pound upon all property, irrespective of the owners' income and commitments, no more satisfactory method has been found for assessing contributions towards the expenses of local government. Its chief merit is its stability. The rateable value and the product of a penny rate are known and are excellent securities for loans.

The distribution of functions between local authorities

The functions of a local authority are clearly shown on the back of a rate demand. The example given is that of Croydon, a county borough situated within fifteen miles of London. It is an all-purpose authority, except that, as it comes within the Metropolitan Police area, it has no Watch Committee, and the cost of police to the borough is included in the rates in the form of a Metropolitan Police precept.

THE COUNTY BOROUGH OF CROYDON
Population: 249,800   Area: 12,600 acres
Rateable value: £2,813,277   Penny rate: £11,380
Year 1955-1956

Services Administered by the Town Council:	s.	d.
*Education	6	7·936
*Public Health (including Health Services under the National Health Service Act, 1946)	1	4·408
*Services for Aged, Infirm and Handicapped Persons		8·363
*Care of Deprived Children		4·397
*Housing		4·993
*Fire Services		6·415
*Highways and Bridges	1	11·118
Public Libraries		6·681
Baths and Washhouses		3·251
Parks and Open Spaces		10·641
Street Improvements (including Town Planning)		3·393
Collection, Disposal and Destruction of Refuse		11·164
*Sewers and Sewage Disposal		9·167
Public Lighting		5·491
Establishment Expenses and Upkeep of Municipal Courts and Offices		8·992
*Other Services and Expenses		6·861
	17	5·271

Deduct in respect of
   Other Credits (not being Government Grants and Moneys) including adjustment of general balance .. ..

	5·410
16	11·861

Services Administered by Precepting Authorities, viz.:

Police (Metropolitan District)			1	11·000
Deduct—	s.	d.	18	10·861
The equivalent in terms of a rate in the pound of any Exchequer Equalisation and Transitional Grants receivable by the Council under Part 1 of the Local Government Act, 1948	—	—		
The equivalent in terms of a rate in the pound of the amount receivable under Section 100 of the Local Government Act, 1948	1	0·360		
The equivalent in terms of a rate in the pound of the proceeds of Local Taxation Licences		·501		
			1	0·861
Rate in the pound payable by ratepayer			17	10

177   G

Note. The asterisks indicate items in respect of which Government grants are received, the rates being calculated after these grants are allowed for. The amount receivable under Section 100 of the Local Government Act 1948 is in respect of hereditaments (i.e. properties) of the British Transport Commission and the British Electricity Authority which have ceased to pay local government rates but in respect of which an annual lump sum is distributed in proportion to rateable values and electricity current consumed in the area. The item in respect of Local Taxation Licences represents the amount collected for dog licences, etc. The Exchequer Equalisation Grant is paid according to a formula to relatively sparsely populated counties; Croydon does not qualify for any grant under this heading.

The chief heads of county council expenditure are: administration of justice, agriculture—allotments and small holdings, civil defence, coast protection, education, fire services, highways and bridges, land drainage, local health authority services, payments to county district councils, police, protection of children, public health, public libraries, registration of electors, town and country planning, water supply, administrative expenses.

The powers and responsibilities of county and county borough councils with regard to police have been explained in chapter XII, page 142.

The chief functions of county districts (including non-county boroughs) are: the raising of a rate (including that demanded by the county), provision of sewers and sewage disposal, open spaces, cemeteries, refuse collection, street lighting, certain health services, housing, and in some cases water supplies and public libraries.

The central government and local authorities

The chief government departments affecting local authorities are the Ministry of Housing and Local Government, which exercises an over-all interest, the Ministry of Education, the Ministry of Transport, the Ministry of Health and the Home Office. Other departments, especially the Treasury and the Ministry of Agriculture, also have relations with local councils. The departments' chief influence is financial, through the system of grants already mentioned. They can also exert influence by support or opposition to private bills promoted by local authorities. They can also introduce public bills affecting local government. The supervision exercised by government

178

departments must be based on an Act of Parliament. For instance the Minister of Education has a statutory duty, through the Education Act of 1944, to promote the education of the people of England and Wales. Though he delegates part of this duty to county councils and county borough councils, he cannot throw off the ultimate responsibility. Similarly the Minister of Housing and Local Government has an ultimate responsibility in respect of loans, housing, water supply and sewerage among other things; the Home Secretary for police, fire services and civil defence. The degree of supervision varies according to the machinery for inspection at the disposal of the minister and the importance of the service. The means adopted may be a gentle call for information to show that the department is awake and interested, or memoranda, based on collected data and experience, may be issued with the object of establishing good practice, or the department may exercise control based on statutory powers. The most potent control is the approval or disapproval of loans or grants. The control of the central government over vital materials for building and other purposes is also an important factor. Still another, and most important, central control is exercised through the district auditors, who in fact are not the servants of any minister, although they are appointed by and paid through the Minister of Housing and Local Government. They are independent, but their services are valuable to the various ministries, since they inspect the accounts which show how grants have been used. The district auditors must disallow every item contrary to law, and surcharge the persons responsible for the negligence or misconduct. A person surcharged for more than £500 is disqualified from membership of any local authority for five years.

Statutory powers of various kinds are given to ministries, especially the hearing of appeals by one local authority against the decision of another, and against the approval or disapproval of local authorities' projects. By-laws made by a local authority must be approved by the appropriate minister, e.g. regarding public health by the Minister of Health, or regarding police and good order by the Home Secretary. Ministries may also require the production of administrative schemes or development plans. Local authorities are affected by the fact that nationally negotiated salary scales are binding on them. The approval of the Minister of Housing and Local Government is required for the appointment or dismissal of certain officers, e.g. medical officers of health and sanitary inspectors. Finally, government departments can exert powerful influence through the regulations they are empowered to issue by the terms of a statute. Control is particularly firm in matters of education, health, police and fire services. The general tendency of the post-war years has been to increase the size of the responsible unit of local government, and to ensure a national minimum of efficiency in the services provided, by means of close inspection and supervision under departmental regulation.

Judicial control

There is yet another restraint upon local authorities—that of the law. They may not exceed the powers with which they are endowed by statute or charter. Thus a local authority may be restrained by an injunction from performing an act which may prove *ultra vires*, i.e. beyond the legal powers conferred on it, or it may be sued for injury to a person or to a body in performance of its duties. In general, the courts endeavour to apply to a corporation the same fundamental principles of law which they apply to individuals. The courts can also, by a writ of *mandamus*, compel a local authority to perform a duty which they hold it is under a statutory obligation to perform.

Summary

There is no regular pyramid of organisation of local government in England. It is true that the county council can exercise its authority over the county districts in some matters, and that there are means by which the central government can influence local authorities, but there is no rigid, uniform control from above. Elections at all stages are free, being conducted in accordance with statutory requirements. Local authorities are at no stage compelled to accept as members nominees of the central government, or in the case of the county districts, of the county council. Councils may set up what committees they please in addition to those required by statute. They have wide powers of co-option; they can make their own standing orders; they can with three exceptions appoint and dismiss their own officers. They can levy and spend their own rates, subject to the supervision of the district auditor.

There remain many anomalies and many possibilities of reform. English local government is no longer the complicated tangle of over-lapping and interlocking authorities it was before the passage of the Acts of 1888 and 1894, but it retains a typically English lack of symmetry and pattern. This may at times lead to some inefficiency, but it provides opportunities for adaptation to local circumstances which are not present in a rigidly centralised system.

CHAPTER XV

THE GOVERNMENT AND THE CITIZEN

One of the consequences of the lack of a written constitution or of any complete codification of the law is that the British citizen has few rights that are defined by statute and few duties that are specifically required of him by law. Most of his rights and freedoms are derived from common law, and from the assumption that he may go where he pleases, and say and do what he pleases, provided that he does not break the law of the land or infringe the rights of others. He is thus free to do what the law does not prohibit.

Important documents in the history of individual rights

Certain documents and statutes have been long venerated by con-stitutional lawyers and historians as vital in the history of the rights and freedoms of the individual citizen. Foremost among these are Magna Carta 1215, the Petition of Right 1628, the Habeas Corpus Act of 1679, the Bill of Rights of 1689 and the Act of Settlement 1701.

All of these have already been mentioned, because of their importance in other aspects of the constitution.

Three clauses of Magna Carta may be quoted in translation from the Latin:

Clause 38 In future no official shall put any one to trial merely on his own testimony, without reliable witnesses produced for this purpose.

Clause 39 No free man shall be arrested or imprisoned or deprived of his freehold or outlawed or banished or in any way ruined nor will we take or order action against him except by the lawful judgment of his equals, and according to the law of the land.

Clause 40 To no one will we sell, to no one will we refuse or delay right or justice.

Magna Carta also set out, among other things, the rights of the various classes of the medieval community. Though it was exacted from King John by the baronage as a guarantee of their privileges, it came to be regarded as a statement of the basis of constitutional government, and above all of the rights of the citizen.

The Petition of Right dealt with matters affecting the private citizen: taxation without the consent of Parliament; the use of martial law in times of peace—the fear being that measures applied to discontented soldiery might soon be applied to all who resisted the government; the billeting of soldiers upon private persons, which could be used as a means of punishing them, and which was a means of exacting a contribution from them; and lastly arbitrary imprisonment without cause shown.

The Habeas Corpus Act of 1679 did not introduce any new principle. The writ of habeas corpus was a common law right long before the passage of the Act, but there were many ways by which it could be obstructed. The Act of 1679 enabled a writ to be obtained by a prisoner or by a person acting on his behalf from the Lord Chancellor or any judge of a superior court requiring the gaoler to produce at a stated place and by a stated time the 'body' of a prisoner who was being detained, and who had not been convicted of a crime or offence. Provision was made for speedy trial or release on bail. Evasion of the writ by transfer of the prisoner to another gaol was prohibited. The important Habeas Corpus Act of 1816 extended the provisions of the earlier Act to imprisonment for debt or as a result of civil suit. The writ of habeas corpus thus protects the citizen by ensuring his discharge if the cause of detention shown to the court is insufficient, and thereafter he cannot be apprehended a second time on the same charge; it also ensures speedy trial, if the cause of detention is held to be sufficient.

Among the many provisions of the Bill of Rights which directly affected the private citizen were the following: that the levying of money by the Crown without the consent of Parliament was illegal; that subjects had the right to petition the King; that the raising or keeping of a standing army within the kingdom in time of peace without the consent of Parliament was against the law; that Protestant subjects might have arms for their own defence; that election of members of Parliament ought to be free; that there should be freedom of speech and debate in Parliament; that excessive bail ought not to be required nor excessive fines imposed nor cruel and unusual punishments inflicted; that jurors might be duly impanelled; that for redress of all grievances and for amending, strengthening and preserving of the laws Parliament ought to be held frequently.

The Act of Settlement did not touch the citizen so intimately as the Bill of Rights, but its provisions affected him indirectly, by enacting that no holder of an office or place of profit under the King or the holder of a pension from the Crown could sit in the House of Commons; that judges should hold office during good behaviour and should be removed from office only on an Address by both Houses of Parliament, and that no pardon given under the great seal of England could stop impeachment by the House of Commons.

The freedom of the individual citizen

The freedoms which we regard as the right of the citizen are freedom of the person, freedom of expression, freedom of association, freedom with regard to religion, freedom to hold property and free elections. Equally essential are the equality before the law of all citizens, and the right to trial by jury on all serious charges. There are, however, no fundamental rights of the individual which cannot be suspended or even taken away by the ordinary processes of parliamentary enactment; for instance, in times of emergency, as will be shown later, the number of things a citizen may do without breaking the law is severely curtailed by the Government's use of emergency powers conferred on it by Parliament.

In modern times the field of state activity has been greatly extended. The Welfare State has brought other rights and freedoms. Freedom from want may be held to be the right of the citizen, together with the right to work or to maintenance by the state and the right to health. The modern state has also brought certain restrictions on the freedom of the citizen, arising from health and welfare legislation.

The whole basis of the British practice governing the relationship of the citizen and the executive is the rule of law, that is, 'the absolute supremacy or predominance of regular law as opposed to the influence of arbitrary power . . . the equal subjection of all classes to the ordinary law of the land administered by ordinary law courts.'

Freedom of the person

It is obvious that there are certain interferences with personal freedom which are necessary for the maintenance of law and order, e.g. arrest and detention if carried out in conformity with the Habeas Corpus Act; detention while serving a term of imprisonment or similar sentence for crime or misdemeanour; imprisonment for debt, which to-day is limited to those of proved ability to pay who have wilfully refused to do so; imprisonment for contempt of court or of either House of Parliament; or detention, again in due legal form, on account of lunacy or mental deficiency; or in the case of a child, because he or she is in need of care and protection. And of course the authority of the parent over the child in normal circumstances is protected by law. When a warrant is issued for an arrest, it must specifically state the name of the person to whom it applies; if an arrest is made without a warrant, it must be justifiable in a court of law as necessary through the commission of a crime, or to prevent the commission of a crime. Search warrants may be issued by a justice of peace if such action appears necessary, or in case of grave emergency by a superintendent of police.

The private citizen may at some time have to take action without the presence of a police officer, if he is satisfied a crime has been committed or that he must act to prevent one. He also has legal remedies, in addition to the writ of habeas corpus, against wrongful arrest. His rights of forcibly resisting a police officer who attempts to arrest him are so limited as to make such an action most unwise under almost all circumstances, but a prosecution for assault or for wrongful arrest against the police may be undertaken.

The right to civil protection is covered by the action of the law and its officers. The citizen may also expect protection or defence against external enemies. This was one of the earliest reasons for the existence of the state. It entails to-day very heavy expenditure and taxation and carries with it duties which will be mentioned in a subsequent section.

Freedom of expression

The limits of freedom of speech and publication are the same as those for other freedoms—whatever is not illegal or can be held to be illegal or is likely to lead to an illegal action is allowable. If the citizen oversteps the mark he may be liable to an action for slander if the words are spoken, or for libel if they are written; he may be liable to an action for inciting a breach of the peace, or for seditious libel, or for blasphemy, or for obscenity. As has been stated in chapter v page 65, *bona fide* reports of parliamentary proceedings are privileged and cannot be held to be defamatory; nor can communications between ministers of the Crown, or military reports, or communications between solicitor and client.

The Press is neither more nor less privileged than a private individual, except that there will be a defence if it is proved that an alleged libel was published without malice, that a full apology was inserted in the newspaper or publication, and that a payment into court was made before the commencement of the action. The Press may print what it pleases without any previous licence, subject to the consequences of the law. Press offences are dealt with by ordinary courts, by judge and jury. These rights are of comparatively recent establishment; as late as the seventeenth century, the privilege of printing was exclusive to 97 London stationers and their successors, and the two University printers of Oxford and Cambridge. The licensing laws were abolished in 1695 but a heavy tax on newspapers continued for many years, and a further restricting influence, the paper duty, was not abolished until 1860.

Actions of blasphemy are now rare; indeed the law has been so far relaxed that it has been allowable for talks to be given on the British Broadcasting Corporation's system defending atheism. Prosecutions for obscene libel are, however, not infrequent and reveal widely divergent interpretations of obscenity by different courts, and some-times lead to fears of unjustifiable censorship. Seditious libel, breaches of official secrets, incitement to disaffection, contempt of court by scandalous behaviour, or by action likely to prejudice the course of justice, are all limitations to free expression by spoken and written word. In war time the Government has such special powers as it requires to prevent publication or prosecute offenders. The licensing of stage plays by the Lord Chamberlain, an officer of the royal household, is an interesting survival of the royal prerogative.

Freedom of assembly

The right to hold public meetings or processions is again limited by what the law allows. The citizen's right to use the highway is the right of passing and repassing, not of loitering or standing still. A procession, which is *bona fide* passing down a thoroughfare, is law-fully using the highway, but limitations can be imposed by the Com-missioner of Police in the London area, and by other local authorities elsewhere, on the application of the chief of police and with the con-sent of the Home Secretary, for a period not exceeding three months, when there is reason to believe that a breach of the peace may occur.

Also by the Public Order Act of 1936, the wearing of uniforms and the formation of societies of a military nature for political purposes were prohibited to prevent disorder arising from processions and public meetings.

Any meeting of three or more persons for a common design, even if it is lawful, may constitute an unlawful assembly if it is likely to involve violence, i.e. lead to riot. For riot to be a misdemeanour there must be three or more persons present, a common purpose, an attempt to execute it, the intent to help one another, and a display of force or violence. By the Riot Act of 1715, such an offence becomes a felony, with a maximum penalty of life imprisonment, if twelve or more persons, having been ordered to disperse by a magistrate, fail to do so within one hour after the reading of the proclamation contained in the Act. It is the duty of every citizen, and the special duty of magistrates and police, to suppress unlawful and disorderly assemblies. Soldiers have the same duty, but should act in subordination to a civil magistrate and should not use arms, unless danger is pressing and immediate (see also chapter XII page 148). The Riot Act was of course passed at a time when there were no police forces, and the Army was far too small to deal with civil disturbances as well as external dangers.

The above-mentioned restrictions cover exceptional circumstances; in general, public meetings are freely held and police action is only necessary in the interests of normal safety among crowds in the open or in crowded buildings.

Freedom of association

The crime and tort of conspiracy are the chief restrictions placed by English law on associations for political or other purposes. A criminal conspiracy is an agreement to do an unlawful act or to do a lawful act by unlawful means. Conspiracy as a tort or civil injury is complex but refers to the effects of conspiracy upon private persons or corporations. The Public Order Act of 1936, already mentioned, makes it an offence to take part in the control or management of any association of persons, organised for usurping the functions of the police or armed forces of the Crown, or for the function of using or displaying physical force in promoting a political object.

Political parties and trade unions and other associations, political and non-political, which do not contravene the law, are allowed to function freely and without interference by the Government, and the individual citizen is free to belong to them.

Free elections

As early as 1275 the Statute of Westminister I provided that there should be no interference with elections by force of arms, malice or menaces. The chief safeguard to-day is the Ballot Act of 1872, which ensures secrecy for the voter. The Corrupt and Illegal Practices Acts provide further protection against bribery and other undue influences.

Freedom of property

The right of freely possessing and using property is difficult to define, as there are many limitations arising from the state's rights under Town and Country Planning Acts, compulsory purchase on statutory authority, requisition of property under Defence of the Realm Acts, use of land for open-cast coal-mining operations, as well as restrictions on use through Acts relating to public health, storage of petroleum and explosives, etc. But with all these limitations and restrictions, it can be said that the right to possess and enjoy property freely remains, and that public and political opinion is a safeguard against abuse of its powers by the executive.

Freedom with regard to religion

Freedom to worship or not to worship, to hold what religious views one wishes, or none at all, is now a commonplace, but it was obtained only after centuries of strife, and many martyrdoms and imprisonments. Civil disabilities on Roman Catholics were not removed till 1829; Jews were not admitted to Parliament till 1858; the Affirmation Act, which allows a member to dispense with an oath altogether, was not passed till 1888. There is one office—that of Lord Chancellor

—for which Roman Catholics are still ineligible. The limitations of the Act of Settlement with regard to the Protestant succession to the throne are, of course, still in force.

Equality before the law and the right of trial by jury

These rights are inherent in the common law and in the system of justice that has been outlined in chapter XI. The independence of the judges is vital to their maintenance. The assumption in the courts is that the prisoner is innocent until he has been proved guilty. The onus of proving the guilt of the accused rests on the prosecution, which must produce evidence to prove the guilt. The accused is further protected by the fact that no reference to any previous criminal record may be made before the verdict is given.

The right of trial by jury for all serious offences dates back to Magna Carta and beyond. Mention of juries and their duties has already been made in chapter XI.

A serious inequality in legal matters has been largely removed by the Legal Aid and Advice Act of 1949. This Act enables people of limited means to apply for aid from the state to assist them to bring or defend legal proceedings in the courts. The Act is designed to cover all courts but it has not yet been fully applied to county courts. The extent of the aid given, when the application has been approved by a committee of solicitors and barristers established for that purpose, depends on the applicant's income and capital. Applicants may choose a solicitor, and if necessary a barrister, and these are paid eighty-five per cent of their costs by the state.

Equality before the law also means that no one may claim the orders of a superior as a defence, that no one is exempt from the ordinary process of law by position or rank.

Emergency powers

As was stated at the beginning of this chapter, no citizen has an absolute right to any of these freedoms. Parliament can take away all or any. By the Emergency Powers Act of 1920 the executive may, if it is satisfied that the life of the community is imperilled, declare a state of emergency by proclamation. It must communicate this to Parliament forthwith, or if Parliament is not sitting, it must be called within five days. The order in council consequent on the proclamation lapses after seven days if it is not renewed by resolution of both Houses of Parliament. The Act of 1920 does not suspend habeas corpus or allow fines or imprisonment without trial.

In time of war more extensive powers may be necessary, including the suspension of habeas corpus. These may be brought about by regulation under Defence of the Realm Acts or further Emergency Powers Acts. The best known of such regulations in the Second World War was Regulation 18B, which empowered the Government to make regulations for detention without trial in the interests of public safety or the defence of the realm. The person detained might attempt to get a writ of habeas corpus, but would have little chance of success. War-time emergency regulations also gave the Government wide powers of property requisition and industrial conscription. The Emergency Powers Act of 1920 is still on the statute book and was invoked last in May, 1955.

The duties of the citizen

The law says little of the duties of the citizen. For this reason this will only be a short section. But duties are implicit in any understanding of government. Without the proper performance of them government is impossible and rights are valueless. The first duty is allegiance to the sovereign, who personifies the state. No oath of allegiance is required of the ordinary citizen, but among those from whom one is demanded are members of Parliament, members of the armed forces, priests of the Church of England, and aliens on naturalisation. Loyalty to the community is inherent in citizenship. The duty of obeying the law and upholding ordered society is incumbent upon the citizen. He knows that the laws can if necessary be changed by the elected representatives of the people, and that without respect for the law order becomes anarchy. It is also part of his duty to contribute, in proportion to his means, towards the expense of government, both national and local.

There is no law in Great Britain which compels a citizen to use his vote. It may well be that he does not feel he can vote for any candidate presenting himself for election, but there is a strong obligation upon him not to neglect using his vote through idleness or indifference. The government of the country, particularly the local government, depends upon the willingness of suitable citizens to come forward and offer themselves for election to posts which entail much hard work and no financial reward.

It is a duty of the citizen under certain conditions to assist in the maintenance of order. It is also a legal obligation on some citizens to serve on juries when called upon to do so. It is also a legal obligation at present for young men to serve in the forces of the Crown, though conscientious objection may be put forward. The duty of participating in the defence of the community in time of war is one that dates back to the earliest societies.

The community of the present is a heritage from the past. It must continue to develop. It is the duty of the citizens of the present to see that the heritage they transmit is worthy of that which they inherited.

PART II: THE EMPIRE
AND THE COMMONWEALTH

INTRODUCTION

In the study of the development of government in the British Empire and Commonwealth the influence of historical continuity must first be borne in mind. The British Empire and Commonwealth has a continuous history of nearly 350 years. Within this time has been gained an ever-increasing experience of the problems and practice of imperial rule. This experience, together with a readiness to profit by mistakes, has enabled many changes and much development in the forms of government to take place, whereby the needs of societies of all races have been provided for. The historical record also shows a readiness to experiment, coupled with the idea that the best results will be obtained by hastening slowly and by consolidating advances made; a belief in the avoidance of extremes and in the supreme importance of law and order; the readiness to discard unsuccessful constitutional experiments and institutions.

Secondly, the various ways in which the British Empire was built up must be remembered. Settlement, conquest and cession account for the greater part of it. By settlement were created colonies of English-speaking emigrants from the British Isles; conquest and cession brought into the Empire colonies whose populations were European, African, or Asian. These different origins complicated the problem of government. It was natural enough for the settled colonies to have a government resembling that of their mother-country, but in the conquered colonies considerable modification was often necessary to adapt British institutions to local conditions and traditions of government that already existed. Thus French Canada, Spanish Trinidad, and Dutch Cape of Good Hope had their own traditions of law and government and the British were bound, for a time at least, to respect and to some extent continue these.

Thirdly, the forms of government that grew up were influenced by the widely different levels of political and economic development that existed among the various peoples. The white populations, with a long tradition of political and economic development behind them, could move relatively quickly from representative government to responsible government and finally to Dominion status. In other parts of the Empire conditions were such that constitutional advance was much slower. Crown Colony government, which is government from above of a direct and authoritarian kind, was, and is, essential in those lands whose populations are politically and economically backward, and where in many cases society is organised on a tribal basis.

The importance of historical continuity to the course of constitutional development has been emphasised. Within this continuity, development proceeds by fairly distinct phases. The first phase runs from the beginnings in the early seventeenth century to the loss of the American colonies in 1783. During this period there was undoubted development of political freedom and representative government in the American and West Indian colonies, within the limits permitted by the old colonial Empire. There was, however, little attempt during this phase to pay much attention to the welfare of the subject peoples.

The second stage appears in the last quarter of the eighteenth century; the change in outlook was decisive and its results have lasted down to the present day. A more considered treatment of the problems of imperial rule becomes apparent, marked by more progressive and humanitarian ideas, together with the acceptance of the trustee concept of empire. In the nineteenth century its results were twofold; for the white colonies of Canada, Australia and New Zealand it brought by stages responsible government under the Crown; for the other colonies with their mixed or wholly native populations the aim was firm and just rule from above, which was achieved through various forms of Crown Colony government.

In the twentieth century, further developments took place. The self-governing Dominions of Canada, Australia, New Zealand, South

Africa, the Irish Free State and Newfoundland, by the Statute of Westminster (1931), received the fuller independence of Dominion status; this, now known as Commonwealth status, after the end of World War II in 1945, was accepted by the three Asian Dominions, India, Pakistan and Ceylon. During this period a new policy for the Crown Colonies emerged, which has become progressively more active since 1946; this aimed at giving them, when conditions justified it, the institutions of representative government, with the further objective of semi-responsible and, ultimately, responsible government within the British Commonwealth of Nations.

CHAPTER XVI

THE CONSTITUTIONAL DOCTRINE OF THE FIRST BRITISH EMPIRE

Formative influences

What ideas of government were carried into the first colonies of North America and the West Indies by the English settlers of the seventeenth century? Because of the different social classes and the variety of political and religious beliefs involved, only an indication of tendencies can be given. From a negative point of view, it seems that some of the settlers were lawless people whose main wish was to get as far away as possible from the restraints of government. Others, like the more extreme Puritan settlers of the New England colonies, affected to despise man-made laws and instead to base their government on God's laws revealed in the Bible. The more responsible and influential settlers of the gentleman class, however, had a strong respect for law. A number of them had received a legal education at the Inns of Court in London, and consequently regarded the problem of government mainly as one of the application of legal forms and processes to the needs of society. The law that these men knew was the common law. This law was much concerned with the property rights of individuals, and although this may have led on occasion to selfish application, the idea of political liberty was intimately connected with that of individual property rights; when individual rights in property were secure, so was the personal liberty of the individual.

Secondly, the early settlers were familiar with representative institutions. We must be careful not to think that these representative institutions of the seventeenth and eighteenth centuries were the same as those of parliamentary democracy to-day. The latter is based on an executive responsible to a House of Commons elected by universal suffrage, male and female; in the seventeenth century, the House of Commons was elected on a franchise, restricted to those males who were freeholders (i.e. those who owned land). The House of Commons thus resulting was representative only in a limited sense, and in spite of the claims it advanced during the seventeenth century to control the executive and dictate policy, its proper function was regarded by many people as that of supporting the policy of the executive and giving its consent to legislation that was introduced. Within these limits, belief in the importance and value of Parliament was widely held by the upper classes of English society, whether Royalist or Parliamentarian, and almost as a matter of course its representative institutions were carried into the new colonies overseas.

Early representative institutions

Virginia in 1618 had been granted by charter some of the benefits of representative government; in 1619, the first meeting of the Virginia House of Burgesses had been summoned. The Bermuda legislature, now the oldest example surviving from the first British Empire, came into being under the following instructions given to the Governor in 1619.

We require you, that as sone as you maye after your arrivall in the Ilands you doe assemble your Counsell and as many of the ablest and best understandinge men in the Ilands, both of the clergie and laitie, as you and your Counsell shall think fitt, wherein we wish you to take too many than too fewe . . . and that in this Assembly you deliberately consult and advise of such lawes and constitutions as shall be thought fitt to be made for the good of the plantation, and for the maintenance of religion justice order peace and unitie among them . . .

The Puritans of Massachusetts hardly required this grant from above of representative institutions, since one of their essential beliefs was that government depended on the consent of the governed. Even in the case of the proprietary colonies of the seventeenth century such as Maryland, New York and the Carolinas, which were in the nature of fiefs granted by royal prerogative to individual proprietors who regarded them as personal possessions, legislation with the consent of a representative assembly was provided for in the royal grant, and assemblies representing the freeholders appeared. As far as the colonies were concerned, the general result of the struggle between King and Parliament was to strengthen their belief in representative institutions. In 1651, the royalist colony of Barbados refused to accept the trade regulations of the Navigation Act passed by the Commonwealth on the grounds that they should not be called upon to obey a Parliament in which they were not represented.

Finally, although there was general acceptance in the English colonies of the seventeenth century of the importance of law and representative institutions, government in actual practice varied from colony to colony. Differences of climate, social organisation, economic activities and religious beliefs were largely responsible for this. Political life was more active in the closely grouped townships of the New England colonies, with their Puritan populations of small farmers, traders and sailors, than in the semi-tropical colonies like Virginia, where the scattered and vast estates with their planters, indentured white servants and negro slaves made for greater social inequality and less political activity. And in colonies such as the Carolinas, the Bahamas and some British West Indian islands the early years were marked by an almost complete contempt for organised government, so turbulent and lawless were their first settlers.

Settled colonies

Private enterprise was responsible for the beginnings of the British Empire in the seventeenth century, but such enterprise needed legal authorisation and also a means of control once the colony had come into being. Both these needs were filled by the Crown acting through its prerogative power.

Two kinds of grant were made by the Crown in the seventeenth century for settlement overseas. One was the grant of a royal charter to a company, and the other a grant to an individual proprietor. Early examples of successful settlement by incorporated companies were Virginia (1606–7), Bermuda (1615), and Massachusetts (1629). The charters for these colonies regulated the scheme of government, the appointment of Governor and Council, the nature of the land grants to settlers, and the rights of shareholders.

Grants to individual proprietors were an equally important method of colonization in the seventeenth century. It had advantages for the Crown as it was often a means whereby royal favourites and courtiers (such as the Earl of Carlisle, who was granted a patent for the 'Caribbee' islands in the West Indies) could be rewarded, or, as in the case of Charles II's grant to William Penn for the plantation of Pennsylvania, it was a means of payment of a royal debt long outstanding. The proprietary colony thus created resembled the fief or grant of land of the feudal society of the Middle Ages, the proprietors making an annual payment to the Crown in recognition of its overlordship. Within their proprietary they exercised the widest powers in the grant of land to their sub-tenants, in the appointment of executive and judicial officials, and in the making of laws with the advice and consent of an assembly representative of the freemen.

The most notable of the proprietary colonies on the American mainland, and the one with the fullest powers reserved to the proprietor, was Maryland, founded in 1634 by grant to Lord Baltimore and his sons. New York, formerly the Dutch colony of the New Netherlands and captured by the English in 1664, was granted by Charles II to his brother James, Duke of York, as a proprietary colony. From this grant arose another proprietary, that of New Jersey, granted by the Duke of York to his friends, Sir George Carteret and Sir John Berkeley. To the south of Virginia, the proprietary colonies of North Carolina (1663) and South Carolina (1670) resulted from the grant by Charles II to eight noblemen and courtiers, including Clarendon, Albemarle, Shaftesbury, Carteret and Berkeley, all of whom were interested in promoting colonial settlement because of its trading possibilities. The Crown in its later grants to proprietors was rather less lavish in the powers it conferred, as is seen in the grant to Penn for Pennsylvania (1682). He, although possessing wide power in the grant of land to settlers and in the internal organisation of his colony, was subject to considerable control from England; his colonists could appeal from the Pennsylvanian courts to the King if they wished, while his control of taxes and customs was not as complete as that of Lord Baltimore in Maryland. The last of the thirteen colonies, Georgia, founded in 1733, was a proprietary for the limited term of twenty-one years, after which it reverted to the Crown; the proprietors' powers were considerably more limited than elsewhere.

In addition to these royal charter and proprietary colonies, there were a few colonies of the seventeenth century founded by independent groups acting without any royal grant. The most celebrated of these was New Plymouth founded in 1620 by the Pilgrim Fathers of the *Mayflower*. Licence to settle had been granted to them by the New England Council, but they had no authority from the Crown to set up a government. Subsequently they worked out their own form of government, which included an oath of allegiance to the King. Connecticut (1635-6) and Rhode Island (1636-44), offshoots of Massachusetts, and Newhaven (1638-40) were also the work of independent groups; like New Plymouth they drew up their own forms of government. Some twenty years afterwards (1663) Connecticut and Rhode Island received royal charters, but Newhaven, which from the start had adopted a radical attitude to outside authority, royal or otherwise, and had recognised only the authority of the Bible, lost its separate existence and was annexed to Connecticut.

Two major principles of constitutional law affecting settled colonies were established at an early date. The first was that the settlers carried with them the right to English law, whenever settlement was authorised by the Crown in its grant to a trading corporation or individual proprietor. This appears in the Charter of Virginia (1606):

And we do declare . . . that all the persons, being our subjects, which shall dwell within any of the said several colonies . . . shall have and enjoy all liberties, franchises and immunities within any of our other dominions, to all intents and purposes, as if they had been abiding and born within this our realm of England or any other of our said dominions.

The charter generally indicated the machinery of law-making in the colony itself; in the grant by the Crown in 1627 to the Earl of Carlisle of a proprietary in the Leeward Islands, the laws were to be made 'with the consent, assent and approbation of the freeholders of the said province, or the greater part of them thereunto called'. The second principle that was now established was that no legislation under the powers that had been granted should run contrary to the laws of England.

Conquered colonies

From the middle of the seventeenth century, European wars had their extensions overseas in the colonial sphere. The Dutch attacked and captured parts of the Portuguese empire. Oliver Cromwell in his 'Western Design' aimed at conquest of Spanish lands in the New World. Colonial gains became increasingly important motives for war, as the colonial clauses of the peace treaties show; conquest and cession of colonies was at its greatest in the period 1713 to 1815.

In the seventeenth century, England conquered Jamaica from Spain (1655) and the New Netherlands (later to become New York) from the Dutch in 1664. The eighteenth century added considerably to Great Britain's colonial conquests. In the Spanish Succession war, Gibraltar (1704) and Minorca (1708) were captured from Spain, and Nova Scotia (1710) from France. At the Peace of Paris (1763), France ceded Canada and Cape Breton Isle in North America; Grenada, St Vincent, Dominica and Tobago in the West Indies and Senegal in West Africa. At the end of the Napoleonic wars in 1815, Great Britain retained numerous conquests, the most important being Ceylon and the Cape of Good Hope from Holland, Trinidad from Spain and St Lucia and Mauritius from France.

The legal doctrines affecting the government of conquered colonies were derived from *Calvin's Case* (1609):

If a King comes to a kingdom by conquest, he may at his pleasure alter and change the laws of that kingdom but until he doth make an alteration of those laws the ancient laws of that kingdom remain; but if a king hath a kingdom by title of descent, then seeing by the laws of that kingdom he doth inherit the kingdom he cannot change the laws of himself without consent of Parliament. If a King hath a kingdom by conquest, as King Henry II had Ireland, after King John had given to them being under his obedience and subjection the laws of England for the government of that country, no succeeding King could alter the same without Parliament.

Briefly, this meant that conquered colonies were at the absolute disposal of the Crown, and that laws existing at the time of conquest would continue in force until the Crown altered them, and that the Crown's power would not remain absolute, if it granted the subjects of a conquered colony English law.

The application of this doctrine to English colonial conquests of the seventeenth and eighteenth centuries varied according to circumstances. Because it was desired to attract English settlers, Jamaica in 1661 was granted English law and the power to legislate. The royal proclamation of 1661 stated:

Children of any of our natural born subjects to be born in Jamaica shall from their respective births be reputed to be and shall be free denizens of England, and shall have the same privileges to all intents and purposes as our own free born subjects of England.

To this grant of English law was added, in the royal instructions to the Governor in 1662, the right of legislation by the usual machinery of Governor, Council and Assembly.

Of the conquered colonies secured to Great Britain by the Treaty of Utrecht in 1713, Gibraltar and Minorca did not receive any grant of English law or representative institutions because they were primarily naval bases with military garrisons and there was no desire to attract English settlers. Nova Scotia, ceded at the same time, was eventually granted an assembly in 1758, as by that time the number of English settlers had so increased as to make this necessary.

Representative institutions were granted by royal proclamation in October 1763 to the conquests of the Seven Years' War in the New World. The grant was carried out in the case of the West Indian islands of Grenada, Dominica, St Vincent and Tobago, conquered from or ceded by France, and also in East and West Florida ceded by Spain. But in Canada the promise of an Assembly was not fulfilled, on the grounds that the French population, who were in a large majority, were totally unaccustomed to representative government, and that there would be danger in introducing institutions of government which would encourage a spirit of troublesome independence such as existed in the American colonies. Eventually the Quebec Act of 1774 gave Canada a form of government which was very different from the representative government hitherto conceded, since it set up no legislative assembly, but instead gave its function to a nominated Council closely controlled by the Governor. This was the pattern followed by many of the Crown Colony governments created in the nineteenth century.

Campbell v. Hall (1774)

A point of fundamental importance during this period was whether the Crown, once it had granted representative government, could revoke this grant. The issue arose in Jamaica between 1675 and 1678, when the Crown attempted to deprive the Jamaican Assembly of its legislative independence and financial control. This attempt, which was strongly opposed by the Assembly, was not persisted in by the Crown after the opinion of its law officers and judges had been taken. Their opinion was against the Crown's intentions, thus first propounding the doctrine that the Crown's right to legislate for a conquered colony disappears if a grant of representative institutions has been made.

Nearly a hundred years later Lord Mansfield's celebrated judgment in the case of *Campbell* v. *Hall* (1774) was decisive. The Crown by letters patent in 1764 had imposed an export duty of $4\frac{1}{2}$ per cent on sugar exported from Grenada, an island recently conquered, and ceded by France at the Peace of Paris. Campbell, a sugar planter, brought an action for the recovery of money collected under the authority of the letters patent by Hall, a customs official. Campbell's case rested chiefly on the point that as the royal proclamation of October 1763 had granted an assembly to the island, the Crown had exhausted its power to legislate by prerogative.

Lord Mansfield gave judgment in favour of Campbell. He held that the grant of an assembly deprived the Crown of the prerogative power to legislate and raise taxes; having once parted with its prerogative, the Crown could not continue to legislate against, and in conflict with, its grant. Under the circumstances, taxation such as that objected to by Campbell could only be imposed by an Act of the Legislature of Grenada or of the Imperial Parliament.

The reception of English common law and statute law

One of the arguments of the English lawyers had been that the common law, the unwritten, customary law of England, went wherever the colonists went. In practice the English colonists of the seventeenth century did not admit it in its entirety, but accepted it to a greater or lesser degree according to their social and political attitudes. One objection against complete acceptance was that English common law had been developed for a better organised and more settled order of society than was found in the new communities planted in America or the British West Indies.

The southern colonies, such as Virginia and the Carolinas, were the most ready to accept the common law; in 1712, the Assembly of South Carolina went as far as to adopt English law by statute. The greatest resistance to English law was found in the New England colonies, where the Puritans looked to the word of God as a superior code of law, but in spite of this a number of legal forms and principles of English law were taken into use from practical necessity. The middle colonies, such as New York, Pennsylvania and Maryland, tended to accept English law; Maryland had done so in 1662 and Pennsylvania had used it (and also the principles of English equity jurisdiction) since 1681. In the more settled phase of the colonies from the middle of the eighteenth century onwards something like an American common law emerged, which was better than its English counterpart because it was simpler, fairer and more rapid in its procedure.

With regard to English statute law the acknowledged rule was that all statutes which had been enacted before the colonies were settled, or had their own legislature, were in force. Statutes enacted since settlement did not apply unless the colonies were specifically mentioned; the Navigation Acts of the later seventeenth century were good examples of statute law which applied to the colonies.

CHAPTER XVII

THE OLD REPRESENTATIVE SYSTEM OF
GOVERNMENT

During the later seventeenth century, a fairly uniform type of government developed, usually known as the 'Old Representative System' by Governor, Council and Assembly. It is found in all the settled colonies of the first British Empire; it was extended to some, but not all, of the conquered and ceded colonies of this period. Granted as a rule by royal prerogative, this form of government commanded general acceptance alike from the aristocratic and royalist colonies such as Virginia, and the more radically minded Puritan New Englanders. By the early eighteenth century it was claimed by the colonists that the functions and powers of King, Lords and Commons were reproduced in their own institutions of Governor, Council and Assembly.

The system is found in both charter and proprietary colonies. When during the later seventeenth and early eighteenth centuries many of these, both in North America and in the West Indies, were taken out of the control of the original chartered companies or proprietors, thus becoming royal provinces, the old representative system still continued. One royal attempt, however, to suppress the assemblies must be noted. James II omitted assemblies from the 'Dominion of New England' (1686–9), formed by the amalgamation of Massachusetts, New Hampshire, Connecticut, Rhode Island, New York and the Jerseys, but after the Revolution of 1688 and the accession of William III, the 'Dominion' was broken up and the assemblies were restored to the individual colonies. The colonial Assemblies regarded the results of the Revolution of 1688 with satisfaction, feeling that they shared its benefits as far as the rights and liberties of the subject and the basis of their own representative institutions were concerned.

The Governor: his appointment and powers

In this system, the Governor was of fundamental importance. He had two main tasks; one as the representative of the Crown, and the other as the executive head of the local government of the colony. The Governor's office was a difficult one because imperial policy on such matters as the trade laws and their enforcement often clashed with the interests of the colonists. Unfortunately it must be said that there were many Governors who were personally unfitted for this responsible post. After 1700, the picture more and more becomes one of Governors at feud with obstinate Assemblies who, by exercise of their power of the purse, were often able to frustrate the policy and encroach upon the powers of the Governor. Besides financial difficulties, Governors were often faced with turbulent and uncooperative assemblies whose members were the most worthless and shiftless of the local aristocracy. Such bodies were almost impossible to work with. Edward Trelawney, Governor of Jamaica (1738-52), showed his disgust, as several of his predecessors had done, with the comment '... managing a Colonial Assembly ... which of all farces is surely the greatest and most stupid'. Under these circumstances, 'Patience, and shuffle the cards' became a guiding rule for many a colonial Governor.

The method of appointment of Governor varied with the status of the colony. In those colonies which were royal provinces he was appointed and given his commission by Order of the King in Council. In the proprietary colonies the proprietor made a nomination which was confirmed by the Crown. The chartered corporate colonies of Rhode Island and Connecticut each elected their Governor, whose appointment was not subject to royal approval.

If the Governor's general authority to act was given by the public commission, the particular and detailed way in which he was to carry out government was usually contained in his instructions; these were private and secret and not disclosed in full to the Assembly. They often contained detailed instructions concerning the kind of laws of the local legislature to which the Governor was to refuse assent.

The Governor's powers were wide and covered every branch of government. In practice, however, they were frequently made ineffective by the opposition and political tactics of the Assembly. The Governor supervised the chief executive officials holding office by grant of letters patent, and could suspend but not remove them for misconduct. He had a general power of appointment, in so far as this was not shared with the Council or limited in various ways by the Assembly, of judges, justices of the peace, sheriffs and minor administrative officials. Wide military powers with regard to the defence and fortification of the colony, and the recruitment, training and command of the militia were possessed by the Governor, but here again his action in these matters was severely limited by the refusal of some of the Assemblies to vote for defence, or if they did so, by their practice of assuming control of the militia by means of commissioners, appointed by, and responsible only to themselves. On the imperial side, as distinct from the internal government of the colony, the Governor had the vitally important duty of ensuring the enforcement of the laws of trade, such as the Navigation Acts of 1660, 1673 and 1696.

The Council: its composition and functions

Membership of the Council was by royal appointment. Councillors were named in the Governor's commission and any vacancies subsequently arising were filled by persons recommended by the Governor. The size of the Council varied; twelve was usual, though smaller and larger ones existed in the West Indian colonies, according to the size of the islands. To these rules Massachusetts was an exception; its Council numbered twenty-eight and was elected annually by a General Court of Council and Assembly, subject to the Governor's veto. The qualifications for membership were loyalty and wealth, it being thought, not without reason, that men with these qualities would be natural allies of the Governor and his policy. In practice, the interests of the Council and Governor tended usually, but not invariably, to be identical; to some extent Council and Governor were both the object of attacks by the Assembly in pursuit of its aim of securing control of expenditure. The Governor had a further means of influencing the Council—he could suspend them from membership and he had also in his gift numerous minor offices as a reward for satisfactory service. In the early eighteenth century an 'official' element, composed of the more important officials such as the Lieutenant-Governor, the Surveyor-General of Customs and others, was given seats in the Council.

When sitting with, and presided over by, the Governor, the Council acted as his Privy or Executive Council, advising him and giving assent to his administrative acts. In a judicial capacity, sitting under the presidency of the Governor, it acted as a court of appeal for the colony, though there remained the general right of further appeal in civil cases to the King in Council. Legislatively the Council appeared as a 'House of Lords' or second chamber with the Governor excluded. In the legislative process it had co-equality with the Assembly, but this was much diminished by the refusal of the Assembly to let it initiate or amend money bills, a practice which was enforced by most of the Assemblies in the first half of the eighteenth century.

In spite of its nominally wide and impressive functions, the Council tended in practice to lose importance, as the struggle between Governor and Assembly intensified during the eighteenth century. It did not develop, as it might have done, as a constitutional shock absorber or 'cabinet' link between the Executive and the Assembly.

The Assembly

In the early history of the colonies the Council and Assembly had often sat as one body, but separation became the rule by the end of the seventeenth century. The Assembly, like the House of Commons in the mother-country, was regarded as representative of the free-holders. Generally, the colonial freeholders had the franchise or right to vote but sometimes this was defined by local act or by charter, as in the case of Massachusetts. There was often disqualification on grounds of alien nationality, colour, race and religion. In general, the franchise was rather limited, and much the same as that in England at this time, though in a few colonies, like Rhode Island, Pennsylvania and Virginia, it was perhaps slightly more democratic. As in England voting was open, by word of mouth, except that in Pennsylvania and South Carolina it was by ballot. In respect of membership, some conflict arose over the presence of the Governor's placemen in the Assembly; Governors, like George III, often tried to build up a party of 'King's Friends' in the Assembly to further official policy there. The Assemblies made attempts to exclude these office holders, but on the whole without much success.

Privileges and legislative powers

In matters of privilege the Assemblies claimed and obtained what the English House of Commons had wrested from the Crown during the constitutional struggles of the seventeenth century. This included freedom of speech, freedom from arrest, freedom of access to the Governor and the right to elect their own Speaker, though occasionally their candidate was rejected by the Governor. The Assemblies also claimed and obtained the right of determining disputed elections. Procedure over legislation generally followed that of the English House of Commons; bills could be introduced by individuals or committees. Three readings were necessary and there were the usual stages of consideration by standing committees or in a few colonies by a Committee of the whole House.

From the time of the first settlements it had been an established principle that, in the exercise of their legislative powers, the colonial assemblies must not make laws repugnant to the laws and statutes of England. A number of cases arose, particularly in the first half of the eighteenth century, where laws passed by colonial assemblies were disallowed, on the grounds that they were contrary to English common law, or statutes of England, or in a few cases because they were contrary to the charter of the colony. The Crown was also quick to disallow any legislation of assemblies, both in North America and in the West Indies, which was contrary to the letter or spirit of the imperial Navigation Acts.

H

Conflict with the executive

In the constitutional conflict between Governors and Assemblies, both sides had means at their disposal either to further their own aims or to frustrate those of their opponents. The Governor, in the majority of colonies, could adjourn, prorogue or dissolve the Assembly as he thought fit, and by using these powers he could often exact compliance over the point at issue from a reluctant Assembly. Again, the Governor had the power of assenting, or refusing his assent, to legislation that had passed through the Assembly and Council. He could also 'reserve' his assent, i.e. neither assenting nor refusing his assent, together with a further device of giving assent provided that there was a 'suspending' clause, whereby the Act would not take effect unless it was confirmed by the King in Council. For the Assembly, control of supply was their best weapon, and was often used to limit or impede the Governor's executive power. Thus the Assemblies, when they made a financial grant, would often make detailed appropriations for its allocation and would appoint commissioners of their own to supervise its expenditure. The Governor's salary was a particular target for the Assembly. In the English Leeward Isles of the West Indies, a permanent revenue existed from the $4\frac{1}{2}$ per cent. duty levied by the Crown on export of produce and in Virginia and Maryland from the quit-rents payable; such revenues secured in part the Governor's salary in these colonies. But in other colonies and especially in Massachusetts, New York and New Jersey no such revenue was available, and the Assemblies there could exert effective pressure on their Governors by refusing them Civil Lists and, where they did make grants, by imposing the conditions mentioned above. The desperate need of the Governors for money also enabled the Assemblies to use the device of 'tacking', i.e. adding on to the supply bill other bills which either had been, or were likely to be, refused assent by the Governor.

Imperial organisation of the first Empire

During this period, imperial control over the Colonies was exercised by a variety of bodies. No special minister or Secretary of State for the Colonies was appointed, and control was often rather haphazard and uncoordinated as between the various departments of state. Colonial affairs had to take their chance with many other matters clamouring for the attention of an executive machine which by modern standards was slow and inefficient. There was also a tendency at the centre to regard the colonies as useful contributors to the wealth and trade of Great Britain but otherwise as remote, unimportant and troublesome.

The constitutional supremacy of Parliament had been established by the Revolution of 1688, and with the consequent restriction of the royal prerogative, Parliament became more influential in colonial affairs, bringing them increasingly under review and legislating for them. The Privy Council, although it had been largely superseded in domestic business after 1688 by the cabinet council, remained important in colonial matters. By order in council it put into force royal policy for the colonies; much of this was based on the advice and suggestions it received from the Board of Trade. The Privy Council also acted in a judicial capacity and received appeals from the colonies.

Until 1768 executive responsibility for the colonies belonged to one of the two Secretaries of State, that of the Southern Department. This office had wide responsibilities at home; abroad it dealt with Great Britain's relations with the states of Southern Europe. This Secretary of State decided matters of defence and foreign affairs relating to the colonies, and also the appointment of Governors; the most distinguished holder of this office during this period was William Pitt the Elder (1757–1761). In 1768 Lord Hillsborough was appointed as a Third Secretary of State with control of colonial business, in addition to his other office of President of the Board of Trade.

The Board of Trade, created in 1691, was descended from the

various Councils for Trade and Plantation appointed by Charles II. Its varied responsibilities included the promotion of English trade, employment of the poor, and the colonies. In the course of time it developed something like a colonial programme of its own, though it could by no means be sure that its advice in this respect would be acted upon by either the Privy Council or the Secretary of State. During the eighteenth century it became a maid of all work, assembling facts and statistics relating to the colonies. It had no executive power of its own and could only pass its suggestions and advice to the Secretary of State and Privy Council.

The colonial agents

In the eighteenth century, when slow communications were the rule, it was advantageous to both Imperial Government and colonies to have representatives of the colonies in London. The West Indian, and later, the American colonies developed a system of agents appointed and paid under Acts passed by the Assembly of the colony concerned. The business of the agent was to further his colony's interests, which he did by attentively watching legislation in the Imperial Parliament which might affect it, by making representations to the Board of Trade, and by gleaning information for dispatch home.

Later history of the 'old representative' system

To this account of old representative system and its working some further comment must be added. Up to the outbreak of the War of American Independence the system was, with very few exceptions, the normal basis of government in English possessions overseas. After 1783, although there were cases of its extension, e.g. New Brunswick (1784), Upper and Lower Canada (1791), Sierra Leone (between 1790 and 1807), Newfoundland (1832-47) and Vancouver Island (between 1856 and 1858), it became discredited and where new colonies had to be provided for was discarded in favour of various forms of Crown Colony government. There were certain points of criticism against the old system; it was not easily forgotten by influential opinion in Great Britain that the Assemblies of the American colonies had been the mainspring of opposition to, and revolt from, the rule of the mother-country; there was the long history of damaging conflict between executive and legislature, which had produced so many deadlocks in government. Finally, as was especially shown by the British West India islands, the system often only represented minorities of white settlers bent on protecting their own particular interests, and indifferent to the humanitarian and trustee concepts which were becoming increasingly influential in the counsels of the Imperial Government. The remnant, however, of the colonies settled in the seventeenth century which still remained in the British Empire in 1783 retained the old representative system. Two of them, Bermuda and the Bahamas, have kept their ancient constitutions down to the present time; a third, Barbados, did so until recently (1946), when by the creation of an executive committee to act as a bridge between executive and legislature, her old representative system was modified in the direction of semi-responsible government.

In retrospect, it is fair to say, that in spite of the various defects and difficulties recorded, it was a major achievement that these representative institutions were transplanted overseas and operated over a long period of time with such vigour. Though constitutional practice in Great Britain and her Empire moved away from the old representative system, many of the ideas of this system were carried over into the constitutional theory and practice of the United States of America, and can be seen in the working of both Federal and State Government in that country to-day.

CHAPTER XVIII

THE AMERICAN REVOLUTION

The American colonies, 1700–63

The old representative system, in spite of the conflict between Governors and Assemblies, gave the colonies considerable opportunity to manage their own affairs. As long as they obeyed the imperial laws of trade and remained politically subordinate, the mother-country, for reasons of economy in administration, was willing that her colonies should be self-reliant in local matters. Such local self-government, however, was not regarded as preparation for subsequent colonial independence of the mother-country.

By the middle of the eighteenth century, the small and struggling settlements of the early seventeenth century in North America had become populous and prosperous colonies. This economic prosperity, together with the power of managing their own local affairs, probably explains why dependence on Great Britain was not greatly resented by responsible colonial opinion. Markets for colonial produce in Great Britain were still indispensable, and in time of war the colonies were largely dependent on the mother-country for defence against the French, Spaniards and Indians.

It is fair to say that the American colonies were ready to enjoy the benefits of the imperial system but were often reluctant to make an equivalent return. Thus in the Seven Years' War (1756–63) they had, in most cases, been very grudging in their military aid to the mother-country and had few scruples in carrying on trade with the enemy in the Caribbean. The rising of Red Indians under Pontiac (1763–4) was chiefly due to their bad treatment by the colonists, but it fell to Great Britain to put down this rising at her own cost.

The beginnings of constitutional conflict 1764–5

The capture of Canada (1759–61) from the French removed an ancient threat which had helped to keep the colonists loyal; hence-

214

forward they were more uncooperative and less amenable to imperial control. Even so it is possible that constitutional conflict might have been avoided for many years, had not Great Britain adopted a policy which was interpreted by the colonists as striking at the very roots of their rights of self-government. The essence of this policy was the assertion of the legislative superiority of the Imperial Parliament over the colonies, and its application was seen in the attempt to raise a revenue by imposing taxation such as that provided for by Grenville's Revenue Act and Stamp Act (1764 and 1765) and Townshend's import duties (1767).

The reaction of the American colonists to this legislation included both thought and action. Able writers such as James Otis attacked the idea of the sovereign power of the Imperial Parliament, maintaining that there was a law above Parliament, a fundamental, natural law, in the light of which the attempts to tax were inequitable and oppressive. Another argument, and one which American opinion seized hold of and returned to time and time again, was that the colonies could not be taxed by a Parliament in which they were not represented—'No taxation without representation.' The Stamp Act, which required the payment of stamp duties on legal documents, newspapers and pamphlets, could not be enforced owing to the non-co-operation of the colonists.

The Declaratory Act and after, 1766–70

In 1766, the Rockingham ministry repealed the Stamp Act, but in the same year passed an Act of great significance. This was the Declaratory Act, which declared that Parliament, in all cases without exception, had the power to make laws for the colonies, and that colonial attempts to question this right were completely without effect. The Townshend Acts of 1767 imposed customs duties on certain British manufactured goods and tea imported by the colonies; its aim (and one which the colonists had always resisted) was to raise a revenue for the payment of colonial governors and judges. Colonial opposition was again aroused, and patriots agreed not to import from Great Britain; in 1770, Lord North repealed all Townshend's duties except that on tea. This last duty remained and was collected together with the others of the Revenue Act, and the colonists had therefore not been quite so successful as in the case of the Stamp Act.

The 'Coercive Acts', 1774

Colonial opinion remained critical and watchful. A new phase started with the 'Boston Tea Party' (December 1773) when a cargo of tea was flung overboard by Boston 'patriots'. Public opinion in England was exasperated by this outrage, which strengthened the position of those, including George III and most of his ministers, who advocated stern repression of the insubordinate colonists. The Imperial Parliament now passed the so-called 'Coercive Acts' (March-June 1774); these were directed at the centre of sedition, Massachusetts. The Boston Port Act closed the port of Boston, until reparation for the losses of the 'tea party' should have been made. The Government of Massachusetts Act made extensive alterations in the government of the colony. It substituted a nominated council for the elective one, increased the power of the Governor to appoint sheriffs and lesser judicial officials, and restricted the meeting and business of the democratic town meetings. The Administration of Justice Act provided that those accused of the murder of customs' officials could, under certain circumstances, be removed to England for trial there. The result was to harden colonial opinion against Great Britain and led to the formation of the Continental Congress (September 1774) at Philadelphia; all the thirteen colonies except Georgia were represented. The Coercive Acts also encouraged radical opinion to demand that the colonies should be removed entirely from the competence of the Imperial Parliament, but that the link of allegiance to the Crown should remain. The radical James Wilson expressed this idea of a self-governing dominion under the British Crown when he wrote in 1774:

Allegiance to the King and obedience to Parliament are founded on very different principles. The former is founded on protection; the latter on representation.

The Continental Congress limited themselves to a statement (October 1774) of what they believed to be their constitutional rights as derived from natural law, English constitutional principles, and their own foundation charters. They emphasised their belief that they alone could tax themselves through their own representative assemblies. They repeated their objections to the 'Coercive Acts', but at the same time declared their willingness to accept the trade laws of the Imperial Parliament such as the Navigation Acts.

Attempts at conciliation

A critical situation existed in 1774–5, but colonial opinion had not yet reached the idea of complete separation. Could or would Great Britain resolve this supreme crisis which had arisen in her relationship with her American colonies? The achievement of a settlement proved impossible chiefly because majority opinion in Great Britain considered that the granting of the demands of the colonists would mean the abandonment of parliamentary supremacy over them. George III, in his narrow yet conscientious way, firmly believed that the colonists were rebels; Lord North and the ministers would not give up the 'Coercive Acts', although they were willing to make a limited compromise over the taxation question; even Chatham and Burke, the advocates of concessions to the colonists, believed that a general parliamentary supremacy over the colonies must be maintained. Both Chatham and Burke worked hard for conciliation, but without success. The 'Speech on Conciliation with America', made by Edmund Burke in the House of Commons on 22 March 1775, is justly famous; in it he urged that Great Britain should not interpret her legal constitutional rights in a narrow and tyrannical way, but that instead she should realise that liberty was indispensable to both colonies and mother-country, and if preserved and nourished would be a powerful and indissoluble bond of empire.

My hold of the colonies is in the close affection which grows from common names, from kindred blood, from similar privileges and equal protection. These are ties which, though light as air, are as strong as links of iron . . . Let the colonies always keep the idea of their civil rights associated with your government; they will cling and grapple to you; and no force under heaven will be of power to tear them from their allegiance . . .

As long as you have the wisdom to keep the sovereign authority of this country as the sanctuary of liberty, the sacred temple consecrated to our common faith, wherever the chosen race and sons of England worship freedom, they will turn their faces towards you. The more they multiply, the more friends you will have; the more ardently they love liberty, the more perfect will be their obedience. Slavery they can have anywhere. It is a weed that grows in every soil . . . freedom they can have from none but you. This is the commodity of price, of which you have the monopoly.

The wisdom of Burke was disregarded. Less than two months after his speech, the first shots were fired at Concord and Lexington (19 April 1775), to be followed in June by the costly victory of General Gage over the American militia at Bunker Hill. In the final attempt to avert general and unrestricted war with Great Britain, the Americans attempted conciliation through the 'Olive Branch Petition' of July 1775; this offered to return to the position of 1763. It was ignored by George III, because he regarded the Congress as an illegal and re-bellious body, and also because return to the position of 1763 meant abandoning parliamentary supremacy over the colonies. In August 1775, a Royal Proclamation of Rebellion was made, followed in December by an Act prohibiting trade with the thirteen colonies. Early in 1776, the feeling grew among Americans that now the only logical solution was complete independence and they were greatly influenced in this direction by Tom Paine's forceful pamphlet *Common Sense*, in which he advocated complete independence and a republican constitution.

The Declaration of Independence, 1776

The preliminaries of American Independence were seen in the opening of American commerce to the world (April 1776) and in the creation of independent state governments, each with its own con-stitution, such as those of South Carolina (March 1776), and Virginia (June 1776). At Philadelphia on 4 July 1776, the Continental Congress made the famous Declaration of Independence. At the beginning of this there was a statement of their political theories, mostly derived from the celebrated English political theorist of the late seventeenth century, John Locke.

We hold these truths to be self-evident, that all men are created equal, that they are endowed by their Creator with certain inalienable rights, that among these are life, liberty and the pursuit of happiness. That to secure these rights, governments are instituted among men, deriving their first powers from the consent of the governed. That whenever any form of government becomes destructive of these ends, it is the right of the people to alter or to abolish it, and to institute new government . . .

The Declaration also contained a recital of the 'injuries and usurpations' inflicted by George III and of attempts by the Imperial Parliament 'to extend an unwarrantable jurisdiction over us'.

For the American colonies the die was now cast; there could be no going back or compromise negotiations. With the course of the war we are not concerned; suffice to say that with the surrender of Lord Cornwallis to Washington at Yorktown (October 1781) Great Britain had lost the war and the thirteen American colonies.

The establishment of state and federal government

It remains to trace the organisation of both state and federal government by the Americans during the period of the war and immediately afterwards (1775–89). Royal government in the colonies ceased to exist towards the end of 1775; the Declaration of Independence of 1776 formally confirmed this state of affairs by proclaiming the withdrawal of all allegiance from the British Crown and the severance of all political ties with Great Britain. The void in government was filled, firstly during 1775–6 by the various congresses and conventions in each of the colonies, which took over legislative and executive authority and drafted state constitutions, and later, after the war and independence had been won, by the creation of a federal constitution.

The establishment of a federal, national government was not easily achieved. The Continental Congress of 1774, acting under the Articles of Confederation of 1777–81, had conducted the war for the

thirteen confederate and allied, yet distinct states. There was reluct-
ance, particularly in the smaller states who feared they might be
under-represented and so dominated by the larger states, to give up
any of their powers to a larger political organisation such as a
federation. A Federal Convention met at Philadelphia in May 1787.
If proof is sought of the extent to which the political consciousness
of the American colonists, and their belief in political freedom and
popular representative government, had grown during the one
hundred and fifty years of their existence, it will be found in the
quality of the debates of this Federal Convention. The larger states,
such as Virginia, Pennsylvania and Massachusetts, proposed in the
'Virginian Resolutions' a national government with representation
proportional to the number of free inhabitants of each state. Smaller
states, like New Jersey, New York, Delaware and Connecticut,
demanded equal representation, such as they had had in the wartime
confederation. The compromise finally reached was that all states
should have equal representation in the Upper House or Senate, but
that in the House of Representatives, representation was to be in
proportion to their population. The federal constitution that resulted
was eventually accepted by all the thirteen states, but only after much
discussion in the various state conventions. There was strong anti-
federalist feeling in some states, particularly Virginia; two states,
Rhode Island and North Carolina, did not join the union until after
George Washington had become the first President of the United
States of America (30 April 1789). Thus was a revolution completed
in the New World; less than a week later, in the Old World, another
revolution began with the meeting of the States-General of France at
Versailles on 5 May 1789.

CHAPTER XIX

CONSTITUTIONAL DEVELOPMENTS, 1763–1815

The rise of the second British Empire, 1783–1815

The period between 1763 and 1815 was a decisive one in the development of the British Empire. A large part of the first Empire had been lost in 1783, but by 1815 the additions of the conquests of the Revolutionary and Napoleonic wars to the nucleus of temperate and tropical colonies remaining in 1783 more than made good this loss. Besides this expansion, Great Britain made a successful readjustment to the problem of government in her Empire; she was able to produce new forms of government for new circumstances, and in addition adopted a more progressive attitude towards her problems of Empire. Before considering these changes, some mention must be made of the historical background.

What remained of the British Empire in 1783? In North America there were the Hudson Bay Company's lands, Newfoundland, Nova Scotia and Canada. In the Caribbean, apart from the loss of Tobago, all the British West Indian 'sugar' islands were retained and also the logwood-cutters' settlement in Honduras. In Europe, Minorca, but not Gibraltar, was restored to Spain. In Africa, France recovered Senegal and Goree, but Britain kept the Gambia settlement. In the East, British India, founded by Robert Clive and consolidated by Warren Hastings, was about to expand further and to take the pride of place formerly held by the thirteen American colonies.

In 1815, at the end of the wars against Napoleon, the British Empire had been considerably extended by conquest and settlement. The shift was noticeably to the East and its strategic approaches. The Cape of Good Hope, an important half-way house on the sea-route to the East, was ceded by the Dutch, who also lost to Great Britain Ceylon with its fine harbour of Trincomalee. The Indian Ocean islands of Mauritius and the Seychelles were taken from France. In India itself, the victories of Sir Arthur Wellesley over the Mahratta princes had extended the rule and influence of the East India Company. Penang in the Malay Peninsula had been leased in 1786 by the East India Company from its native Sultan, while Singapore and Malacca were acquired by negotiation in 1819 and 1824 respectively. In Europe, the naval base of Malta was retained, together with the less important island of Heligoland in the North Sea and the protectorate over the Ionian islands off the west coast of Greece. In the New World, the island of St Lucia, 'the Gibraltar of the Caribbean' was taken from France; Trinidad, a Spanish island off the mouth of the Orinoco river, conquered in 1797, was retained because of its possibilities for trade with the Spanish American colonies, soon to become independent. Great Britain also kept the Dutch colony of Demerara which had been ceded by capitulation in 1803.

Settlement also played a part in the building up of the British Empire during this period. We must notice the beginnings of Australia, with the establishment in 1787 of the penal colony of New South Wales; the resettlement in Ontario and Nova Scotia of the 'United Empire Loyalists' from the American colonies; the founding of Sierra Leone (1787) with negro emigrants from England, who had gained their freedom there by virtue of Lord Mansfield's judgment in the case of *Sommersett v. Stuart* (1772) that slavery could not exist on the soil of England. This settlement was the advance guard of a much greater emigration from Great Britain and Ireland in the nineteenth century to Australia, New Zealand, Canada and South Africa.

The lesson of 1783

The loss of the American colonies was calmly accepted by Great Britain, ready as she was to cultivate her garden elsewhere. The American Revolution had certainly triumphed, but there was little or no official admission by Great Britain that her policy of coercion had been wrong. Although in 1782 she had repealed the Irish Declaratory Act of 1719 and so given Ireland her legislative independence, she did not repeal the very similar Declaratory Act of 1766; the idea of parliamentary supremacy over the colonies, founded jointly

on the judgments of Lord Chief Justice Mansfield and the juris-
prudence of Blackstone, was not repudiated. Nevertheless, Great
Britain learnt certain lessons from the loss of the American colonies.
It was realised that parliamentary supremacy, although retained
intact, must be used rarely and cautiously in the case of those
colonies remaining which possessed the old representative system
of government. Secondly, in retrospect, this old representative
system appeared to bear much responsibility for the revolt of the
American colonies and, in the different circumstances of a conquered
and ceded colony, it also had drawbacks, as the case of *Campbell* v.
Hall revealed. Accordingly, the doctrine of the first Empire, whereby
settlers took with them, as it were, representative institutions, and the
related practice of a grant of these institutions under the prerogative
to conquered colonies, now fell into disfavour, and its application in
the old way was greatly curtailed.

The Quebec Act, 1774

Constitutional events in Canada between 1763 and 1815 illustrate
this change in outlook. By a royal proclamation of October 1763, the
conquered colony of Quebec was promised representative institutions such as prevailed in almost all the other colonies of the first
Empire. The keeping of this promise seemed unwise to the British
Government on the double grounds that the French Canadians were
totally unaccustomed to such representative institutions and that the
old representative system, judged by its workings in the American
colonies, was getting out of control. Therefore, in 1764, a provisional
government for Quebec was provided by a Governor who had full
executive and legislative powers; there was an advisory council of
officials and the more substantial inhabitants to give advice to the
Governor in the exercise of the legislative powers.

Ten years later, government was more clearly defined by the
Quebec Act of 1774. Thus a colony was constituted by Act of Parliament in order to get round the difficulty occasioned by Lord Chief
Justice Mansfield's judgment in *Campbell* v. *Hall*, where it was held
that, after a grant of representative institutions had been made, the

Crown had no further power to legislate by prerogative: only Parliament or the colonial legislature could do this.

The Quebec Act did not grant an Assembly. Instead, legislative power (which did not include the right to tax) with the consent of he Governor, was given to a nominated Council of not less than eve nteen or more than twenty-three colonial residents. Besides its egis lative functions, this Council had an executive quorum of five, and it also acted as a court of civil appeal. French civil law and the civil rights of the French Canadian Roman Catholic population were recognised; for criminal causes English law was introduced.

The Canada Constitutional Act, 1791

The government set up by the Quebec Act was acceptable to the French Canadians, but not to the increasing number of British immigrant loyalists who, as supporters of George III, had been forced to leave the American colonies. These men thought their loyalty was ill rewarded by being placed under a rule which was much less free than the old representative system they had known in their original colony of settlement. A solution was attempted by William Pitt the Younger in the Canada Constitutional Act of 1791. By this, Canada was divided into Upper and Lower Canada, thus separating the British, i.e. Empire Loyalist, element of Ontario from the French of Quebec. The government created was a development of the old representative system: Governor, Council and Assembly. The important change was that the Governor's Executive Council was quite separate from the Upper House or Legislative Council, both as regards its composition and functions. Its members held office at pleasure, whereas the members of the legislative council were appointed for life.

Apart from solving a definite problem, this Act was a reassertion of belief in free representative institutions and in the expediency of their extension to non-British settlers. Perhaps also, set against the background of the upheaval of the French Revolution, it was also an act of faith that British political institutions could give both freedom and order without anarchy and bloodshed.

The doctrine of trusteeship

During this period the doctrine of trusteeship emerged. Responsible opinion had been much exercised over the problem of controlling the rule in India of the East India Company. Lord North's Regulating Act of 1773 had not succeeded; Fox's Bill had been rejected (1783), but Pitt's India Act of 1784 set up a Board of Control in London as the deputed authority of the British Government, to which the East India Company remained accountable until the abolition of the Company's rule in 1858. Although Warren Hastings had been acquitted in 1795 of the charges of oppression and extortion while he had been Governor-General in India, on which he had been impeached in 1788, his trial helped to develop the idea of trusteeship.

Edmund Burke was the leading spokesman in the matter. Speaking during the debate on Fox's India Bill (October 1783) he said:

All political power which is set over men . . . ought to be in some way or other exercised ultimately for their benefit. If this is true with regard to every species of political dominion, and every description of commercial privileges, none of which can be original, self-derived rights or grants for the mere private benefit of the holders, then such rights, or privileges, or whatever else you choose to call them, are all in the strictest sense a trust; and it is of the very essence of every trust to be rendered accountable; and even totally to cease, when it substantially varies from the purposes for which alone it could have a lawful existence.

Opening for the House of Commons in the impeachment of Warren Hastings (February 1788) Burke declared:

We call for that spirit of equity, that spirit of justice, that spirit of protection, that spirit of lenity, which ought to characterize every British subject in power; and on these, and these principles only, he will be tried.

Thus the guiding principle of trusteeship was that Great Britain had a positive duty towards those non-European peoples she ruled. This duty could not be avoided; Imperial government must be based on principles of right rather than mere expediency; it must be just and never tyrannical. This concept and its application were greatly helped by the humanitarian movement which, by bringing about the abolition of the slave trade and slavery, not only ended a great wrong, but also something that was directly opposed to the ideas of trusteeship. The official medium through which Great Britain applied these new ideas was Crown Colony government; in the sphere of private activity, much was done by the work of missionary organisations.

CHAPTER XX

CROWN COLONY GOVERNMENT

The problem of government, 1763–1815

The colonial conquests made between 1763 and 1815 brought under British rule European but not English-speaking peoples such as the French Canadians, the French Creoles of the West Indies and Mauritius, the Spanish Creoles of Trinidad and the Dutch colonials of the Cape of Good Hope and Demerara. In addition, and much more numerous, were the Asian peoples of British India and Ceylon, together with a rising African population. The old representative system of the first Empire could not be applied automatically to these peoples with their different languages, traditions, and cultures. The immediate requirement was for a system of government which would rule strongly and justly under widely different conditions; the Governors must have ample, even unrestricted, powers in the colonies they ruled, and yet at the same time be subject to strong control from Great Britain to prevent any abuse of authority and to ensure that, as far as possible, humanitarian and trustee concepts of Empire were fulfilled.

Nature of Crown Colony government

The solution to this problem was provided by the development of what, about the middle of the nineteenth century, became known as Crown Colony government. Although this type of government did not conform to any one identical pattern, and proved itself capable of many variations, two main features distinguish it. Firstly there is a concentration of the powers of government in the hands of the Governor and his Council, whatever form this last may take. Secondly, Crown Colony government is essentially flexible, since it can move forward and expand its basis of government by the introduction of representative elements to the Legislative Council: conversely, it can move backwards to a less representative constitution by restoring the old supremacy of the executive. Because of this flexibility and adaptability it has become the instrument whereby dependent colonies can progress, by stages, to more representative, and ultimately semi-responsible and fully responsible, government. The majority of the constitutional changes since 1815 have been in this forward direction, but there have been occasions when it has been necessary to regress, e.g. Cyprus, Malta, and British Guiana. The adaptability of Crown Colony government is shown by the widely different kinds of dependencies which came under its 'umbrella' in the nineteenth and twentieth centuries.

Conquered and ceded colonies

In its original form the Crown Colony was the conquered colony of the late eighteenth and early nineteenth centuries. Early examples are Senegambia (1765) and Quebec (between 1764 and 1791), followed by the conquests of 1793–1815 such as Trinidad, St Lucia, Mauritius, Ceylon, Demerara, and the Cape of Good Hope.

In the second half of the nineteenth century were added those colonies, lying in the tropics, which were either conquered or ceded. Ashanti (1895–1901) was conquered; Lagos (1862) and Fiji (1874) are examples of Crown Colonies gained by cession.

The British West Indies

The British West India islands, after the abolition of slavery in 1833 and the loss of preference for their sugar in the British market, due to the adoption of a free trade policy by Great Britain, suffered serious economic decline. Politically the old representative system of Governor, Council and Assembly had become unsatisfactory; it now represented only an embittered, impoverished and dwindling white planter population. In Jamaica, there were less than 2,000 electors; in some of the smaller islands the number of electors barely exceeded the number of Assembly men elected. The agrarian rising in Jamaica of negro squatters on Crown Lands around Morant Bay in October 1865, and its suppression by Governor Eyre, led to drastic changes. The Jamaica legislature was compelled by these events to surrender its powers to the Crown, which was then authorised by the Imperial Parliament to provide for the government of Jamaica. This it did in 1866, when a nominated Legislative Council was set up. The Windward islands followed suit; in the Leeward islands the constitutional modifications were made by acts of the local assemblies by virtue of their constituent powers. The general result was that, although the process was delayed in a few of the islands by the retention of an elected majority in a single chamber, one by one they passed to Crown Colony government by Governor and Council with a wholly nominated majority. Only in Barbados, the Bahamas and Bermuda did the old representative system survive. There is little doubt that Crown Colony government was the best solution at a time when representative government could not be based on either the planter minority or the uneducated ex-slave population. Crown Colony government filled the gap and gave effective government for the long period necessary before a more representative form of government could be introduced.

Tropical settlements of chartered companies

There were a few colonies which although undoubtedly settled could not, because of their tropical location and very small white population, be given institutions of the old representative kind. Sierra Leone and the Gambia in Africa and the Straits Settlements in Asia came into this class; they had originally been administered by chartered trading companies. When the rule of these companies ended and the settlements became part of the dominions of the Crown, government of the Crown Colony type by a Governor and nominated Council was introduced.

British settled colonies of the nineteenth century

The tide of emigration from Great Britain and Ireland during the nineteenth century led to new settled colonies in Australia, New Zealand, Natal, and British Columbia. The constitutional doctrine of the old Empire, which would have given these settled colonies representative institutions from the start, was now inoperative. Instead their government was provided for by Act of the Imperial Parliament and their first institutions were those of the Crown Colony with Governor and Council. This phase was of relatively short duration; all these new colonies made rapid constitutional advance, firstly to representative, and then, responsible government.

Protectorates

During the latter part of the nineteenth century the dependent Empire was greatly extended by the creation of protectorates. The protectorate brought territories under British control without that annexation which would have made them legally British territory. In a number of cases protectorates followed the pioneer action of chartered companies, e.g. the British East Africa Company (Uganda) and the British South Africa Company (the Rhodesias).

The legal basis of the protectorate is the Foreign Jurisdiction Acts of 1843 and 1890, which conferred on the Crown the power to exercise jurisdiction (which included justice and administration) over protectorates as if they were territories of the Crown acquired by conquest or cession. It should be noted that protectorates are not part of the dominions of the Crown nor are their inhabitants British subjects in the full sense of the word, although entitled to diplomatic protection when in foreign countries.

Protectorates have developed along the following lines: (i) Some have been brought under the Colonial Office; they have been assimilated to Crown Colonies, and have been given Governors and the various forms of executive and legislative councils found in Crown Colonies; examples are Uganda, Northern Rhodesia and Nyasaland. Others, such as Bechuanaland and Swaziland, are under the Commonwealth Relations Office and are ruled by a High Commissioner, who legislates by proclamation.

(ii) Other protectorates are semi-independent 'protected states' where their rulers by treaties have accepted British protection and control of their foreign relations, but have retained to a greater or lesser extent control of their internal domestic government. Some examples are Zanzibar, Aden Protectorate, and Tonga.

Trustee territories

The trustee (formerly mandated) territories held by Great Britain are dependencies which resemble in many respects the protectorates. The mandated territories were originally created in 1919 by Article 22 of the Covenant of the League after World War I; in 1946, under Article 77 of the United Nations Charter these became trustee territories. Great Britain's trustee territories are all in Africa: the Cameroons, Togoland and Tanganyika Territory. The jurisdiction of the Crown over these territories is, as in the case of protectorates, exercised under the Foreign Jurisdiction Act. The power of the Crown, however, is limited to the extent that there is the international supervision of the Trusteeship Council of the United Nations.

The dependent Empire

The term 'dependent Empire' is in common use to-day, and it will be worth while to investigate its meaning. One obvious test is that of constitutional status: those territories which have not attained internal self-government and external independence from Imperial control are members of the dependent Empire. Another way of approaching the problem is to consider how external relations are transacted: territories which are represented internationally by Her Majesty's Government in the United Kingdom likewise belong to the dependent Empire. Finally, we may note that the test of Colonial Office control is only approximately correct, since some parts of the dependent Empire are controlled by other departments of state, e.g. the Commonwealth Relations Office is responsible for Basutoland, Bechuanaland Protectorate, and Swaziland.

The Governor

Throughout the British Empire and Commonwealth, the executive government is carried on in the name of the Queen. The representative of the Crown and the head of the executive government in the dependent Empire is, with few exceptions, the Governor. The office of Governor is constituted by letters patent issued by the Crown in Council under the great seal. The Governor's personal appointment to fill this office is contained in his commission from the Queen, and his powers and duties are defined in the royal instructions under the sign manual.

In the Governors of the Crown Colonies and similar dependencies there is a remarkable concentration of power, subject only to their responsibility to the Imperial Parliament and the instructions issued to them by the Secretary of State for the Colonies at the Colonial Office. The Governor is supreme in the civil sphere and although his title usually includes that of Commander-in-Chief he is essentially a civilian Governor and does not, save for one or two exceptions like Gibraltar, command the regular forces in the colony. The Governor is responsible for the exercise of the royal prerogative of mercy; this power is delegated directly to him by the sovereign. In relation to his Executive and Legislative Councils the Governor is advantageously placed. Thus he can disregard the advice of his Executive Council, though in practice this rarely happens. Through his power of nomination he can influence the composition of the official and nominated unofficial elements of the Legislative Council. He usually presides in this council; he initiates legislation; he has a reserve power of legislating on issues of special importance and he has a veto on legislation.

Finally, much of the dignified ceremonial associated with the duties of the monarchy in Great Britain has been carried over into the Crown Colonies with the office of Governor. This is shown by the exalted position the Governor holds, with his personal staff and bodyguard, and the ceremonial attending his public activities in the colony.

The Oversea Civil Service

The detailed work of government, under the Governor, is done by the various public services. These are staffed by the officials of the Oversea Civil Service; recruitment for this is carried out partly locally and partly outside the colony. The public services divide broadly into two classes; firstly, those concerned with general administration and, secondly, the specialist services such as medical, education, veterinary, mines, forestry etc. In any particular colony, members of the Oversea Civil Service working there are public servants of that colony and their salaries are paid out of local revenue. In cases of discipline, where investigation of charges or complaints against officials is concerned, the Executive Council of the colony is the competent body.

The Executive Council

The modern Executive Council of the Crown Colony is derived from the advisory council of the early years of the nineteenth century; it also has some links with the Council of the old representative system. In the 1820's and 1830's the constitutions of conquered colonies such as Trinidad, Ceylon and the Cape of Good Hope were changed from Governor and advisory council to Governor and Legislative and Executive Councils. This pattern of the two Councils was also applied to the new colonies created in the 1830's and 1840's in Australia and New Zealand, while the Executive Council was added where it was lacking in a few of the older established colonies such as British Honduras and Sierra Leone, which already had a Legislative Council.

Originally membership of the Executive Council was entirely official, but this was modified by the gradual inclusion of some unofficial members. Of the official members, certain officials, such as the Chief Secretary, the Attorney-General, and the Financial Secretary, are members *ex officio* (by virtue of their office); other officials, such as the heads of important departments and senior provincial commissioners, are usually added. Unofficial members are sometimes appointed by the Governor, acting under his instructions; sometimes, as in Gibraltar, the Executive Council has been constituted by letters patent which provide for unofficial representation.

The presence of unofficial members in the Executive Council is connected with constitutional progress. When they join the Council, the expression of the opinion of colonial society by other than official members becomes possible, thus making the government more representative. Again, when unofficial members who are already members of a representative Legislative Council are nominated to the Executive Council, there is the possibility that in course of time a cabinet will result. This last development largely depends on the social structure of the particular colony, e.g. its chances seem slight in dependencies like Kenya, where there are the complications of a plural society and communal representation.

Though the Governor, in all but exceptional circumstances, is bound to consult his Executive Council and thereby receive their advice, he is not bound to accept and act on this advice; he has overriding powers. This situation, however, is exceptional and as a rule the advice of the Executive Council on policy is accepted and furnishes the basis of executive action or of legislative ordinances.

The Legislative Council

The modern Legislative Council is the result of much constitutional experiment and growth. Its beginnings go back to that early autocratic stage in the Crown Colonies' history when the Governor, although he may have had an advisory council, was both the sole executive and legislative authority. The constitutional advance from this phase was the creation of a Legislative Council which, with the Governor, now became the legislature. It must be noted that not all Crown Colonies received Legislative Councils; a number remained at the level where the Governor was the sole legislative authority.

The most important feature of the new Legislative Council as it developed was that it was mixed; i.e. it had official and unofficial members sitting together. It lent itself to constitutional progress because the proportions of official and unofficial members could be altered. By increasing the nominated unofficial members, the legislature could be made more representative and this process was aided by the later development of the election instead of nomination of unofficial members. In this changing balance between official, nominated unofficial, and elected unofficial members is reflected the constitutional progress that has been and is taking place throughout the dependent Empire.

The legal origins of the Legislative Councils are varied. Those of Bahamas, Bermuda and Barbados derive from the constitutional doctrine of the first British Empire and the royal commissions and instructions to the Governor; others, like the conquered or ceded colonies such as Trinidad, Ceylon, St Lucia, Fiji and Hong Kong, are constituted under the prerogative. Acts of the Imperial Parliament account for others, notably Jamaica and British Guiana. Protectorates such as Northern Rhodesia, Nyasaland, Uganda, or trustee (mandated) territories like Tanganyika, have received legislative councils under the authority of the Foreign Jurisdiction Act, while those of Gambia, Sierra Leone and the Falkland islands derive from the authority of the British Settlements Act.

The instruments by which the legislative councils have been set up are, as a rule, either letters patent or orders in council. These constitute the legislative council in the colony, while the royal instructions to the Governor elaborate the details of its composition and its powers of making ordinances. The Legislative Council has power to pass those ordinances and to constitute those courts and officers for the administration of justice necessary for the peace, order and good government of the colony. Its powers of legislation, however, are subject to considerable limitations. The Legislative Council is limited by the legislative powers of the Imperial Parliament, expressed through an Act of Parliament or by order in council. The Crown can disallow ordinances that have been passed, and there are certain bills that must be reserved by the Governor for signification of the Crown's pleasure through the Secretary of State for the Colonies. There are also such limitations as the Governor's power of initiation of all legislation, his reserve power of legislation on matters of exceptional importance, and his veto on legislation. In the all-important matter of finance, the enactments of the colonial legislature cannot take effect until the sanction of the Secretary of State has been given. These limitations appear formidable and hampering, but in practice they are largely a reserve power to prevent undesirable measures. The legislatures of the dependent Empire have, with the encouragement of the Colonial Office and with the aid given under the Colonial Development Acts, plenty of opportunity of passing measures which will advance the economic development and social welfare of their particular colony and much has been done in this respect by enterprising Governors and legislatures working together in harmony.

The electorate

Constitutional progress within a Crown Colony is closely connected with the changing balance between the official, the nominated unofficial and the elected unofficial elements of the legislature. Something must be said about the problems and difficulties involved in this progress.

In Western Europe there is sufficient similarity of outlook and interest, based on a common national consciousness and tradition, to enable all the voters to be organised in territorial constituencies to elect their representatives. In much of the dependent Empire, such uniformity is lacking: instead society is plural in character and great difficulties would be caused if peoples of different races and religions were divided up into constituencies like those of Great Britain. In the Crown Colonies of the nineteenth century, other than those of

British settlement, the lack of such a unified electorate has made progress from nominated unofficial representation to elected unofficial representation slow. One way round the difficulty has been to use electoral bodies representing various interests, organised on a corporate or communal basis.

Corporate and communal representation

Corporate representation is representation according to function, i.e. occupation or profession within the community. In the British Empire, where trading interests are strongly present, the trading communities organised themselves in Chambers of Commerce which provided a convenient basis for giving unofficial representation to commercial interests. Later corporate representation was extended to labour organisations and educational bodies. The corporate members can be elected or nominated. Until recently examples were found in the Gold Coast, where the mining and commercial interests had members in the Legislative Assembly, and in Singapore, where the European, Chinese and Indian Chambers of Commerce were represented in the Legislative Council. Although corporate representation is not now regarded with much favour by democratic theorists it may well have its uses in the more complicated social structures of some lands of the dependent Empire as an alternative to the disadvantages of communal representation.

Communal representation is representation of the various cultural or racial communities that are found in plural societies. There are many examples of plural societies within the Empire: in Kenya there are African, European, Indian, and Arab communities; in Mauritius there are the descendants of the original French settlers, together with Indians and Chinese; in Malaya there are Malays, Chinese and Indians. In such societies, where the various communities each have their own language, customs and religion, political representation can only be done at present on the basis of the racial or cultural community. Progress to more representative forms of government depends considerably on the extent to which a single electorate can be built up to take the place of the various community electorates. This

236

will be difficult as the differences of race, religion and culture go very deep: in themselves they are all manifestations of separateness. Communal representation perpetuates these differences and the tensions that inevitably arise from them: how are communal differences to be resolved so that something like a national unity takes their place? We may note that, where the problems of a plural society are not so pronounced, constitutional progress has been greater, as is shown by a comparison of the Gold Coast and Nigeria with the British East African territories.

The advance to representative and responsible government

The possibilities for constitutional development contained in the institutions of Crown Colony government have already been mentioned. What is the aim of this development? It is the eventual attainment of self-government within the British Commonwealth of Nations. In each Crown Colony this involves internally a change in the old relations between the executive and the legislature, whereby the latter controls the former; externally it means the gradual disappearance of the old subordination to the Imperial Government.

The whole process, like others of the British constitutional tradition, is a gradual one. At first nominated, and later elected, or partly elected and partly nominated, the unofficial members grow steadily in importance and influence in the legislative council. Eventually, when half or more of the legislative council are elected, a representative legislature has been attained. Difficulties may occur at this stage with the legislature in conflict with the executive, as happened in the old representative system of the first Empire. The deadlock may be solved either by the exercise of the Governor's reserve powers or by a constitutional advance whereby the executive in the person of ministers becomes responsible to the legislature. This development is the beginning of responsible government, but it is not quite the fully responsible government attained by Canada, the Australian colonies and New Zealand in the nineteenth century. Modern authorities have named it semi-responsible because the Imperial Government still exercises external control either through its own direct legislation or in certain cases by legislation through the reserve powers of the Governor. The tendency is for internal control through exercise of the Governor's power to disappear first, leaving only the powers of external control of the Imperial Government. These powers are principally the following:

(1) the power of legislation, which may be used for (a) general purposes, (b) emergency purposes, (c) control of the vitally important matters of foreign affairs and defence, and (d) amendment or revocation of the colonial constitution;

(2) the limitation of the power of a colonial legislature, originally written into its constitution. This is found in a few cases to prevent any discriminatory legislation against cultural minorities or native populations;

(3) the power of disallowance of legislation, which becomes inoperative when the frontiers of responsible government have been crossed.

When this external control by imperial legislation, or by limitation of the legislation of the colonial legislature, has been removed, the constitutional status becomes that of responsible government. This, however, complete as it is in sovereignty over internal affairs, falls short of that independent status enjoyed by members of the Commonwealth such as Australia or Canada. It is only when the colonial government has acquired a sovereignty over matters concerning it outside its boundaries and is so able to control its foreign relations, make treaties and appoint its own ambassadors, that it reaches the goal of independent status within the Commonwealth.

CHAPTER XXI

FEDERATION

The idea of federation

Federation is the formation of a larger political unit by the closer political association of those states who have agreed to form such a union. In a federal state there is a sharing of authority between the federal government and the confederating states. The instrument which sets up the federation will be as precise as possible about the respective powers of the federal government and the states. Even so, constitutional disputes between the federal government and the states will arise and as a rule these will be referred to a Supreme Court which will interpret the constitution and give judgments ·binding on both sides. One conspicuous merit of a federal constitution is that it makes political unity and strength possible without extinguishing the separate existence of the states who have agreed to federate.

Older examples of federation are those of the Dominion of Canada (1867) and the Commonwealth of Australia (1901) the development of which is explained in Chap. XXII. Since 1945 the idea of federation has been of importance in parts of the dependent Empire. One federation, that of Rhodesia and Nyasaland, has been set up (September 1953-February 1954). Another, that of the British West Indies will be constituted under the powers given by the British Caribbean Federation Act of August 1956. In both cases the larger political unit brought by federation gives the prospect of greater strength and the possibility of working out a common policy for such matters as defence, external affairs, economic development and communications. The present constitution of Nigeria is of federal character and is an interesting attempt to solve the political difficulties which had arisen under the constitution of 1951.

The Federation of Rhodesia and Nyasaland

The Federation of Rhodesia and Nyasaland is made up of the colony of Southern Rhodesia, the Protectorate of Northern Rhodesia and the Protectorate of Nyasaland. Before 1950 there had been some tentative moves towards closer association between Southern and Northern Rhodesia. The war of 1939–45 emphasised the need of an organisation for dealing with common problems, and as a result the Central African Council, a consultative and advisory body, was set up for the three territories in 1945. This body pointed the way to closer political association in a federation with powers to deal with major problems common to all three territories. Proposals for such a federation were drawn up in 1951: these were approved in Southern Rhodesia by the two-thirds majority necessary for constitutional amendment and by the Legislative Councils of Northern Rhodesia and Nyasaland. In 1953 the Federation was formally authorised by an Act of the Imperial Parliament; under the Act the Crown by order in council set up the constitutional machinery necessary for the federal government.

The Queen is represented in the Federation by a Governor-General, who is invested with the executive power of the Federation. He exercises his powers on the advice of his Prime Minister and Executive Council except in matters where the constitution has given him discretionary powers, e.g., where a proposed law conflicts with international agreements. The Federal Legislature has a Speaker and 35 members; of these, 26 are elected members: 14 from Southern Rhodesia, 8 from Northern Rhodesia and 4 from Nyasaland. The remaining 9 consist of 6 specially elected African members, two from each territory, and 3 European members, one from each territory, with special responsibility for African interests. This responsibility is discharged through the African Affairs Board, a standing committee of the Federal Assembly, composed of the three European members representing African interests and one of the elected African members from each territory. The Board can make representations to the Federal Government about legislation which it considers affect

African interests adversely and which it thinks should be reserved for the signification of Her Majesty's pleasure.

The Federal Government has exclusive power over such external affairs as are entrusted to it by the Imperial Government, defence, immigration and emigration, financial and economic policy, roads, railways, posts and telegraphs, European education and agriculture. A few matters such as health are within the competence of both federal and territorial governments, though federal law will prevail in case of conflict. Apart from these matters specified in the constitution as federal all other functions of government remain with the territorial governments, viz., African administration, education and agriculture, land, mining, irrigation, local government and housing.

There is a Federal Supreme Court with a chief justice assisted by federal justices varying in number between two and five: the court has exclusive jurisdiction in matters of interpretation of the federal constitution. Financial arrangements include an apportionment of the money raised by the income-tax levied by the Federal Government between itself and the territories: of this the Federal Government gets 64 per cent., Northern Rhodesia 17 per cent., Southern Rhodesia 13 per cent., and Nyasaland 6 per cent. The territories can also surcharge up to 20 per cent. on the income-tax levied in their areas.

Federal elections have been held; the first Federal Assembly met in February 1954 and a Prime Minister and six other ministers have been appointed by the Governor-General. In 1956 the Federation sought to determine its constitutional status when it asked the British Government for independence within the Commonwealth.

The British Caribbean Federation

Federation is not a new idea in the British West Indies, where examples of federation of groups of islands such as the Leeward islands are found from the early eighteenth century onwards. The success of these federations was very limited, chiefly because of strong local patriotism. Each island, however small, was intensely proud of its own history and separate government, while the difficulty

of inter-island communication increased this separatism. The conditions of the twentieth century, with their emphasis on the needs for
improving standards of government and for raising living standards,
gave strong impetus to the idea of a British Caribbean Federation
with the eventual aim of Dominion status.

At a conference held at Montego Bay in Jamaica in 1947 the intention of the representatives of the island governments there
assembled was to consider closer association only, but they ended by
accepting the principle of federation. A Standing Closer Association
Committee resulted from this Conference and reported in March
1950. It recommended a federation with Dominion status as the
final aim. The matter was carried a stage further at the London
Conference of April 1953 at which nearly all the British West Indian
islands were represented; British Honduras and British Guiana, who
were critical of the scheme, sent observers only. The delegations
pledged support of their respective governments for a British Caribbean Federation; the British Government promised to make a suitable financial grant-in-aid.

The legislature planned for the Federation is a Senate of 19
members nominated by the Governor-General, and an elected House
of Assembly in which the confederating islands are represented
approximately according to their populations. The Crown will be
represented by a Governor-General, who will act as chairman of the
Council of State, which will include the Prime Minister, seven
members nominated by the Prime Minister and three members
appointed by the Governor-General in Council. The Governor-
General, when he appoints or dismisses members of the Council
of State, will do so in accordance with the accepted constitutional
conventions of the United Kingdom.

In February 1955, the British Colonial Secretary announced
further steps towards the setting up of this Federation. These
included the appointment of a Commissioner for the preparation of
the federal organisation, of commissions to plan the financial
arrangements, the civil service and judiciary of the Federation,
and of a conference on freedom of personal movement within the

Federation. The London Conference of February 1956 confirmed the constitutional plans of 1953 and decided that the constitution was to be drafted by the end of 1956 and that federal elections should be held as soon as practicable after 1 January 1958. By an Act of the Imperial Parliament (2 August 1956), the Crown was empowered to constitute the Federation by order in council.

The Federal Constitution of Nigeria (1954)

In 1951 the Colony and Protectorate of Nigeria received a constitution giving semi-responsible government. The Central Government included a Council of Ministers with a majority of Nigerian ministers and a Central Legislature of 148 members; 136 of these were elected by the Nigerian members of the three Regional Legislatures. The Central Legislature had full powers of legislation subject to reservation at the discretion of the Governor. The Northern, Eastern and Western Regions each had an Executive Council and a Legislature whose powers were subject to direction and approval of the Council of Ministers at the centre. It was this supervision from the centre that led to trouble in 1953. Riots at Kano in the Northern Region clearly showed the political dislikes and fears of a population of 11 million Moslems which saw the likelihood of being brought under the rule of 14 million Christians and pagans of the two southern Regions 'if and when full self-government came about'. The Eastern Region had also run into difficulties with its government owing to party feuds; a Government commission had revealed corruption in the municipal government of Lagos.

The decision was taken by the Imperial government soon after the Kano riots to redraft the constitution so that there would be much greater self-government for the Regions and so that the Central Government would lose its powers to interfere in matters which had been entrusted to the Regions. A federal constitution which would break down the rigidity and over-centralisation of the previous system was planned. This constitution, drafted by conferences held at London and Lagos between July 1953 and February 1954, gave certain specified functions to the central government, the remaining ones going to the Regions. The principal functions of the central government include external relations, defence, immigration and emigration, customs, finance, railways, harbours, posts and telegraphs. Education, agriculture, police, security, roads and local government are among the more important functions of the Regional governments. There are also certain subjects common to both but in case of conflict central legislation prevails.

The constitution which came into force in October 1954 provides for a single-chamber Federal House of Representatives of 184 elected members together with a Speaker, 3 *ex-officio* and 6 nominated members. Of the elected members 92 are returned by the Northern Region, 42 by the Eastern Region, 42 by the Western Region, 6 by the Southern Cameroons and 2 by Lagos. There is a Cabinet of 10 Ministers: the Governor-General and the Governors in each of the Regions retain certain reserve powers. The Eastern and Western Regions both have a single-chamber House of Assembly; the Northern Region has a bi-cameral system—House of Chiefs and House of Assembly. There are Regional Executive Councils of Ministers.

Some time must elapse before the results of federation in Nigeria can be fully judged. In its favour it can be said that the alternative unitary form of government would be difficult to carry out because of the three distinct regional groupings of peoples with different religions, traditions, and history who are at different stages of economic development. Under such conditions federation can give a working balance and safeguard the rights of the large minority group in the Northern Region. It is interesting that the Bourne Report of December 1955 recommends that in the Gold Coast, where regional differences and difficulties are present, though on a lesser scale than in Nigeria, the unitary principles of government should be preserved by the devolution of powers to regions. The proposed devolution would give considerable power to the regional assemblies to raise money for local government services which would be under their own control. Legislative power for the Gold Coast, however, would remain at the centre, thus preserving the unitary principle and so avoiding the fragmentation which federation would cause in a territory such as the Gold Coast.

CHAPTER XXII

THE SELF-GOVERNING COLONIES

Colonial self-government

Chapter XX traced the development of Crown Colony government and its gradual change during the last hundred years into more representative forms of government. Something must now be said about constitutional development during the nineteenth century in those newer colonies whose settlers were of British or European descent. In Canada, the Australian colonies and New Zealand there was a fairly rapid movement towards responsible government. This responsible government bore a general resemblance to the state of government in Great Britain, where parliamentary democracy with a cabinet of ministers (executive) dependent on and responsible to a majority in Parliament (legislature) had developed. It would be wrong to assume that responsible government in the colonies was an exact copy of the constitutional situation that existed in Great Britain, and that all the British constitutional usages and conventions were automatically transferred overseas. In practice, what responsible government did give these colonies in the nineteenth century was internal self-government, which included control of finance and all matters of domestic government. Externally, however, the imperial relationship imposed certain limitations on the legislative and judicial powers of these self-governing colonies; these will be referred to in the next chapter.

The basis of the old representative system

The starting point of this forward movement was sometimes, as in the case of Canada, a representative form of government resembling that of the first Empire, or, in most other cases, a Crown Colony system which has been modified by the grant of a legislative council. The old representative system, in spite of its concentration of executive power in the hands of the Governor, had kept alive the idea of popular participation in the work of government. Such participation was usually limited to the elected assembly giving its consent to legislation (which was often refused assent by the Governor), to criticism of the Governor and his policy and to some control over grants of public money. Because of her unfortunate experience with the thirteen American colonies under the old representative system, Great Britain preferred the alternative of Crown Colony government, but, in the light of her own constitutional development and beliefs, she could not completely disown and abandon this old representative system. Thus the representative government given to the two Canadas by the younger Pitt in 1791 was not very different from that of the old representative system. New Brunswick, after its formation as a separate colony, received representative government, and as late as 1832-47 Newfoundland adopted it. It is perhaps significant that Canada was the first to become a self-governing Dominion within the British Empire.

Colonial demands for self-government

The second point is that in those newly settled colonies where the settlers were of British origin, Crown Colony government became the object of increasing criticism from those it governed. The free emigrants who went from Great Britain in the 1840's and 1850's to the new Australian colonies regarded Crown Colony rule as a denial of popular democratic rights. They even attributed those financial and economic difficulties which were inevitable in the pioneer stage of these colonies to this form of government. Self-government, it was said, would bring prosperity. Many of these settlers had left Great Britain because of a deep dissatisfaction with their poverty and lack of political rights. In the freer atmosphere of a new land they were eager to alter both these conditions and they were very sure of their ability to manage their own government. There was also a small number of the emigrants who came from the upper and professional classes of English society. These settlers considered they had a prescriptive right to take an active part in government and regarded Crown Colony rule as a denial of this right.

The attitude of Great Britain

The attitude of Great Britain to this demand from her colonies for greater self-government was a cautious one. Great Britain herself had made a modest step towards democracy by the passing of the Reform Bill of 1832 and it was felt that she could not logically withhold these benefits from the new settled colonies. But there was much distrust of setting up a full-blooded democracy, which was what the colonies seemed to want. If democratically elected assemblies were introduced, British opinion thought there should be an upper house to act as a constitutional check. The idea of letting these colonies have full control of all their affairs was considered unwise; it was thought essential that some subjects of Imperial interest such as foreign affairs and defence should be withheld from the colonies' control. Thus Lord Durham in his Report, while advocating responsible government for Canada, proposed to keep in Imperial hands control of foreign affairs, external trade, disposal of unoccupied lands, and the power of amending the colonial constitution. Again, in the granting of self-government to the Australian colonies the Imperial Government did not want to surrender its control of the unoccupied lands to the individual colonies, because retention of this control was thought essential for the successful working of the policy of 'systematic colonisation'.

Upper and Lower Canada, 1791-1837

The circumstances in which the Canada Constitutional Act of 1791 was passed have been told in chapter XIX. By this Act each of the provinces, Upper and Lower Canada, received a legislature consisting of an elected Assembly and a nominated Legislative Council. At the head of the executive over both provinces was a Governor-in-Chief; each province had its Lieutenant-Governor and nominated Executive Council.

247

Under this representative form of government the Assemblies had a limited control of taxation, but they could neither remove the executive nor enact laws without its consent, which was not given unless the legislation was acceptable to the British Government in London. Nevertheless, for the first twenty years or so this constitution worked reasonably well and both English and French Canadians energetically and loyally repulsed American invasions during the war of 1812-15. After 1815, however, trouble developed in both provinces. The French Canadians became increasingly politically minded and racially hostile to the English executive in Lower Canada (Quebec). In 1834 the Assembly of Lower Canada, led by Louis Papineau, put forward extensive demands which if conceded would have given them complete financial control and partial control of the executive. In Upper Canada (Ontario) the monopoly of political power so tightly held by the descendants of the original United Empire loyalists was attacked by a growing Liberal party, chiefly drawn from recent emigrants from the British Isles. Led by William Mackenzie they demanded that the Executive should be responsible to the Assembly. The demands of both Papineau and Mackenzie were rejected by the Imperial Government. In protest both leaders in 1837 led small armed rebellions which were quickly suppressed.

The Durham Report, 1839

These danger signals were recognised by the Imperial Government. In Lower Canada the Constitution of 1791 was suspended and Lord Durham was sent out to make a thorough investigation in both the Canadas. In his 'Report on the affairs of British North America', Durham made two important recommendations. The first was that Upper and Lower Canada should be reunited into one province, in order that English and French Canadians might forget their racial animosities and become united in a common Canadian citizenship. The second was that self-government of a responsible kind which would give the Canadians full control over their internal affairs must be granted. Durham, however, proposed to keep such matters as foreign relations, constitution-making powers and external trade relations in the hands of the Imperial Government.

Canada Act, 1840

The proposal for union of the two Canadas was accepted, and by the Act of Union or Canada Act of 1840 a united Parliament was created. It consisted of a Governor-General, a Legislative Council of twenty nominated by the Crown for life, and an elected Assembly of eighty-four, in which Quebec and Ontario were equally represented. But this constitution was like that given in 1791 and so did not bring the responsible government advocated by Durham. The Whig Government when in power in Great Britain thought that (in 1840) responsible government was impossible on the grounds that if granted, the Imperial Government would lose all political control of the colony, and the break-up of the Empire would follow. But within ten years of the Report, Canada had achieved responsible government. Several factors contributed to this result. One was the realisation in Great Britain that responsible government if freely granted to the colonies was likely to win their loyalty and keep them in a united Empire. Another was the movement to give the colonies economic freedom by abolishing what remained of the restrictions of the old Empire such as the Navigation Acts (repealed in 1849). If the colonies were to be given this economic freedom, then, it was argued, it was inconsistent to withhold the political freedom which responsible government would give. In Canada much was due to the common sense and political moderation shown by both sides and to the skill and courage of Governor-General Lord Elgin.

Responsible government, 1847

Durham had said in his Report that the change from representative to responsible government could be brought about by an instruction from the Secretary of State to the Governor-General authorising him 'to secure the co-operation of the assembly in his policy, by entrusting its administration to such men as could command a majority'. This is what actually happened in Canada and in many other colonies in the representative stage. It is yet another illustration of how constitutional advance has sometimes grown out of an existing situation and developed locally by the application of constitutional conventions rather than being formally imposed from above by an Act of Parliament. After 1840 the Governors-General in Canada, with one exception (Sir Charles Metcalfe), began to choose their Executive Council from the majority party in the Assembly. It was in 1847 under Lord Elgin, Durham's son-in-law, that the final step was taken and responsible government, with a party cabinet and party Prime Minister, started. The Governor-General's position, under the new order of things, in time came to resemble the impartial and detached position of the Crown. By the same process, responsible government was brought about in the other British North American colonies of Nova Scotia (1846), Prince Edward Island (1851), New Brunswick (1854), and Newfoundland (1855).

The British North America Act, 1867

The establishment of responsible government in Canada was followed twenty years later by the British North America Act of 1867, which created a federal union. The foundation members were Canada (Ontario and Quebec), New Brunswick and Nova Scotia. Prince Edward Island, the North-west Territory (taken over from the Hudson's Bay Company in 1869) and British Columbia had joined this union by 1873; Newfoundland joined in 1949, when she gave up Dominion Status.

The Dominion of Canada had been created, within which a united nation could grow up. The movement for Canadian union had been fostered by several forces. One was the remarkable economic growth of the various colonies; another was the building of railways, which not only drew tighter the links between Canada and the 'Maritimes' of Nova Scotia and New Brunswick but also held out the prospect of a trans-continental link with British Columbia and the Pacific coast. The American Civil War of 1861-5 had led to strained relations between Great Britain and the northerners (Federals); if war broke out the Canadian colonies would be the first to be attacked. Canadian union was the obvious answer to this threat from the south.

The chief characteristics of this union were its application of the principles of federation and adoption of the principles of the British parliamentary system. At the head of the Dominion or Federal Government was the Governor-General: the Dominion legislature consisted of the Senate and House of Commons. As in Great Britain, the Prime Minister and cabinet were dependent on the support of the House of Commons. Each of the colonies which had federated together in this union had provincial governments with Lieutenant-Governors, appointed Legislative Councils (except Ontario) and elected Legislative Assemblies. Responsible government, with Prime Minister, cabinet, and party majority, was the rule. The Dominion had its powers declared in the Act; these were extensive and included all matters of national importance such as defence, trade, posts, currency and taxation. The intention of the Act was to make the Dominion government a strong one, so avoiding the situation in the U.S.A., where the extent and strength of state rights often hindered and embarrassed the federal government. Consequently the powers of the Canadian provincial governments, relating chiefly to matters of local government, were strictly specified in the Act. Any residuary powers belonged to the Dominion, and not to the provinces.

The Australian colonies

British settlement in Australia started with the penal colony of New South Wales. In 1786 the Crown, acting under authority given it by the Transportation Act of 1784, named New South Wales as the new penal colony. The Governor was given very full powers and ruled without any council. Special courts with power and procedure resembling those of military courts-martial were authorized for the colony by an act of 1787; there was no trial by jury.

The character of this convict colony was soon changed by the arrival of free settlers, who by the early years of the nineteenth century had started an agitation for representative institutions and trial by jury. It was urged that, under the harsh restraints of a penal colony, free settlers would not be attracted. If the numerically small white settlements of the British West Indies had representative institutions, why should they be withheld from New South Wales? In 1819 the British Government appointed a Commissioner to investigate the situation and in particular the administration and acts of the Governor. His report led to the New South Wales Judicature Act of 1823 which, besides introducing constitutional improvements to end the unrestrained autocracy of the Governor, also showed that Great Britain was coming to regard New South Wales as a settled colony and not merely as a convict settlement. The chief reform was the creation of an Advisory Council of not more than seven or less than five members appointed by the Crown. This Council was to assist the Governor in legislating, but the Governor in certain circumstances could legislate against its advice. If he did so he had to give written reasons for his action, while the dissenting members of the Council could record their protests in writing. A further check on too much high-handedness by the Governor over legislation was provided by the chief justice, who had to certify that proposed legislation brought before the Council, was not repugnant to the laws of England. Another reform was the introduction of trial by jury in civil but not criminal cases. In 1825 an Executive Council, whose members also sat in the Legislative Council, was added to assist the Governor. Legislation of the Imperial Parliament in 1828 enlarged the Legislative Council to fifteen nominated members, eight official and seven unofficial, but did not grant a Legislative Assembly as had been petitioned for in 1827. Legislation now required a majority vote in the Council; the Governor's former power of legislating on his own with the support of one member was abolished.

Much agitation for representative government took place in the 1830's; a petition asking for a Legislative Assembly of fifty members for New South Wales was presented to the Imperial Parliament in 1833. It failed chiefly because of the great bar to the granting of freer institutions at this time—the continuance of the transportation of convicts; Great Britain thought it unwise to give the vote and power of legislating to ex-convicts who had served their sentences or had been pardoned. When, however, transportation to New South Wales was ended in 1840 a more representative form of government became possible. By an Act of 1842, New South Wales was granted a Legislative Council of thirty-six members, 12 nominated by the Crown and twenty-four elected on a moderate franchise. This representative government, although an advance on its predecessors and probably as much as was warranted at the time, came under much criticism. Some of this was noisy and misinformed, the product of irresponsible newspapers and radical agitation, much of which had been introduced by Chartist emigrants from England. Among the constitutional grievances were the Governor's control of administration through his Executive Council and also the fact that he had a fixed and guaranteed Civil List which made him financially independent of the legislature. Another grievance was the control of the waste lands of the colonies by the Imperial Government, who fixed the price and conditions of their sale. By 1850, the demand was strong for responsible government such as Canada had achieved. The Imperial Government was cautious; it did not want to give up its control of the waste lands and emigration, and it did not like the prospect of 'raw' democracy in these colonies. Nevertheless the Australian Colonies Government Act was passed in 1850. This Act formed a new colony, known as Victoria, out of the southern part of New South Wales and gave it, together with South Australia and Van Diemen's Land (Tasmania), the kind of representative government existing in New South Wales. More important, the Act gave power to these colonies to draft for themselves new constitutions which could then be submitted to the Imperial Parliament for enactment.

The constitutions drawn up by these colonies between 1851 and 1855 differed in some particulars but in the main they followed the British constitutional pattern. In all of them there was a Governor representing the Crown and a legislature of two chambers; the importance of an upper house as a brake on hasty legislation was insisted on by the British Government. In New South Wales the upper house was nominated; in South Australia, Tasmania and Victoria it was elected, while all four lower houses were elected on a democratic franchise. To show its good will towards constitutional progress in the Australian colonies the Imperial Government in 1852–3 gave up its control of waste lands, which were now placed under the colonial legislatures. By 1856, all the Australian colonies, with the exception of Western Australia, were on the threshold of responsible government with cabinets supported by popular majorities in the lower house. In 1859 the colony of Queensland was formed out of the northern part of New South Wales; it was given responsible government immediately on foundation without passing through any intervening stage of representative government. Western Australia, where development was slower than the other colonies, and where transportation of convicts was not abolished until 1868, did not attain responsible government until 1890, having passed through the representative stages of a Legislative Council first with elected minority (1867) and later with elected majority (1870).

The Commonwealth of Australia (1901)

The achievement of a federal union of the Australian colonies was, as in the case of Canada, beset by many difficulties—among these were inter-state jealousies, long distances, conflicting economic interests and little sense of a common nationhood. The British Colonial Secretary, Earl Grey, had made proposals for federal union as early as 1847 and the draft of the Australian Colonies Government Bill of 1849–50 included provision for federation. A federal legislature was proposed; its members were to be elected by the legislatures of the four colonies: New South Wales, Victoria, South Australia and Van Diemen's Land. Tariffs, posts and communications and a Supreme Court were the most important subjects proposed for federal activity. But realising the colonial opposition and lack of enthusiasm the Imperial Government finally withdrew the federal clauses.

For the next twenty-five years the Australian federation movement was inactive, although the inconvenience caused by the different customs tariffs of the colonies emphasised the benefits a federal customs union or tariff agreement would bring. After 1880, French and German colonial activities in the Pacific and the growing realisation

of the relative defencelessness of Australia stimulated the movement for union. A shadowy federal council (which New South Wales
and New Zealand did not join) was formed in 1883 but it had very
little power to do anything and lacked executive or revenue. In the
1890's New South Wales, who hitherto had held aloof, became more
favourably disposed towards federation. A Convention, attended by
representatives from the various states, was held at Sydney in 1891
and outlined a scheme of federation. It took another eight years
to get acceptance by all the states of these proposals. When this was
done the Imperial Government in 1900 passed the Commonwealth of
Australia Constitution Act which created, on 1 January 1901, the
Commonwealth of Australia.

Six states joined this federation: New South Wales, Victoria,
South Australia, Tasmania, Western Australia and Queensland. The
federal Parliament consists of the Queen, the Senate and the House of
Representatives; it sits at the federal capital, Canberra. The Queen is
represented by a Governor-General, who is appointed on the advice
of her Australian ministers. The Senate has 60 members: regardless
of population each state has 10 senators who are elected for six years
by universal suffrage; every three years 30 senators retire. The House
of Representatives originally had 75 members, but as members are
proportionate to the population it now has 123.

The federal judicature is the High Court of Australia with a chief
justice and 6 justices: it has original and appellate jurisdiction.
Appeals go from this court to the Judicial Committee of the Privy
Council by special leave of the Committee, except in certain constitutional cases where special certification by the High Court is
necessary.

The constitution resembles the federalism of the U.S.A. rather
than that of Canada. Thus Commonwealth powers are specified in
some forty matters, the most important being trade, commerce,
taxation, ports, telegraphs, banking, immigration and emigration,
defence and foreign affairs. All remaining powers belong to the state
government, whose rights are fully safeguarded. When, however, a
state law is inconsistent with a Commonwealth law, the latter prevails

and the former is invalid to the extent of its inconsistency. Amendment of the Commonwealth Constitution requires the support of a majority of electors in a majority of states.

New Zealand

The systematic colonisation of New Zeaiand started with the activities of the New Zealand Company in 1839. In 1840 New Zealand was constituted a colony and given Crown Colony type of government with a Governor, Executive Council and nominated Legislative Council. Government in the early days of the colony was considerably influenced by the geography of the two islands and the long distances between the chief areas of settlement. Thus in the New Zealand Constitution Act of 1852 there was a certain measure of federation introduced; New Zealand was divided into six provinces with elected provincial councils having legislative powers. At the centre there was a General Assembly of two chambers, the upper nominated and the lower elected. It was not originally intended that this constitution should confer responsible government, but this was demanded by the first Assembly, which met in 1854, and it was conceded by 1856, apart from control of Maori affairs, which was retained by the Imperial Government for some years. Improved communications and an increasing sense of unity led to the abolition of the provincial councils in 1875; the government now became unitary and local needs were met by elected county councils. New Zealand was one of the first countries to give the vote to women, this being done in 1893.

South Africa

The capture of the Cape of Good Hope from the Dutch in 1795 and its subsequent retention in 1815 gave Great Britain control of an essential naval base on the route to India and the East; it also placed under her rule the Dutch Boer inhabitants. As in the case of other conquered colonies of this period, the early governments concentrated power in the hands of the Governor, while maintaining the ancient laws and institutions of the Boers. In 1825 an Advisory

Council was created, followed in 1834 by nominated Executive and Legislative Councils, in which there was a small unofficial element, which in 1849–51 considerably helped the movement towards representative government in the Cape by their refusal to accept nomination, unless the Governor agreed to choose his unofficial members from those who had been elected by various popular bodies. Representative government came in 1853 with a legislature of two houses, both elected. The upper house was the first example of an elected house in the new Empire; hitherto the Imperial Government had greatly mistrusted such an idea: the example, however, was soon followed by Tasmania, Victoria and South Australia. Twenty years later, in 1872, responsible government was attained by Cape Colony.

Natal, lying between the Drakensberg mountains and the southeast coast of Africa bordering the Indian Ocean, was penetrated in the late 1830's by Boers trekking away from British rule in Cape Colony; a Boer Natal Republic was set up. Natal, however, was proclaimed a British colony in 1843, chiefly in order to control the Natal Boers in their dealings with the native tribes inland. By 1847, disliking this British control, the Natal Boers left the country and trekked northwards into the Transvaal in search of new homes. Natal was first under the control of Cape Colony but had its own Lieutenant-Governor and nominated council. In 1856 it became entirely independent of Cape control and was given representative government with a Legislative Council with a three-quarters elected majority. Responsible government was reached in 1893.

The Transvaal Republic and Orange Free State were founded by Boers of the Great Trek (1836–52) who were dissatisfied with British rule in Cape Colony. Great Britain, after trying to assert her control over them, agreed to their independence by the Sand River Convention of 1852 (Transvaal) and the Bloemfontein Convention of 1854 (Orange Free State). At the end of the Anglo-Boer War of 1899–1902, both these Voortrekker republics lost this independence and were annexed to the British Empire. British policy sought after this war to conciliate the Boers, and giving self-government as soon as possible was part of this policy. Thus after annexation the Transvaal and Orange River Colony both received Crown Colony government of the nominated council kind, but made a rapid advance to responsible government, the Transvaal in 1906 and the Orange River Colony in 1907.

The Union of South Africa Act, 1909

By the South Africa of 1909 a legislative union under the British Crown was formed of the self-governing colonies of the Cape of Good Hope, Natal, the Transvaal, and the Orange River Colony. This union has a unitary constitution and all original authority is held by the Union government. The four self-governing provinces upon union became subordinate provinces and such powers of government as they now possess were delegated to them by the Union government.

The executive government of the Union is made up of a Governor-General, appointed by the Queen on the advice of the South African Prime Minister, and an Executive Council of ministers who, in accordance with British constitutional practice, form a cabinet possessing the confidence of the House of Assembly. The House of Assembly has 158 members distributed as follows: the Cape province 54, Natal 15, Transvaal 68, Orange Free State 13, South West Africa 6, with 2 European members representing native interests. The maximum life of the Assembly is five years.

By the Senate Act passed by the Union Parliament in 1955, the number of senators was increased from 48 to 89. The aim of this Act was to give the government the two-thirds majority in a joint session of the Union Parliament necessary for legislation to alter the 'entrenched clauses' of the South Africa Act of 1909 relating to the electoral rights of coloured voters. Provincial representation in the Senate now is: the Cape 22, Transvaal 27, Orange Free State 8, Natal 8: South West Africa has 2 elected and 2 nominated senators. There are also 4 elected senators representing native interests and a further 16 nominated for the same purposes. The election of senators, which was formerly done on the basis of proportional representation of the parties has now been abolished: the majority party in each province now takes all the senatorial seats in that province.

THE SELF-GOVERNING COLONIES

The judicature consists of a Supreme Court, with provincial and local divisions. Appeals from these two divisions go to the Appellate Division of the Supreme Court. By the Appeal Court Quorum Act of 1955 the number of judges of this Appellate Division required to hear appeals in constitutional cases was raised from six to eleven.

In the provinces of the Union there are elected provincial councils with power to legislate on certain specified subjects delegated by the Union government. Executive powers in each province are held by an administrator, assisted by an executive committee of four, elected from the provincial council.

Southern Rhodesia

The foundations of Southern Rhodesia were laid by the energy and vision of Cecil Rhodes and by the work of the British South Africa Company. The period of the Company's rule from 1890 to 1923 witnessed considerable settlement by British subjects and these settlers made frequent demands for increased representation on the Legislative Council, which had been set up as early as 1894. In 1899 a minority of elected members was added: in 1903 there were 7 elected representatives of the settlers and 7 official members: by 1914 there was an unofficial majority with 12 settlers and 6 officials.

In 1914, the original term of the Company's charter of twenty-five years expired but was renewed for another ten years; the growing body of settlers had demanded self-government, but recognised that some time must elapse before the Company could satisfactorily transfer its power to them. In 1920 the Legislative Council passed a resolution asking for the establishment of responsible government in the very near future. Before this could be done, a decision had to be made about the provision in the South Africa Act of 1909 whereby Southern Rhodesia could, if she wished, become a fifth province in the Union of South Africa. By a plebiscite, incorporation in the Union was rejected; the majority vote was for a self-governing constitution for Southern Rhodesia. The Company's charter and rule were ended and in October 1923 the new constitution was established by letters patent, the territory having previously been annexed to the British Crown.

The constitution of 1923 gave responsible government short of Dominion status. There is a Legislative Assembly of 30 members, representing single-member constituencies; since 1933 this body has assumed the style of Parliament. Powers exist under the constitution for the establishment by the assembly of a Legislative Council or second chamber. Subject to certain economic and educational quali-fications the franchise is open to all Southern Rhodesian citizens over 21, irrespective of colour. The Queen is represented by a Governor; there is a Prime Minister and cabinet of five ministers in all.

There are certain restrictions on the powers of the Southern Rhodesian legislature which must be mentioned. The Crown can disallow legislation which discriminates against the native popu-lation, i.e. which imposes disabilities to which Europeans are not also subjected. Originally there were other matters such as Rhodesian railways, unalienated lands, and mineral rights, legislation on which the Crown could, if necessary, disallow. The existing constitution thus places Southern Rhodesia very close to the status of a Common-wealth country such as Australia or New Zealand.

When the Federation of Rhodesia and Nyasaland was set up certain powers previously exercised by the Southern Rhodesian government were transferred to the Federation, viz., external affairs and defence, commerce and industry, immigration and emigration, European education and agriculture. The powers retained by Southern Rhodesia were over police, land, mining, irrigation, local government, housing, and African administration, education and agriculture.

CHAPTER XXIII

THE DOMINIONS IN THE TWENTIETH CENTURY

Constitutional limitations

Responsible government had given the colonies concerned full self-government in their internal affairs; it had also helped the formation of federal unions such as the Dominion of Canada and the Commonwealth of Australia. To keep this picture of constitutional development in balance it must be remembered that at the beginning of the twentieth century all those colonies who had achieved responsible government (and who were officially known as 'self-governing Dominions' from 1907 onwards) were in certain respects constitutionally subordinate to Great Britain. This subordinate status is illustrated by the following limitations upon the legislative and judicial powers of the self-governing Dominions.

Reservation and disallowance

The power of reservation was exercised by the Governors-General over legislation of the Dominion Parliaments: i.e. the Governor-General declared he reserved the bill for the signification of the sovereign's pleasure. The sovereign, upon the advice of his United Kingdom ministers, had power to declare his pleasure by giving or refusing assent to the bill. This power of reservation was discretionary, or, in the case of certain specified subjects, obligatory. Instructions to reserve were given in instructions to Governors under the prerogative, or by statute. Obligatory reservation under instructions had virtually disappeared by 1900, but obligatory reservation under statute, e.g. Merchant Shipping Acts, was regularly used down to the 1920's. Such a veto was generally used with the aim of deferring the legislation in question, so as to secure amendment which would enable it to be passed on a future occasion.

Power of disallowance made it possible for acts passed by Dominion or colonial legislatures and assented to by Governors-General or Governors to be annulled by the sovereign acting on the advice of his responsible ministers in the U.K. Such disallowance was rarely used, and by 1900 the constitutional convention existed that it would not be used in respect of Dominion legislation.

The Colonial Laws Validity Act, 1865

Further Imperial control over Dominion legislation was secured by the Colonial Laws Validity Act of 1865, which affirmed the doctrine of the supremacy of the Imperial Parliament over colonial legislatures. It enacted that any colonial law which was repugnant to the provisions of any Act of the Imperial Parliament extending to that colony was, to the extent of such repugnancy, void and inoperative. It should be noted that this Act, while asserting the supremacy of the Imperial Parliament, was chiefly passed to assist colonial legislatures by telling them what they could do and not what they ought not to do. Again, the Imperial Government never legislated under this Act on matters of exclusively domestic concern to any colony, except at the request or with the consent of the colony itself. In the wider field of Imperial affairs the United Kindgom Parliament legislated for all parts of the Empire on such matters as control of merchant shipping, copyright, and naturalisation of aliens. By the early twentieth century the constitutional convention was established that new Imperial legislation required consultation and discussion with the Dominions and that its application in whole or in part to the Dominions depended on their consent.

Extra-territorial legislation and foreign relations

Colonial and Dominion legislatures had no power of extra-territorial legislation, i.e. the jurisdiction of their legislatures could not go beyond their respective territorial limits.

In the conduct of foreign relations and all that this involved, e.g. foreign policy, declarations of war and the making of peace and international treaties, the Dominions were dependent on the Imperial Government. This dependence remained until immediately after

World War I (1918) when they began to acquire the right of treaty making, and their own ambassadorial representation in foreign countries.

Appeals to the Judicial Committee of the Privy Council

Restriction of the judicial powers of the self-governing colonies existed because of appeals to the Judicial Committee of the Privy Council. These appeals were either appeals as of right or as of grace: in the former case the subject has the right to appeal, subject to any legal restrictions existing, without asking special leave of the Judicial Committee; in the latter case he has the right to ask for special leave to appeal and this may be granted or refused by the Judicial Committee.

The constitutional limitations described above appear considerable, but in practice they were not burdensome or restrictive to the Dominions. They did not prevent increasing co-operation between Great Britain and the Dominions from 1887 onwards. At the same time, however, the growing sense of independent nationhood in the Dominions led to a demand for the removal of these remains of subordination and for a redefinition of their constitutional status in terms of equality with Great Britain.

Imperial Conferences

Co-operation between the self-governing Dominions and Great Britain was brought about by the Imperial Conferences. They were originally known as Colonial Conferences and the first one met in 1887 on the occasion of Queen Victoria's Golden Jubilee, which celebrated fifty years of her rule. Ten years later a similar Conference met for the Diamond Jubilee and it was then decided to hold periodic meetings at intervals of four or five years. At these early Conferences there was consultation between the Prime Ministers of the Dominions and the British Colonial Secretary, and later the British Prime Minister, who presided. Discussions in the pre-1914 era were chiefly about tariffs, the possibility of Imperial federation and, because of the threatening international situation, the needs of Imperial defence. In

1911, Dominion representation on the Committee of Imperial Defence was conceded, but the making of policy for Imperial defence and the whole conduct of foreign policy remained firmly in the hands of the British cabinet.

The Imperial War Cabinet

When war was declared in August 1914 by Great Britain on Germany the declaration included the whole Empire, although the Dominions had no share in the diplomacy leading up to this. Without hesitation the Dominions informed the Imperial Government that they would support her in this war and proceeded to mobilise their naval and military forces. As the war proceeded it was recognised that there was urgent need for machinery which would give the Dominions a share on a basis of equality in the conduct of the war and eventually in the making of the peace. Early in 1917 by the action of Mr Lloyd George, then British Prime Minister, an Imperial War cabinet was formed. Its task was making decisions for the successful conduct of the war. Presided over by the Prime Minister, it included five members of the British War Cabinet, the Dominion Prime Ministers, a representative of British India, and the Colonial Secretary representing the dependent Empire. As far as the conduct of the war was concerned the Dominions now shared responsibility for this on a basis of equality with Great Britain, for the Imperial War Cabinet was largely concerned with executive decisions. At the same time there was also the Imperial War Conference, which dealt with Imperial problems of a general nature not connected with the war; it was in many ways a war-time version of the normal Imperial Conference. It made an important contribution to constitutional development by its Resolution IX of 1917. This strongly recommended that after the war the constitutional relations of the various parts of the Empire should be adjusted, so that the self-government already possessed by the Dominions in domestic affairs should be extended to include foreign policy and external relations, and that there should be consultation and common action on important matters of Imperial concern.

International status of the Dominions, 1919–26

The making of the peace treaties in 1919 and the creation of the League of Nations showed clearly the extent to which the international status of the Dominions had improved. They were not willing to be represented at the peace conferences by the Imperial Government. The Dominions felt that, if the smaller allied nations who had put less men in the field than the Dominions were to have separate representation at these conferences, then they must have the same. This demand for separate representation was supported by the British Prime Minister and was granted by the Supreme Council of the Allied Powers. Thus Canada, Australia, South Africa and India (though not a self-governing Dominion) received two delegates each; New Zealand had one. In addition there was the British Empire delegation of five members covering the interests of the other parts of the Empire.

At the signing of various treaties of peace with the defeated powers further proof was given of the advancing status of the Dominions. The Dominions signed the treaties separately, though it should be noted that Great Britain signed for 'the United Kingdom of Great Britain and Ireland and the British Dominions beyond the sea', so that the Dominions were not entirely independent signatory powers. Each Dominion Parliament formally gave its approval of the various treaties and finally the Crown ratified them on behalf of the whole Empire.

Next followed separate representation in the Assembly of the League of Nations; Canada, Australia, South Africa and New Zealand each received a seat in its own right. Originally it had been thought that there would be a single united British Empire representative in the League. When the disposal of the enemy colonies was done by the creation of League mandates some of these went directly to the Dominions; thus South Africa received a direct mandate for German South West Africa and Australia for German New Guinea.

By 1926 the right of legation, i.e. to have separate diplomatic representation, had been conceded to the Dominions. In 1920 Canada, because of her frequent relations with her neighbour the U.S.A., had wished to appoint her own ambassador at Washington. The Irish Free State soon after its foundation sent a diplomatic representative to Washington in 1924; in 1926 Canada did so. By 1936 there were eleven representatives from Canada, South Africa and the Irish Free State in various capitals.

Equality of status

The period between 1921 and 1926 proved decisive in Imperial relationships. Imperial unity, which had been strong during the War and immediately after, tended to weaken, and growing Dominion nationalism did not favour the project of a centralised Imperial federation which had influential support in Great Britain. In particular the attempt of an Imperial 'Peace' cabinet to carry out a common foreign policy for the whole Empire was unsuccessful, and it was the events described below connected with this that led to the demand, particularly from Canada, South Africa and the Irish Free State, for a definition of their constitutional and international status.

(i) In 1921 the Dominions, in spite of their independent representation at the Versailles Peace Conference, did not at first get separate invitations from the U.S.A. to the Washington Conference on the limitation of armaments, but by insisting on their right to this, it was conceded.

(ii) In 1922, the British Empire was brought to the verge of war by the Chanak 'incident' caused by the need of protecting Constantinople and the Straits area against attack from Mustapha Kemal and his revolutionary Turkish government, who did not accept the peace settlement of the Treaty of Sèvres. The question now was: could Great Britain declare war and call on the Dominions to support this policy? In this case the Prime Minister Lloyd George issued somewhat prematurely an appeal to the Dominions for military aid. Australia and New Zealand gave immediate support but South Africa and Canada disowned responsibility for what might be regarded as a British-made war developing out of a British-made foreign policy.

(iii) At the Conference of Lausanne held in 1923 a new peace treaty was made between Turkey and the Allied powers. Canada refused to accept responsibility for it on the grounds that she had not been represented at the conference, though as Great Britain had signed the treaty in the name of the British Empire, Canada recognised that legally she was bound by it. From this arose the idea of 'passive responsibility', i.e. active obligations in foreign affairs could not be placed on the Dominions by Great Britain without their consent. In 1925 the Locarno Treaty between the European powers carried this idea a step further, as far as Great Britain and the Dominions were concerned. Great Britain, because of her strong local interest in European peace, signed for herself only; under Article 9, however, the Dominions could, if they wished, become parties to the treaty and acquire an active responsibility.

Besides a clear definition of their constitutional status certain of the Dominions (Canada, South Africa and the Irish Free State) wanted the removal of those legal forms which dated from an earlier era and which were reminders of constitutional inferiority, even though constitutional usage and convention had greatly modified their working.

The Imperial Conferences of 1926 and 1930

Influenced by events of the previous five years the Conference of 1926 stated the theory of the Empire as affecting the self-governing Dominions.

They are autonomous communities within the British Empire, equal in status, in no way subordinate one to another in any aspect of their domestic or external affairs, though united by a common allegiance to the Crown and freely associated as members of the British Commonwealth of Nations.

The Conference, and also that of 1930, dealt in detail with certain legal inequalities that existed. It did this in two ways: firstly by the statement of constitutional conventions which then existed in respect of these inequalities and which were constitutionally binding, and secondly by the recommendation of legislation (later enacted in 1931 as the Statute of Westminster).

Examples of the first procedure were seen over the status of the Governor-General in a Dominion. The Conference adopted the convention that his status was the same as that of the King in Great Britain in relation to his ministers. With regard to disallowance, the Conference in 1930 recognised the convention that this power could no longer be exercised in respect of Dominion legislation.

Reservation of Dominion legislation was more complicated as there were three kinds of this:

(i) The Governor-General's obligatory reservation under Statute. This was mostly exercised under Imperial Statutes such as the Merchant Shipping Act and Colonial Admiralty Courts Act. As regards the inequality arising the Conference recognised that only statutory enactment could remove it. This was done by the Statute of Westminster, 1931.

(ii) Obligatory reservation under instructions from the United Kingdom government. The Conference declared the convention that such instructions would not be given.

(iii) Discretionary reservation. The convention was now recognised that this must be exercised by the Governor-General in accordance with the advice of his Dominion ministers.

The Conference of 1930 dealt with other legal inferiorities remaining, and recommended that they should be removed by enactment of the Imperial Parliament; such legislation should give the Dominions full power to make laws having extra-territorial operation, should annul the application of the Colonial Laws Validity Act to the Dominions and should give the Dominion Parliaments power to legislate for merchant shipping and Admiralty Courts.

The Statute of Westminster, 1931

The Statute of Westminster may be regarded as carrying the work of constitutional definition begun in 1926 a stage further on its road, and as a statutory removal of such legal inferiority as remained in the Dominions relationships with Great Britain.

In the preamble or preliminary part of the Statute, two constitutional conventions are declared. The first is that in view of the great importance of the Crown as the symbol of free association of the members of the British Commonwealth of Nations, and because of their common allegiance to the Crown, any changes in the law of succession or the Royal Style and Titles henceforth will require the assent of the Dominion Parliaments as well as that of the Parliament of the United Kingdom. The second convention is that

it is in accord with the established constitutional position that no law hereafter made by any Parliament of the United Kingdom shall extend to any of the said Dominions as part of the law of that Dominion otherwise than at the request and with the consent of that Dominion.

In the main body of the Act the sections are:

Section 2: No law made after the commencement of this Act by the Parliament of a Dominion shall be void or inoperative on the ground that it is repugnant to the law of England or to the provisions of any existing or future Act of the Parliament of the United Kingdom. (Removed application of Colonial Laws Validity Act of 1865 to Dominion legislation.)

Section 3: It is hereby declared and enacted that the Parliament of a Dominion has full power to make laws having extra-territorial operation.

Section 4: No act of the Parliament of the United Kingdom passed after the commencement of this act shall extend, or be deemed to extend, to a Dominion as part of the law of that Dominion unless it is expressly declared in that act that that Dominion has requested, and consented to, the enactment thereof. (Reinforced the constitutional convention to this effect recited in the preamble of the Statute.)

Sections 5 and 6: Certain sections of the Merchant Shipping Act, 1894, and Colonial Courts of Admiralty Act, 1890, were no longer applicable to the Dominions.

Sections 7 and 8: Enacted that the Act did not confer powers to repeal, amend or alter the British North American Acts 1867 to 1930 and their working (Section 7), or powers to repeal or alter the Constitution Acts of Australia or New Zealand otherwise than in accordance with the law existing before the commencement of this

Act of 1931. (Aimed chiefly at safeguarding the interests of the provinces and states which had federated into Canada and Australia.)

Section 10: Enacted that Sections 2, 3, 4, 5 and 6 of the Statute will not extend to the Commonwealth of Australia, the Dominion of New Zealand and Newfoundland unless these are adopted by the Parliaments of these Dominions, who can do so either with retrospective effect to 1931 or from a later date. The Parliaments of these Dominions are given power to revoke subsequently their adoption of any of these sections.

Section 11: Enacted that after the commencement of the Act, the expression 'Colony' shall not in any future United Kingdom Act be used to include a Dominion or any province or state forming part of a Dominion.

At the time of its coming into force the Statute applied in full only to the Union of South Africa and the Irish Free State, and apart from Section 7, to Canada. The extent of the excepted sections named in Section 10 and the method of their application to Australia, New Zealand and Newfoundland have been noted above. It must be emphasised that Australia did not adopt these sections until 1942 and New Zealand only in 1947: Newfoundland had not adopted any of them when in March 1949 she gave up her Dominion status and became the tenth province of Canada. The delay of Australia and New Zealand in adopting the Statute seems due to their belief that it was not really necessary, when the existing constitutional conventions gave them virtually all the freedom they desired and because Great Britain would always legislate specially for them at their request and with their consent.

World War II (1939–45)

The strength of the relationship which had developed between Great Britain and the Dominions was shown in 1939. Common allegiance to the same King as Head of the Commonwealth, free association, and equality of status united all of them (the Irish Free State excepted) without formal treaties of alliance, in World War II.

The British Commonwealth of Nations since 1945

Since the end of World War II in 1945 there have been important developments in the constitutional history of the self-governing nations of the British Empire and Commonwealth. Thus in 1947 the term 'Dominion' gave way to that of 'Member of the British Commonwealth of Nations'. The self-governing nations of the British Empire had reached such maturity and independence that the term 'Dominion', which to some slight extent conveyed the idea of dependence, was now thought unsuitable. This change was also emphasised by renaming the Dominions Office the Commonwealth Relations Office, while the Secretary of State for Dominion Affairs became Secretary of State for Commonwealth Relations.

The membership of the British Commonwealth was increased when in 1947 India and Pakistan became independent Dominions. In 1948 Ceylon, a classic example of the advance through the various stages of Crown Colony government to responsible government, became a fully self-governing member of the Commonwealth. Burma, however, rejected Dominion status and became an independent state outside the Commonwealth (1947). The flexibility of British Commonwealth practices was shown when the new Dominion of India decided to adopt a republican constitution. In April 1949 at a Prime Minister's Conference in London this matter was considered. India declared her wish to continue full membership of the British Commonwealth and her acceptance of the King as the symbol of the free association of its independent member nations, and, as such, Head of the Commonwealth. The other Governments then accepted and recognised India's continuing membership of the Commonwealth. When Pakistan adopted a Republican constitution her status within the Commonwealth was decided, in the same way as India, at a British Commonwealth Prime Ministers' meeting held in February 1955. Pakistan, like India, declared her wish to continue membership of the British Commonwealth of Nations and her acceptance of the Queen as Head of the Commonwealth, and was accepted and recognised by all the other members of the Commonwealth. At a Commonwealth Prime Ministers' meeting held in June 1956 the Prime Minister of Ceylon stated that his country would eventually become a republic but would remain in the Commonwealth.

The right to secede, i.e. to leave the British Commonwealth, has appeared important to two Dominions, South Africa and the Irish Free State: this right to leave the Commonwealth at will seemed proof positive that they were independent. Since 1945 one Dominion has seceded. In April 1949 Eire (the Irish Free State) repealed the External Relations Act of 1936 and declared its separation from the British Commonwealth. The United Kingdom Parliament then passed the Ireland Act (June 1949) which recognised that Eire, henceforth known as the Republic of Ireland, was no longer part of his Majesty's dominions.

POSTSCRIPT

We may conclude with some brief comment on the position of the British Empire and Commonwealth to-day and its future prospects.

Two streams of development can be seen: one is that of the self-governing members of the British Commonwealth of Nations, associating freely together and dealing with Commonwealth interests on a basis of consultation and discussion; the other that of the dependent Empire whose many members, starting from widely different stages of constitutional development, are moving towards greater self-government within the British Commonwealth. Providing there are no set-backs some of the present members of the dependent Empire should within reasonable time attain full self-government and perhaps Commonwealth status.

The prospect for the future development and association together of the British Commonwealth of Nations is a hopeful one. The constitutional progress to date of members of the dependent Empire has been remarkable, but there remain numerous difficulties to be overcome, some of which are ignored or treated too lightly by political opinion in the countries concerned. There is often insufficient realisation of the difficulties that will be encountered on moving from representative to responsible government, when the practice of self-government rather than its theory will impose a severe test. The belief that the establishment of self-government automatically solves all problems may prove a dangerous illusion. The following extract from the Report of the British Caribbean Standing Closer Association Committee, in connexion with the drafting of their federal constitution, is highly relevant in this matter:

Problems are never automatically solved by new constitutions, but only by the efforts of men to whom new constitutions may give appropriate powers and responsibilities which did not exist before.

There are serious difficulties in those countries (such as Malaya and Kenya) where plural societies exist, whose different outlooks and interests must first be harmonised before even a minimum political unity can exist. Further, a sufficiently educated electorate is essential for the working of a parliamentary democracy and this is, at present, not always found in the dependent Empire. It is also clear from recent experience in the Gold Coast and Nigeria that the recognition and safeguarding of the rights of minority groups at a less advanced stage of development will test to the utmost the powers of statesmanship of those who have received power on the attainment of self-government.

Finally, when all the heat and talk of politics has subsided, there remains the everyday task of government. It is essential to realise how exacting is the task of giving honest and competent government. Administrators and judges who are capable, efficient, and incorruptible will be needed to take over government and they will need both experience and technical knowledge. To acquire such experience and knowledge will take time, and once again it seems clear that the old rule, so often seen in British constitutional practice, of hastening slowly, is the best one for the circumstances in which the members of the dependent Empire are advancing towards self-government. And if undue haste and inexperience in control should weaken the processes of government, so that standards of administration and justice in central and local government alike are lowered, the success of a great and novel political experiment will be seriously endangered.

THE ADVANCE TO REPRESENTATIVE AND RESPONSIBLE GOVERNMENT

Since 1945 changes in the constitutions of Crown Colonies have taken place with great rapidity. The Gold Coast, whose constitutional advance to representative and then responsible government is summarised below, is a good example of such changes. The Gold Coast state is made up of four components, each of different status, viz.

Gold Coast Colony (settled colony).
Ashanti (conquered colony).
Gold Coast Northern Territories (protectorate).
Togoland (ex-German colony, formerly mandated, now trustee territory).

(1) From 1925 to early in 1946 the Gold Coast was governed under the Constitution of 1925. This gave a Legislative Council with an official majority. Of the unofficial minority, 9 were elected African members, 2 elected Europeans for corporate representation of Chambers of Mines and Commerce and 3 nominated European representatives of commerce, banking and shipping.

(2) In March 1946 the Gold Coast was given a Legislative Council with an unofficial African majority, thus being the first British African colony to have an unofficial African majority in its legislature.

Composition of the Legislative Council:
President: the Governor (without vote).
6 official members.
9 provincial members. (Elected by the Joint Provincial Council on the basis of 5 for the Eastern Province and 4 for the Western.)
4 Ashanti members. (Elected by the Ashanti Confederacy Council.)
5 municipal members. (Accra, 2; Cape Coast, Kumasi, Sekoradi-Takoradi, 1 each: elected by ballot.)
6 nominated by the Governor. (Representing mining and commercial interests.)

(3) In 1951 a new constitution, based largely on the recommendations of the Coussey Report, was introduced and this gave the Gold Coast semi-responsible government.

Legislative Assembly: 84 members: 75 Africans
                                    3 ex-officio
                                    3 mining interests
                                    3 commercial

Election to this Assembly was for the most part indirect, through electoral colleges.

Executive Council, with the function of cabinet:
                    Governor
                    3 European Ministers (ex-officio)
                    8 African Ministers

The Governor retained certain powers of reservation and of independent legislation.

(4) In March 1952 the Constitution was revised and formal recognition was given to the office of Prime Minister. Dr Kwame Nkrumah, hitherto known as Leader of Government Business, became the first Prime Minister of the Gold Coast. The Executive Council was renamed 'Cabinet' and the Prime Minister submitted names to the Governor for the eight African Ministers to sit in this Cabinet.

(5) The constitutional reforms of April 1954 provided for an enlarged Legislative Assembly chosen by direct election, the total being 104 members.

The cabinet now became one of 9 African ministers—the first all-African cabinet in British Africa. It was presided over by the Prime Minister, Dr Nkrumah, who as leader of the Convention People's Party had won at the election 71 of the 104 seats.

This cabinet was responsible for all internal government; the Governor was responsible for defence, external affairs, and Togoland. These constitutional changes brought the Gold Coast in sight of Dominion status, which was asked for in a resolution moved by Dr Nkrumah in the new Legislative Assembly soon after it met.

(6) In April 1956 the Gold Coast government outlined its proposals for independence within the British Commonwealth; the name of the new state was to be Ghana. The Colonial Secretary in May 1956 announced that H.M.'s Government would grant independence if after a general election a reasonable majority for independence was obtained in the Gold Coast Legislature.

GLOSSARY

(Reference should also be made to explanations of terms in the text).

Ad hoc. For this (i.e. for a special) purpose.

Appellate jurisdiction. The power of a superior court to review the decision of an inferior court. After judicial examination, the decision of the inferior court may be upheld, or the appeal may be allowed, by the superior court.

Assizes. Courts presided over by High Court judges and held several times a year in certain provincial towns in England. The judges sitting with a jury have power to hear criminal cases of all kinds.

Ballot. Secret voting, made general in parliamentary elections by the Ballot Act, 1872.

Bar of the House. The line in the House of Lords and the House of Commons beyond which non-members may not pass, e.g. members of the House of Commons, headed by the Speaker, attend at the Bar of the House of Lords to hear the Queen's Speech.

Behind the Speaker's Chair. A phrase used to denote discussions between Government and Opposition Whips about the timetable of the House of Commons with the object of working out an agreed programme.

Bona fide. In good faith, genuine.

Black Rod. An official (Chief Gentleman Usher) of the Lord Chamberlain's department of the royal household who is also the Usher of the House of Lords. He summons the members of the House of Commons to hear the Queen's Speech.

Budget. The word is derived from a French word meaning a 'pouch' or 'wallet'; the annual review of the country's finance, with the estimates and taxation proposals for the coming year. It is usually ·put before the House of Commons in April.

Burgess. An inhabitant of a borough; also a member of Parliament for a borough.

By-election. An election caused by the death or resignation of a member held at a time other than a general election.

By-law. A regulation having the force of law, made by a local authority or other body under the powers conferred on it by a private Act of Parliament.

Canon law. The law of the church having a basis in the principles of Roman law.

Case-law. Judge-made law resulting from the interpretation of statutes and common law.

Chiltern Hundreds. A district in Buckinghamshire. The Stewardship of the Chiltern Hundreds is an office of profit under the Crown, the holding of which disqualifies a member from sitting in the House of Commons. A member wishing to resign therefore applies for the Chiltern Hundreds.

Civil List. The sum allocated for the expenses of the Queen and her household, and those of the members of the royal family. It is not the subject of an annual vote and is a charge on the Consolidated Fund.

Clerk of the Parliaments. The Clerk of the House of Lords.

Closure. The method of ending a debate by the carrying of the motion that 'the question now be put'. This must have the support of at least 100 members. It is the Government's method of getting its business through.

Common law. 'The unwritten law of the Kingdom.' Customary law dating back to Anglo-Saxon times, embodied in the decisions of judges. Regarded as the basis of English liberties.

Communal representation. Representation in a legislature based on voting by cultural and racial communities separately organised for electoral purposes (Plural Society).

Consolidated Fund. The fund into which all taxes, etc. are paid and out of which all authorised payments are made.

Conventions. Constitutional customs of importance and often of antiquity, unwritten but regarded as having the force of law.

County districts. Rating areas with their own councils within the administrative area of a county council—urban and rural districts, and (non-county) boroughs.

Crimes. Nowadays are divided into the main categories (i) the more serious or indictable crimes, i.e. those which require a written indictment and (ii) the less serious or non-indictable crimes, which can be dealt with in courts of summary jurisdiction. The old categories—felonies and misdemeanours—are largely superseded.

Delegated legislation. Legislation by order in council, or departmental regulation. Now grouped under the heading 'Statutory instruments'.

Dispensing power. The sovereign's power of dispensing with the penalties imposed by a law, exercised only on the recommendation of the Home Secretary. It cannot be used in such a way as to affect the life or property of a third party.

277

Dissolution. The ending of a Parliament by royal proclamation—done on the recommendation of the Prime Minister. All uncompleted bills are wiped off the parliamentary slate.

Established Church. The Church of England (Anglican) in England; the Church of Scotland (Presbyterian) in Scotland.

Equity. A body of decisions based on natural justice filling in the gaps in, and mitigating the effects of, statute and common law. When law and equity conflict, equity prevails.

Executive. The side of government responsible for administration; restrained in Great Britain by the supremacy of Parliament and the rule of law.

Exempted business. Matters to which the time limit imposed by Standing Orders does not apply

Ex officio. By right of office held.

Fiat (Latin: Let it be done). Permission to proceed, e.g. with an appeal.

Fief. A term of feudal law. An estate granted by a superior lord (usually the King) to a tenant, and held by the latter on certain conditions of service.

Franchise. The right to vote; also in earlier times the right to send a member to Parliament.

Fundamental law. A constitutional law which can only be changed by special process, e.g. after a referendum to the electorate. In the British Constitution there are strictly speaking no fundamental laws.

Gavel. The chairman's hammer, his emblem of authority.

Guillotine. A means of cutting down discussion in the committee stage of a bill by strict allocation of time to clauses or groups of clauses.

Habeas corpus, Writ of. A writ obtained from a High Court judge ordering a gaoler to 'produce the body' of a prisoner in a certain court at a certain time. An ancient right of Englishmen protecting them against arbitrary imprisonment.

Hansard. The name given to the printed proceedings of Parliament. Derived from the name of a nineteenth-century publisher of the proceedings.

Impeachment. Prosecution of an individual by the House of Commons before the House of Lords—last used in 1806.

In camera. In private, i.e. without the public's being present.

Judiciary. The whole body of judges.

Kangaroo. The passing over by the Chairman of a Committee of some amendments and the selection of others for discussion.

Knights of the shire. The term formerly used for members of Parliament for the shires (counties).

Legislature. The supreme law-making body. In Great Britain this is the Queen-in-Parliament, i.e. the House of Commons, the House of Lords with the Queen signifying assent.

Letters patent. A document sealed with the Great Seal of England giving authority to an individual or corporation to do or enjoy something they otherwise could not. The name is derived from the form of the document which is open with the seal affixed. (Latin: 'litterae patentes' = open letters.)

Long title. The title of a Bill, e.g. as given on the Order Paper, defining its purpose.

Mace. The symbol of the authority of the House of Commons.

Mandamus, Writ of. A writ from a superior to an inferior court, or to a corporation, etc., ordering some specific thing to be done.

Natural law. Unwritten law, which is the basis of natural justice; the inherent rights of man. It played a great part in the philosophy of the eighteenth century from which the American Constitution and the doctrines of the French Revolution were derived.

Office of profit. A salaried appointment under the Crown. By the Place Act, 1707, holders of such offices with the exception of a few specified ministers were barred from membership of the House of Commons. The number of Ministers and Parliamentary Under-Secretaries who can claim exemption from the action of the Act is now fixed by the Ministers of the Crown Act, 1937.

Order in council. An order made by the Queen 'by and with the advice of her Privy Council' either under statutory authority or under the royal prerogative.

Petty Sessions. Courts at which minor offences can be dealt with summarily by two or more magistrates, or by a stipendiary magistrate.

Plural society. The population of a state or territory made up of communities differing in race, language, religion, customs, etc. E.g. East Africa with African, Arab, Asian and European communities.

Pocket borough. A term used for boroughs which before the Reform Act of 1832 were virtually personal possessions of some magnate.

Prayer. The moving of an address to Her Majesty the Queen, e.g. for the annulment of an order in council or for the confirmation of a draft order.

Precepting authority. An authority, e.g. a county council which has the right to make a precept or demand for the levying of a rate upon a rating authority, e.g. a county district.

Prerogative. Originally the ancient customary powers of the Crown, now the rights remaining to the Crown, e.g. the royal prerogative of pardon which, however, is duly exercised on the advice of the Home Secretary.

Prima facie (Latin). At first sight or appearance.

Privileges, Committee of. A committee of the House of Commons which watches over the privileges of the House and takes action in the event of any breach, e.g. disrespect to the House by any member or non-member.

Proclamation. An executive document by which the sovereign makes known to her subjects her wishes and commands on various matters of government, e.g. summoning or dissolving of Parliament, declaring war or peace, calling attention to provisions of existing laws etc. A proclamation cannot make new law, unless authorisation has been given by statute, nor can it make provisions contrary to existing law.

Prorogation. The ending of a session of Parliament which nevertheless remains in being. Like a dissolution this puts an end to all measures still before Parliament. This can be avoided by the adjournment, instead of prorogation, of the House.

Quarter Sessions. Quarterly meetings of county justices of the peace presided over by an experienced lawyer and having considerable jurisdiction.

Quorum. The minimum number of members, e.g. of the House of Commons or any committee, required for the conduct of business.

Recorder. A barrister who acts as sole (paid) judge in a Borough Quarter Sessions.

Referendum. A vote by the electorate on a special matter referred to it.

Repugnant to. Contrary to, or inconsistent with, the principles of existing laws.

Rotten borough. A borough before 1832, where there was only a handful of voters and where bribery was easy and usual.

Rule of law. The supremacy of the ordinary law of the land, administered by the ordinary courts. Thus there is no special protection for the official, the policeman or the soldier.

Secretary of State. Originally the King's Secretary. From 1540 two Secretaries of State were appointed. In 1782 Secretaries for Home and Foreign Affairs were appointed. The other Secretaryships have developed from these. There are now seven in all.

Select Committee. A committee set up by the House of Commons for a special purpose. It usually makes a report to the House and has power to summon witnesses and hear evidence.

Session. A parliamentary year ended by prorogation or adjournment.

Short title. All bills coming before Parliament have a short title by which they may be cited.

Sign manual. The autograph signature, especially of the sovereign.

Sovereign. The supreme authority. Applied to the monarch as the embodiment of the state and of authority within it, and also to Parliament because it is supreme in the Constitution. A sovereign state is one whose authority is unfettered by allegiance to another power.

Standing Committee. Each Standing Committee of the House of Commons (except the Scottish Committee) consists of forty to fifty members—quorum fifteen. The Scottish Committee is composed of all members for Scottish constituencies and may include others.

Standing Orders. Rules made to ensure the proper conduct of business in Parliament or a council or a committee. In both Houses of Parliament the Standing Orders can be suspended when necessary and they are supplementary to customs, usages, Speakers' rulings, etc.

Stipendiary. A paid magistrate who acts instead of (or with) justices of the peace. He can act as a court of petty sessions, i.e. he has the power of two justices.

Supply, Committee of. The Committee of the Whole House which considers the estimates. It is concerned with policy rather than details of expenditure.

Ten Minute Rule. A means by which a private member may bring in a Bill and introduce it with a short speech at the commencement of public business in the House of Commons.

Tort. A wrong (apart from breach of contract) whereby the person suffering the wrong acquires a right of action in the civil courts (e.g. for damages).

Ultra vires (Latin). 'Beyond the powers' of an authority.

Unitary state. A state whose central government exercises full and undivided sovereign powers (contrast a federal state).

Usual channels. In parliamentary matters, conversations between the Party Whips with a view to co-operation to facilitate the programme of Parliament.

Ways and Means, Committee of. A Committee of the Whole House dealing with (i) taxation proposals (ii) proposed payments from the Consolidated Fund.

Ways and Means Resolutions. These are passed when the estimates have been voted in the Committee of Supply and reported to the House. They are ultimately gathered together and passed in the Appropriation Act.

Whip. (i) A party official whose business it is to see that members vote, and vote according to party instructions. (ii) The weekly note issued by the party Whips to members giving information, instructions with regard to the coming programme in Parliament.

Whole House, Committee of. The House sitting under the Chairman of Committees as Committee of Supply, Committee of Ways and Means, Committee to consider an important measure etc.

Woolsack. The scarlet-covered sack of wool on the Lord Chancellor's Chair; it recalls the days when wool was the chief source of England's wealth.

Writs for Parliamentary Elections. Issued by the Crown office to returning officers, giving time and place at which nomination papers are to be delivered, and the date of the poll, if the election is contested.

Writ of summons. The individual summons to Parliament received by a peer.

BOOK LIST FOR FURTHER READING

PART I

Shorter Books

CHRIMES, S. B. *English Constitutional History* (Home University Library, 2nd edition, 1953).

COLE, M. *Servant of the Country* (Dobson, 1956).

CRITCHLEY, T. A. *The Civil Service To-day* (Gollancz, 2nd edition, 1951).

GILES, F. T. *The Magistrates' Courts* (Pelican, revised edition, 1955).

HANBURY, H. G. *The English Courts of Law* (Home University Library, 1953).

HART, J. McK. *The British Police* (Allen and Unwin, 1951).

HICKS, U. K. *British Public Finances* (Home University Library, 1954).

ILBERT, SIR C. and CARR, SIR C. *Parliament* (Home University Library, 3rd edition, 1948).

JACKSON, W. ERIC. *Local Government in England and Wales* (Pelican, revised edition, 1949).

KENNET, LORD *The System of National Finance* (out of print), (Murray, 1936).

MAUD, SIR J. and FINER, S. E. *Local Government in England and Wales* (Home University Library, 2nd edition, 1953).

TAYLOR, E. *The House of Commons at Work* (Pelican, 2nd edition, 1955).

TILLETT, N. R. *The Law and the People* (Harrap, 1950).

WHEARE, K. C. *Modern Constitutions* (Home University Library, 1951).

Books for Reference

AMERY, L. S. *Thoughts on the Constitution* (Oxford University Press, 2nd edition, 1953).

ANSON, SIR W. *Law and Custom of the Constitution.* Vol. II. *The Crown,* ed. A. B. Keith (Oxford University Press, 4th edition, 1935).

283

BAGEHOT, W. *The English Constitution* (World's Classics, 1952).

CAMPION, LORD (and others). *British Government since 1918* (Allen and Unwin, 1950).

CAMPION, LORD (and others). *Parliament—a survey* (Allen and Unwin, 1955).

CARTER, BYRUM E. *The Office of Prime Minister* (Faber, 1956).

DICEY, A. V. *The Law of the Constitution* (Macmillan, 9th edition, 1939).

EMDEN, C. S. *The People and the Constitution* (Oxford University Press, 1956).

JEFFERIES, SIR C. *The Colonial Office* (Allen and Unwin (New Whitehall Series), 1956).

JENNINGS, SIR W. IVOR. *Cabinet Government* (Cambridge University Press, 2nd edition, 1951).

JENNINGS, SIR W. IVOR. *The Law and the Constitution* (University of London Press, 4th edition, 1955).

JENNINGS, SIR W. IVOR. *Parliament* (Cambridge University Press, 1939).

KEITH, A. B. *The British Cabinet* (2nd edn. by N. H. Gibbs, Stevens, 1952).

MAITLAND, F. W. *A Constitutional History of England* (Cambridge University Press, 1905).

MCKENZIE, R. T. *British Political Parties* (Heinemann, 1955)

MORRISON, HERBERT. *Government and Parliament* (Oxford University Press, 1955).

NEWSAM, SIR F. *The Home Office* (Allen and Unwin (New Whitehall Series), 1954).

REPORT OF THE COMMITTEE ON MINISTERS' POWERS (H.M. Stationery Office, CMD 4060, 1932).

SMELLIE, K. B. *A Hundred Years of English Government* (Duckworth, revised edition, 1950).

STRANG, LORD, *The Foreign Office* (Allen and Unwin (New Whitehall Series), 1954).

WADE, E. C. S. and PHILLIPS, G. G. *Constitutional Law* (Longmans, 5th edition, 1955).

WARREN, J. H. *Municipal Administration* (Pitman, 2nd edition, 1954).

WHITE PAPER ON LOCAL GOVERNMENT (H.M. Stationery Office, July 1956, CMD 9831).

PART II

BAILEY, S. D. (editor). *Parliamentary Government in the Commonwealth* (Hansard Society publication, 1951).

BARKER, SIR E. *Ideas and Ideals of the British Empire* (Cambridge University Press, 2nd edition, 1951).

CARRINGTON, C. E. *The British Overseas* (Cambridge University Press, 1950)

DAWSON, R. McG. *The Development of Dominion Status* (out of print), (Oxford University Press, 1937).

HARVEY, H. J. *Consultation and Co-operation in the Commonwealth* (R.I.I.A., Oxford, 1952).

JENNINGS, SIR W. IVOR and YOUNG G. M. *Constitutional Laws of the Commonwealth* (Clarendon Press, 2nd edition, 1952).

KEITH, A. B. *The First British Empire* (out of print), Oxford University Press, 1930).

MANSERGH, N. *The Commonwealth and the Nations* (R.I.I.A., 1948).

WHEARE, K. C. *The Statute of Westminster and Dominion Status* (Oxford University Press, 5th edition, 1953).

WIGHT, M. *The Development of the Legislative Council 1606–1945* (Faber, 1947).

WIGHT, M. *British Colonial Constitutions (1947)* (Clarendon Press, 1952).

INDEX OF ACTS OF PARLIAMENT

GENERAL INDEX

Adjournment, motion for, 81–2, 83
Agents, Colonial, 212; Election 50–1
Aldermen, 161
Aliens, oath, naturalisation, 109
American Constitution, 21–2
American Revolution, 214–20
Armed Forces, 144–8; command of, 145; parliamentary control, 145–6; discipline of, 146; Mutiny Acts, 146–7; Articles of War, 147; Army Act (1881), 147; duties in aid of civil power, 148
Ashanti, 227, 274
Assembly, the Colonial, 207, 208–10
Assizes, 127, 131, 134, 135, 161
Attorney-General, 98
Australia, Commonwealth of, 254–6

Bagehot, Sir W., 24, 99
Bahamas, 213, 228
Bank of England, 43, 108
Barbados, 198, 213, 228
Barristers, 129–30
Bermuda, 197, 213, 228
Bill of Rights (1689), 18, 34, 181, 182
Black Rod, 66
Board of Trade, 99, 105, 211–2
Boroughs, 149; municipal, 156; county, 157–8; metropolitan, 159
Brass Crosby, Alderman, 65
British Broadcasting Corporation, 64, 74
British Columbia, 229
British Commonwealth of Nations, 267, 271–2
British South Africa Company, 229, 259
Budget, 100, 120–1
Burke, Edmund, 217–8, 225
By-elections, 50

Cabinet, *passim:* main reference, 92–104; historical development, 92–4; Prime Minister and, 96–7; membership, 97–9; business and procedure, 99–100; Committees, 100–1; collective responsibility, 101;

secrecy and procedure, 101–2; Secretariat, 98, 102; War, 98; minutes, 101; Office, 102, 157
Calvin's Case (1609), 201
Campbell v. *Hall* (1774), 203, 223
Canada, 57; Act (1840), 249; Constitutional Act (1791), 224; Dominion of, 250–1; Upper and Lower, 212, 224, 246–7
Canon law, 127, 129
Cape Colony, 201, 226, 256
Carolina, North, 197, 199, 220; South, 197, 199, 204, 209, 218
Central Criminal Court, 134
Central Statistical Office, 102, 107
Ceylon, 57, 201, 221, 226, 227, 271
Chairman of Committees, 60, 71, 76; of Standing Committees, 61, 77, 79
Chancellor of the Exchequer, 98, 101, 107, 108, 119
Chancery, Court of, 128; Division, 131, 132, 133, 134, 136
Channel Islands, 103, 110, 138
Charles I, 18, 34, 40, 63, 144
Charles II, 34, 40, 57, 88
Chartists, 36, 253
Chequers, 95
Chiltern Hundreds, 52
Church of England, 27, 34, 40
Church of Scotland, 27
Churchill, Sir Winston, 41, 56, 97, 98, 100
Citizen, duties of, 190–1
Civil List, 29, 118
Civil Service, 18, 104, 105, 107, 110–15; organisation, 110–11; evolution, 111–12; work of grades, 112–13; code of conduct, 113–14; pay and conditions, 114–15
Civil War, 18, 34, 40
Clergy, estate of, 86
Clerk of the House, 60, 69, 71, 75, 77; of the Parliament, 61, 73
Closure, 78
Cobbett, Wm., 65
Colonies, conquered, 201, 227; settled, 198, 229

287

Finance Bill (annual), 26, 66, 69, 72, 73, 117

Finance, public, 116–24; scope of, 116–17; general principles, 117; expenditure, 117–18; estimates, 118–19; Committee of Supply, 119; Ways and Means, 119–20; National Budget, 120–1; payments from Consolidated Fund, 122–3; control of public expenditure, 123–4: local government, 174–180; rates, 175–6; rate demand, 177; central government grants, 178

Financial Resolution, 71

Fire Services, 109

Five Members, 63, 64

Fortescue, Chief Justice, 126

Franchise, 33, 34, 37

Freedom, 183–9; of individual citizen, 183–4; of person, 184–5; of expression, 185–6; of assembly, 186–7; of association, 187–8; of elections, 188; of property, 188; of religion, 188–9

Gambia, 221, 229

George I, 93

George III, 25, 40, 94

George V, 25

George VI, 23, 29, 30, 57

Georgia, 199–200, 216

Gibraltar, 201, 202

Gladstone, W. E., 40, 43, 97

Gold Coast, 236, 274–5

Government, passim; and the citizen, 181–91

Governor, the, 206–7, 210, 231–2

Great Council, 32, 126

Grenada, 201, 202, 23

Guillotine, 78

Hansard, 65, 79

Hastings, Warren, 225

Henry II, 126

Henry IV, 88

Henry VII, 85

Henry VIII, 27, 33, 53, 85

Hewart, Lord, 138

High Commission, Court of, 127

Home Affairs, Secretary of State for, 98, 108–10, 142, 178, 179

Home Office, 107, 108–10; diagram opp. p.108

Honours, bestowal of, 27–8, 96

Impeachment, 87, 182

Imperial Conferences, 263–4, 267

Imperial War Cabinet, 264

India, 221, 226, 271

Inns of Court, 129, 196

Ireland, Northern, 38, 87

Irish Free State, 39, 85, 272

Irish Nationalists, 40

Iron and Steel Nationalisation Bill (1948), 90

Jamaica, 202, 206, 228

James I, 33–4, 63

James II, 34, 40

Journals of the House of Commons, 61

Judges, 20, 26, 57, 118, 127, 128–9, 183

Judicial Committee of the Privy Council, see Privy Council

Juries, 130–2, trial by jury, 189

Justice, High Court of, 134

Juvenile Courts, 136

Kangaroo, 78, 79

Kenya, 233, 236

King's Bench, Court of, 127

King's Council (Curia Regis), 126, 127

King's Friends, 25, 40

Lagos, 227

Law, Courts of, 126–37, the courts today, 132–4; Magistrates' Courts, 135; Petty Sessions, 135; diagram of Courts and Appeals, 136; County Courts, 137; Coroners' Courts, 137; rivals to Courts, 138–9; Scottish Courts, 139–40

Law, English, origins of, 26; Criminal, 132; Civil 132

Law Officers of the Crown, 99, 130

League of Nations, 230, 265

Leeward Islands, 200, 210, 228

Legal Education, Council of, 129

Legislation, disallowance of, 261; reservation of, 210, 261, 268

Lloyd George, D., 96, 100

Orders of the Day, 69, 76, 78
Oversea Civil Service, 232

'Pairing', 83
Pakistan, 271
Parliament, *passim;* main references:
  origins and development, 31–39;
  House of Commons 53–84; House
  of Lords, 85–92
Party System, 39–53
Parties, Conservative, 37–46, 84, 99,
  103–4; Labour, 38–46, 89, 90;
  Liberal, 38–46, 89; Communist,
  44
Patronage, 82
Peace, Justices of the, 135–6, 149
Peel, Sir Robert, 38, 40, 43, 95–6,
  141
Peers, Scottish representative, 85;
  Irish representative, 85
Pennsylvania, 199, 204, 209, 220
Petition of Right (1628), 18, 144, 181,
  182
Petitions, to Commons, 67; to
  Queen, 156
Petty Sessions, 135–6
Pilgrim Fathers, 200
Pitt, Wm. the Younger, 94
Police, 140–4; organisation in Eng-
  land and Wales, 142; County and
  County Borough forces, 142–3;
  City of London, 143; Metro-
  politan, 143, 160; constitutional
  importance of tradition, 143–4;
  and freedom of citizen, 185–6;
  English tradition, 185–6
Polling, 49
Poor Law, 150
Post Office, 107
Prayer Book Measure (1928), 74
Prime Minister, *passim;* main refer-
  ence, 92–104
Prison Commission, 109
Private bills, 66–7, 73, 89
Private Members' bills, 70, 72–3
Private notice questions, 68
Privy Council, 76, 93, 102–3, 161,
  211; Judicial Committee of the,
  103, 128, 133, 138, 263
Privy Purse, 29
Proclamation of Queen Elizabeth II,
  23–4

Proportional representation, 42
Proprietary Colonies, 197–9, 206
Protectorates, 229–30
Provisional Order Bills, 73
Press, The, 65, 185–6
Public Bills, 70–3
Public Works Loans Board, 174

Quarter Sessions, 131, 134, 135, 149,
  151, 156
Queen, Her Majesty, *see* Sovereign
Queen's Bench Division, 132–4, 136
Queen's Counsel, 130
Queensland, 254
Question-time, 60, 68, 69
Quorum, 80–1

Recorder, 134, 156; of London, 134
Referendum, 20
Register of electors, 46–7
Regulation 18B, 190
Representative government, 237–8
Requests, Court of, 127
Responsible government, 237–8, 245,
  249–50
Revolution of 1688, 34, 93, 116, 205,
  211
Revolutionary and Napoleonic Wars,
  35
Rhode Island, 200, 206, 209, 220
Rhodesia, Northern, 239–41; South-
  ern, 259–60
Rolls, Master of the, 129, 130, 133
Rolls of Parliament, 64
Roses, Wars of the, 85
Royal Assent, 25, 32, 72
Royal Household, 29–30
Royal Prerogative, 110
Royal Robing Room, 57

St Lucia, 201, 222, 227
St Stephens, 53, 56
St Vincent, 201, 202
Salisbury, Lord, 95, 97
Scotland, appeals from, 87; Courts of
  Law, 139–40; local government,
  160; Standing Committee for
  Scottish Affairs, 20, 77; Secretary
  of State for, 20, 98; Union with, 35
Separation of Powers, 17
Serjeant-at-Arms, 57, 61
Settlement, Act of (1701), *see* Acts

Lightning Source UK Ltd.
Milton Keynes UK
UKHW012239300720
367458UK00001B/29